Acta Universitatis Upsaliensis
Uppsala Studies in Education 81

Valdy Lindhe

Greening Education

Prospects and Conditions in Tanzania

UPPSALA 1999

Dissertation for the Degree of Doctor of Philosophy in education presented at Uppsala University in 1999

ABSTRACT

Lindhe, V. 1999: Greening education. Prospects and conditions in Tanzania. Acta Universitatis Upsaliensis. *Uppsala Studies in Education* 81. 251 pp. Uppsala. ISBN 91-554-4511-X.

Environmental education in Tanzania after independence takes the Education for Self-Reliance policy as its starting point. This policy dominated the curriculum from 1967 to the 1980s.

The study explores the development of environmental education components in the curriculum in a historical, political and economical context and maps out frame factors in the teaching situation. It describes and analyses the differences between the formulated and the realised curriculum of environmental education in the formal Tanzanian education system. These external factors are supplemented by an analysis of primary and secondary school teachers' ways of experiencing the concept of the environmental education.

Among the frame factors for the teaching in schools, important elements are teachers' access to syllabi, teaching resources, the content of the questions in the national examinations, pupils' language proficiency in Swahili and English and pupils' access to textbooks. The teachers' socio-economic status and professional training background are other important frame factors. On a macro level, non-governmental actors such as the International Monetary Fund, the World Bank and aid organisations have played an important role in influencing the educational policy.

There are a large number of environmental education components in the syllabi for primary school and less in secondary. These components are strongly related to the Education for Self-Reliance policy in the syllabi developed before the mid 1980s. However, it seems that the impact of environmental education has been minimal due to several frame factors.

Teachers' ways of experiencing the concept of environmental education constituted three qualitatively different categories: environmental education is about natural and social surroundings; about how the environment supports human beings through its resources and about conservation and improvement of the environment.

The outcome suggests that the prospect of education for sustainability in the least developed countries is complex but also that the use of Western research tools in a non-Western cultural context is not fully satisfactory.

Keywords: Environmental education, education for sustainability, frame factors, Education for Self-Reliance, teachers' thinking, developing countries, Tanzania.

Valdy Lindhe, Department of Education, Uppsala University, Box 2109, SE-750 02 Uppsala, Sweden

© Valdy Lindhe

ISSN 0347-1314
ISBN 91-554-4511-X

Cover design: Jerk-Olof Werkmäster
Typesetting: Editorial Office, Uppsala University
Printed in Sweden by Elanders Gotab, Stockholm 1999
Distributor: Uppsala University Library, Box 510, SE-751 20 Uppsala, Sweden

To my grandchildren

Martina, born on 14 May 1997,
Elias, born on 25 July 1998,
Axel, born on 17 May 1999,
and ...

Contents

Acknowledgements	11
Tanzania—General information	13
CHAPTER 1: Introduction	15
Mrs Mema, a Tanzanian school teacher	15
Environmental education	18
A short history of environmental education	18
Research on implemented Environmental Education	21
Research in Tanzania	21
Research in South Africa	22
Research in Western countries	24
Aims and objectives of the study	29
Limitations of the study	30
The structure of the study	31
CHAPTER 2: Theoretical and Methodological Points of Departure	33
Introduction	33
The researcher	34
The Frame Factor Theory Approach	35
The formulation and realisation of curriculum	37
What determines and limits the teacher's realisation of the curriculum?	38
Field investigation approaches	39
Teachers' thinking and reasoning	39
Phenomenography—a research approach	40
Interviews as a research method	43
CHAPTER 3: Realisation of the study	45
Introduction	45
Empirical procedure	45
Collection of field data	46
Procedure	46

Data processing	56
Transcription of the interviews	56
Ways of experiencing and ways of finding categories of descriptions	57
CHAPTER 4: Education in Tanzania	**61**
Introduction	61
Historical background	61
Development of the educational system	63
Current educational system and policy	69
The frame factors in the Tanzanian educational system	75
Governing factors	75
Regulating factors	78
Constraining factors	84
Summary of frame factors	90
CHAPTER 5: Environment and Education	**92**
Introduction	92
The expectations on environmental education	92
Curriculum analysis	97
Curriculum emphases	98
The planning of the syllabi	102
Analysis of syllabi for Primary Schools	104
Summary of analyses of curriculum for primary school	109
Analysis of syllabi for Secondary Schools	110
Summary of analyses of curriculum for secondary school	115
Teacher training	117
Conclusions	119
The role of Education for Self-Reliance as a transition tool	119
On the impact of Education for Self-Reliance	120
Summary	123
CHAPTER 6: The conditions for teachers' lives and work	**125**
Introduction	125
Teacher qualification	125
Teaching methodology	126
The teachers' working conditions	127
Summary	132
CHAPTER 7: Classroom accounts	**134**
Introduction	134
Visits to classrooms	134
Primary school	135
Secondary school	137
Teacher Training College	140
Summary and personal reflection	141

CHAPTER 8: Teachers and environmental education 144
   Introduction. 144
   Teaching conditions for environmental education—answers from
      a questionnaire 144
   Teachers' ways of experiencing environmental education—outcome
      of the interviews 149
      Three different ways of experiencing environmental education. . . . 149
      Why is environmental education important? Two ways of
         experiencing 154
      Learning and teaching strategies. 155
      Content of environmental education. 160
      Summary and conclusions. 164

CHAPTER 9: What do pupils understand about the environment? 168
   Introduction. 168
   A questionnaire study 168
      Summary and discussion of results. 177

CHAPTER 10: Summary, conclusions and reflections 181
   Introduction. 181
      Critical view of the researcher 182
   Social transition through education. 183
      Environmental components in the curriculum 184
   Frame factors and teachers' thinking 185
      The difference between the formulated and
         the realised curriculum 186
      How teachers understood environmental education 189
   The impact of environmental education 195
      Factors of importance for the learning outcome of environmental
         education. 195
   Theoretical and methodological approaches versus findings 198
   The prospects of education for sustainability in the least developed
      countries 201

References. 205

Appendix. 219

Acknowledgements

One of the questions that one has to face now and then is, 'How did I become involved in this'? In my case, I think my interest for the environment developed while I was growing up. To me, the outdoors—farmland, forest land, mountains, streams, rivers and lakes—was a natural place for work, play and recreation. When I decided to involve myself in the research for this thesis, environmental education was an issue that came naturally to me. At that time, I was about to move to Tanzania, so the setting was given.

I would like to thank all the teachers in different Tanzanian primary and secondary schools who revealed their thinking to me. You all gave me vital information! I also want to thank all the educational staff at central, regional and district levels who assisted me in implementing the interviews. More than 1,400 pupils answered my questionnaire—thank you all and thanks to your head teachers (mistresses/masters)! A special thanks to Ms Laisha Said, who acted as my assistant and translator in Dar es Salaam, and to Professor A. S. Sumra, Faculty of Education, University of Dar es Salaam, who introduced her to me. Professor F. L. Mbunda from the same place gave me valuable advice in selecting the schools. I would also like to thank my friend Ms Joyce Msolla, principal of Iringa Teachers College, for her co-operation. My gratitude also goes to my friend Professor Carl James of York University, Toronto, for his viewpoints and kind asssistance.

I have had two supervisors. Professor Karl-Georg Ahlström, 'Atis', my supervisor for an earlier thesis in 1960s, and who, from the start, gave me unlimited encouragement. During the last few years, Professor Sverker Lindblad took over the supervising. Thank you, Sverker, for your indefatigable support and for pushing me forward—always asking, 'When are we going to see each other next'? My thanks also include the members of the thesis reading group, Professor Donald Broady and research assistant Hector Prieto Peréz. Research fellow Olle Österling and (at that time) doctoral student Michael A. A. Wort read parts of manuscript at an early stage and gave valuable criticism.

Mr Dag Kyndel, librarian at the Department of Education, has given invaluable assistance in searching for books and articles. Thank you, Dag! When not even Dag could help me with a certain document, one of my former students, subject teacher Johan Stenkula, was of infinite help. Mrs Barbara Rosborg has scrutinised and improved my English—thank you, Barbara, for smooth co-operation! My friend since many years, lecturer Ulla Håkanson, has proof-read the manuscript, for which I am deeply grateful. Thank you, Ulla!

Last, I would like to give deep thanks to my family. I am in debt to my eldest younger brother, research fellow Hans-Erik Uhlin, for his constructive criticism. My two sons, Örjan and David, have taught me how to use a computer since their early school years and have watched over my performance until now. Growing older, but always a step ahead of me in this field and able to teach their mother. Thank you both! And, finally, my heartfelt gratitude to my husband, Bosse, for his undying encouragement, support and love.

Tanzania—General information

Location: Eastern Africa, borders on the Indian Ocean between Kenya and Mozambique. National capital: Dar es Salaam (Dodoma).
Area: 945,090 sq. km.
Natural resources: Hydropower potential, tin, phosphates, iron ore, coal, diamonds, gemstones, gold, natural gas, nickel.
Land use: Arable land: 3%, permanent crops: 1%, permanent pastures: 40%, forests and woodland: 38%, other: 18% (1993 est.).
Environment—current issues: Soil degradation; deforestation; desertification; destruction of coral reefs threatens marine habitats; recent droughts affected marginal agriculture.
Environment—international agreements: Party to: Biodiversity, Climate Change, Desertification, Endangered Species, Hazardous Wastes, Law of the Sea, Nuclear Test Ban, Ozone Layer Protection, Whaling. Signed, but not ratified: none of the selected agreements above.
Population: 30,608,769 (July 1998 est.); 29.6 mil (Sida 1997).
Population growth rate: 2.14% (1998 est.); 3 % (Sida 1997).
Life expectancy at birth: Total population: 46.37 years (1998 est.); 51 years (Sida 1997).
Total fertility rate: 5.49 children born/woman (1998 est.).
Ethnic groups: Mainland[1]—native African 99% (of which 95% are Bantu, consisting of more than 130 tribes), other 1% (consisting of Asian, European and Arab) Note: Zanzibar—Arab, native African, mixed Arab and native African.
Religions: Mainland—Christian 45%, Muslim 35%, indigenous beliefs 20% Note: Zanzibar—more than 99% Muslim.
Languages: Kiswahili or Swahili (official), Kiunguju (name for Swahili in Zanzibar), English official, primary language of commerce, administration, and higher education, Arabic (widely spoken in Zanzibar), many local languages (the first language of most people is one of the local languages).

---

[1] The United Republic of Tanzania consists of Mainland Tanzania and Zanzibar.

Literacy: Total population: 67.8%; male: 79.4% ; 78.8% (Sida 1997); female: 56.8% (1995 est.); 54.3% (Sida 1997).

Administrative divisions: 25 regions; Arusha, Dar es Salaam, Dodoma, Iringa, Kigoma, Kilimanjaro, Lindi, Mara, Mbeya, Morogoro, Mtwara, Mwanza, Pemba North, Pemba South, Pwani, Rukwa, Ruvuma, Shinyanga, Singida, Tabora, Tanga, Zanzibar Central/South, Zanzibar North, Zanzibar Urban/West, Ziwa Magharibi (Kagera).

Economy—overview: Tanzania is one of the poorest countries in the world. The economy is heavily dependent on agriculture, which accounts for 57% of GDP[2], provides 85% of exports, and employs 90% of the work force. Topography and climatic conditions, however, limit cultivated crops to only 4% of the land area. Industry accounts for 17% of GDP and is mainly limited to processing agricultural products and light consumer goods. The economic recovery program announced in mid-1986 has generated notable increases in agricultural production and financial support for the program by bilateral donors. The World Bank, the International Monetary Fund, and bilateral donors have provided funds to rehabilitate Tanzania's deteriorated economic infrastructure. Growth in 1991–97 has featured a pickup in industrial production and a substantial increase in output of minerals, led by gold. Natural gas exploration in the Rufiji Delta looks promising and production could start by 2002. Recent banking reforms have helped increase private sector growth and investment.

GDP—per capita: USD 700 (1997 est.) .

Proportion of poor people (< 1 USD/per day): 16,4 % (Sida 1997).

Inflation rate—consumer price index: 15% (1997 est.) .

Budget: Revenues: USD 959 million. Expenditures: USD 1.1 billion, including capital expenditures of USD 214 million (FY96/97 est.).

Industries: Primarily agricultural processing (sugar, beer, cigarettes, sisal twine), diamond and gold mining, oil refining, shoes, cement, textiles, wood products, fertiliser, salt. Agriculture products: coffee, sisal, tea, cotton, pyrethrum (insecticide made from chrysanthemums), cashews, tobacco, cloves (Zanzibar), corn, wheat, cassava (tapioca), bananas, fruits, vegetables; cattle, sheep, goats.

Debt—external: USD 7.9 billion (1997 est.).

Exchange rates: Tanzanian shillings (TSh) per USD 1—631.61 (January 1998), 612.12 (1997), 579.98 (1996), 574.76 (1995), 509.63 (1994), 405.27 (1993).

Telephones: 137,000 (1989 est.).

Radios: 720,000 (1993 est.).

Televisions: 55,000 (1993 est.).

Sources: World Fact Book. Central Intelligence Agency, United States, 1998. http://www.cia.gov/cia/publications/factbook/tz.html (30 January 1999)

Country Information. Swedish International Development Authority (Sida, 1997). http://www.sida.se (30 January 1999).

---

[2] Gross Domestic Product.

CHAPTER 1
Introduction

Mrs Mema was a primary school teacher. She told me about her life as a teacher. I relate her story in the way and the order she told it. It is not a verbatim account but it reflects her language and her way of reasoning. Her story will give you an introduction to the school system in Tanzania during the last decades.

Mrs Mema, a Tanzanian school teacher[1]

Mrs Mema started her teaching career at Diriki practising school in 1973. She had completed a two-year training as a primary teacher at Aminika Teacher Training College (TTC). It was a good school with good administration and good pupils. All the teachers were trained professionally. She did not experience any problem—the school had almost everything. 'These were the golden days.'

In January 1975, she was transferred to Ganda Teacher Training College. They had a shortage of staff and she acted as a tutor in Swahili and science. It had previously been a mission school but the government had taken over. Still, everything was new—buildings, equipment etc. She was part of the beginning staff of the new Teacher Training College. There was a shortage of staff—and of water. They had to walk very far to get water. She stayed only nine months. In September or October 1975 she was transferred to Diriki Teacher Training College. At that time it was situated in a secondary school and they trained grade B and C[2] teachers. Diriki did not have as serious a problem with water as Ganda at that time. She walked only two kilometres to get it. She still taught Swahili but had to teach history also because of the shortage of tutors.

In 1976, the training college started 'crash courses' in order to supply the demand of Universal Primary Education (UPE). The teacher students of this course were Standard VIII or VIII leavers[3]. They were selected by their ward to work in a primary school and met three times a week at the ward centres. The ward centre teachers were the best primary school teachers in the area and they already had teacher training. Those students who were considered to be capable, were sent to a Teacher Training College. There, the teaching was arranged in short seminars, mostly to show that they had knowledge of the syllabus and the examination questions and also to go through the books that they had studied. Then they went back to their schools and returned again

---

[1] All names of people and places are changed.
[2] Primary school teachers were categorised as grade A, B or C teachers, with C as the lowest, depending on educational training background.
[3] From primary school.

later for the next seminars. This enabled them to obtain one week of teaching methodology after which they were sent back to practice teaching.

After nine months of this type of shift training at the local and Teacher Training College level, the students took the same examination as those attending the two year course. Most of them passed the examination. They were very eager, says Mrs Mema.

Mrs Mema said that some of these teachers were better qualified than those in the ordinary two year course. They were given an opportunity to become teachers and they worked hard to succeed. After the training they were employed as grade C teachers.

In 1979 the college moved to new buildings just opposite the old ones. The facilities were larger and the Teacher Training College started to train grade A and C teachers.

The work at Diriki was not very bad, said Mrs M. They had a hospital, a church, a bank and a post nearby. It was not necessary to include transport to the nearby town in one's budget. In October 1980, she followed her husband to the Bweni region. He changed from working for the Ministry of Education to another ministry. She had to ask permission to go to Aminika Teacher Training College. There they had full staff but she was offered a job at the primary school and she was not even disappointed. In primary school the Saturdays and Sundays were free and you finished your work at 4 or 4.30 p.m. By contrast, in the college you would have to act as teacher on duty on weekends and evenings. Being a woman she would even have had to cook when the work load was high for the domestic science staff.

Education for Self-Reliance started in 1972 at Aminika Teacher Training College. Mrs Mema was a student teacher there back then and it was discussed and decided that the students should clean their own rooms and do their own washing. Shamba (agricultural) work was introduced on a small scale with gardens only. In the beginning the Education for Self-Reliance projects had some extra funds, or so Mrs Mema believed. But in the following years they (the ministry) asked that the schools contribute up to 25 percent of their expenses through the self-reliance project. Not many schools were able to do that.

When Mrs Mema returned to Aminika Teacher Training College in 1980, she found that it was one of those that had succeeded. As a result of the Education for Self-Reliance projects, the students were given eggs for breakfast besides tea with sugar, milk and half a loaf of bread. At tea time in the morning, they got tea with milk, sugar and ground nuts. For lunch and supper they got a balanced diet, and sometimes they got chicken to eat. They even got afternoon tea. She envied the students; they got a better diet than she did in 1971–72. This was a result of the Education for Self-Reliance projects, for which the college was, as she put it, 'an example of colleges.' They received a lorry (the same one that they were using at the time of the interview in 1995) as a first prize for cleanliness. This you cannot believe when you see the college today, she said. (And I agree—the place is falling into pieces.) The college had money at that time.

At Aminika Mrs Mema did not notice the effect of the war with Uganda, since the projects were running so well. But in 1987–88, the Education for Self-Reliance projects collapsed. There was no medicine and food for the chickens and prices had gone up. She remembers that that is why the college had to close the poultry project. They were running at a loss. Of the original six cows and the pigsty, only one cow remained. The student teachers got very poor food, ugali and beans day out and day in. This meant that there were no more balanced diets. The primary school which Mrs Mema first walked into in 1980 was quite different then from what it appeared today. The teaching staff then had more matured teachers than the school at the time of my interview. Most of them then were married and had children. Today the staff was young. The old teachers were better trained. They had teaching practice for one and a half months twice a year, which added up to six months in total. The young teachers of the day were lucky if they had one month. And just then teaching practice was non-existent. It was almost like running a crash programme even though they stayed for two years at the college.

Mrs Mema said that there were 'born' teachers and 'made' teachers. In 1980, there were more 'born' teachers on the staff. And they were working better than the young ones.

The pupils had also changed. In 1980 they were attentive and challenging. They were able to ask questions. Now, they did not have any why-questions but just sat and waited to be fed. She thought that it was caused by poorly trained teachers and poor facilities. They did not have exercise books; only two were given each year by the government and not all parents could afford to buy more for their children. She said that the learning atmosphere was not good. They used to have pictures on the walls and materials in the classrooms. Now the teachers drew poor pictures and the pupils made bad copies—if they had an exercise book. Recently the Standard I and II children finally got their two exercise books. At the end of their first years! What have they learnt? Mrs Mema believed that the reason behind all this was limited funds. But she said, 'Look at how little the government is spending on education! The young teachers are poorly taught pupils that have become poorly trained teachers and they will produce even poorer taught pupils.'

Further, Mrs Mema pointed out, 'the Teacher Training College might prepare student teachers with the theoretical content but what is missing is practice in classes. The student teachers teach each other but how can they be prepared to create motivation among the pupils? If a child has no exercise book and the parents cannot afford to buy them, what do you do? Do you give them a piece of paper every day during the whole year? What do you do? How do you teach them?' Mrs Mema became quite agitated when she talked about the poor teacher training. She believed that practice in schools was very important.

The administration at Elimika, too, was different in 1980. It had an experienced and mature head teacher. She was offered the position in 1990, but she was pregnant and was not prepared to do the work. The person who was appointed instead was a young man with no previous administrative experience. But she believed that he was talented. There had not been much trouble with the staff.

Respect for teachers was much greater in 1973 when Mrs Mema started to teach. It changed in the mid-1980s. Maybe it was political. Pupils became free to question the teachers and they started to argue. They did not greet the teacher outside school. Also parents had changed their attitudes toward teachers. They looked down at the teachers as very poor people since some parents had TV sets and videos. A teacher could not afford such items. In 1973, however, a teacher was among the most highly paid.

In Aminika the majority of the parents were peasants and a minority were businessmen. The peasants thought the Education for Self-Reliance activities were good, since it gave their children some practice. But the business parents did not see the meaning of it. Class differences were shown in dress; some pupils had shoes and talked about things that a teacher could not afford. When the school went to do shamba[4] work seven times a year, the 'rich' children brought soft drinks, bread and fruits and the 'poor' children brought pieces of sugar cane and something light to eat. These social differences were one reason why needle work at school had to stop. Some children could not afford to contribute to the material that was needed.

Since 1973, a teacher's salary has declined dramatically. In 1973 a teacher did not have to engage in agricultural work but today they need some kind of projects which might include a cow, some chickens and a shamba to make ends meet. Pay was maybe 500 shillings a day but they spent 1050 shillings. Where did they make up the difference? A teacher ate a poor breakfast and most could not afford anything to have with their morning tea. Then they had a poor lunch and a poor dinner. The result was poor health and poor work.

---

[4] Field for cultivation.

The teaching resources were good in 1973. Mrs Mema said that there were fewer schools then but now there were many more schools and less funds. The textbooks and the teachers' guides were also better in 1973. Back then the authors had a pedagogical interest in their subject and they were proud. Now they published books just for the sake of doing so and to get some money. 'They are not interested in doing something good,' Mrs Mema feels. Mrs Mema went on to show some grave errors in one textbook.

Mrs Mema said that she liked the idea of Education for Self-Reliance. But the result depended on the implementer. If the programme was implemented in a good way, then the result was good and the pupils were interested. At Elimika it was quite successful. The children knew that the ugali[5] was made from the maize at the shamba. Mrs Mema had one garden for Standard VI A and one for VI B. The profit from the gardens was used to buy ingredients for cookery in domestic science. This made the pupils interested. She only wished that they could have at least two meals per year using the harvest from the banana plants, but it was all sold.

Mrs Mema was teaching English and domestic science in a primary school at the time. She appeared to be a resourceful woman with good knowledge of what was happening in the school and the surroundings. She told me that she did not restrict her teaching to the school compound only but made study visits with her classes to the local homes and surroundings, to study for example health and hygiene aspects.

After this introduction to the educational setting in Tanzania, I will continue with the issue in focus of this study, environmental education. After a presentation of the development of the concept, as steered by international agencies in the Western countries, a research overview will follow. The chapter concludes with the aims of the study.

Environmental education

A short history of environmental education

After the Second World War the United Nations started to arouse an international interest in the environment and organised a Scientific Conference on the Conservation and Utilisation of Resources in 1949. In the same year UNESCO funded a foundation called the International Union for the Conservation of Nature.

The Biosphere Conference in Paris in 1968 promoted an environmental education programme with a focus on the development of environmental study material for curricula at all levels, the promotion of technical training and stimulation of global awareness of environmental problems. An important step was taken from environmental studies towards environmental education as a concept.

The creation of the United Nations Environment Programme (UNEP) was initiated at the UN conference on Human Environment in Stockholm, Sweden in 1972. UNEP was to supervise and protect the global environment and

---

[5] Maize porridge.

spread information. The importance of education was stressed and in 1975 the International Environmental Education Programme (IEEP) was created. One of its offices was established in Nairobi, Kenya.

The First Intergovernmental Conference on Environmental Education was held in Tbilisi (Georgia, in then USSR) in 1977. The conference was attended by delegates from 70 member states. The declaration and recommendations of this conference were later endorsed by 150 countries and have been the guideline for further development.

The declaration stated that environmental education (EE) is a continuous and lifelong process where individuals and society become aware of their environment and develop knowledge, values, skills, experiences and action orientation to be able to solve present and future problems. Furthermore environmental education must consider the economical, social and ecological realities of each society. Some goals, however, are general and global by nature. Knowledge should be developed through observation, discovery and practical experiences of the actual environment. The pupils should participate in the planning of activities and decision making. Special emphasis should be given to the nearby environment for younger pupils; as they grow older they investigate local, national and international environmental issues. The complex nature of environmental issues should be pointed out and it is necessary to develop a critical thinking. The most important aspect of environmental education is the problem-solving approach. This necessitates a multi-disciplinary approach to the issue.

In 1981, the International Union for the Conservation of Nature and Natural Resources (IUCN), together with UNEP, and World Wide Fund for Nature (WWF), presented a 'World Conservation Strategy' (IUCN, UNEP, WWF 1980). This strategy emphasised three major goals for sustainable development:

– the maintenance of essential ecological processes and life-support systems.
– the preservation of genetic diversity.
– sustainable use of species or ecosystems.

The strategy also emphasised the need of an environmental education that permits people to live in harmony with nature. Today's generation should not leave behind lesser resources to the coming generation than those that it inherited itself. This is the meaning of a sustainable development that was first launched in the so-called Brundtland Report (World Commission on Environment and Development 1987).

IUCN, UNEP and WWF presented a development of the World Conservation Strategy called Caring for the Earth: A Strategy for Sustainable Living (IUCN, UNEP, WWF 1990). Here a world ethic for living sustainably is given prominence. Within the formal educational sector it is necessary to develop an understanding for the relationship between the human being and nature. Children and adults alike must acquire knowledge and attitudes that lead to a sustainable way of living. Environmental education should be related to social studies, including knowledge and understanding of human behaviour and the value of a multi-cultural society.

In chapter 36 of Agenda 21 adopted by the United Nations Conference on Environment and Development (UNCED) in Rio de Janeiro, Brazil, in 1992 environmental education was reoriented towards sustainable development. The International Conference on Environment and Society: Education and Public Awareness for Sustainability[6] (UNESCO 1997) was held in Thessaloniki, twenty years after the first conference in Tbilisi. Little had been achieved during these years, according to the Director-General, Mr Fredrico Mayor (ibid. pp.1). There is still a strong need to promote sustainable development integrating considerations pertaining to population, health, economics, social and human development, and peace and security. The conference suggested a focus on problems which the general public experiences in everyday life in order to build public awareness. The conference members agreed that education (including both formal and non-formal schooling and traditional learning acquired in the home and the community) is the most effective means that society possesses for confronting the challenges of the future. Lifelong learning in a changing world was stressed, as well as concentration on basic education in the developing world. They suggested that there was a need to reform curricula and educational policies and structures at all levels. The importance of teacher education and training and higher education was highlighted. It was also pointed out that there is a need to develop interdisciplinary studies. It is the role of education to communicate the moral imperative of sustainability.

Environmental education as such is nothing new—traditionally it has been a part of the informal education from one generation to the next (Sterling 1992, Brock-Utne 1994, Gough 1997a). The relation and interdependence between the human being and the environment has been very clear in most societies. Land has always been cultivated in various manners and the concept of carrying capacity has been known from a practical point of view around the world.

The following quotation[7] from an interview with a female agricultural officer, born in the 1940s, tells about the use of indigenous practices related to soil conservation.

> I think this custom originates from the Zulus ... that when you have harvested your crops ... you shouldn't burn the residues ... you have to lay out ridges ... put them into a straight line and then ... when it comes during rainy season ... you cover with the soil ... they believe that all the ground all over the world are graves ... I mean which you can't see ... so the ancestors would never like someone to burn grass or trees above their graves ... it is a sign of respect ... so actually all over the place now there are ridges ... we cultivate on ridges ... so you bury the residues and respect them ... this increases the production of crops ... because it is like manure

---

[6] Sustainability: 'Meeting the needs of the present without compromising the ability of future generations to meet their own needs' (definition from 'Our common future,' the 1987 report from the World Commission on Environment and Development—the so-called Brundtland report).

[7] The quotation is a transcription of her own words from a tape recording. The dots indicates pauses in speech but not the length of the pauses.

or compost ... nobody will tend to burn it ... if anyone does ... he will be summoned by the elders ... if you break the rules of conserving wild trees ... plants ... or all that ... the tribe had very strict rules ... the first time you commit ... you get strokes by the chief ... made out of hippopotamus tail ... soaked and salted and that is very painful ... if you repeat then you are going to be ... speared ... yes ... you die ... everybody was very keen of obeying ... the rules ... actually at home [Songea district, Rovuma region, Tanzania] ... if you are a girl and you reach about the age of seven and onwards ... you are given a plot as a member of the family ... and then there is a communal one for the whole family ... so when you know you have got this type of plot ... you have to be told what things to do and which time you should do it ... so the elderly women they will tell you that ... you know you have got a field ... and on your field there is a river passing across ... you should know how you should treat your field ... there are some sacred trees growing along that river and you should never, never cut them down in your life because ... those sacred trees they have a name ... and they have got very sweet fruits ... it should not be cut down because it attracts water ... wherever it is ... I mean the river will always flow ... that is one reason ... another reason is that ... when you grow up and you have babies ... when the baby drops down its navel ... the navel is taken by an elderly woman ... and she will bury it under that tree ... so this type of trees are very, very precious ... they should never be cut down ... another type you have to preserve is ... when a girl or a boy has reached the puberty ... whenever you go maybe you are going to cultivate at the shamba or to look for fire wood the mother or the grandmother will always show you plants which are used as medicines ... this is a plant for diarrhoea or for headache and this plant is useful for this ... so you start to know different types of trees or plants which are useful ... when you have reached puberty then you will be shown more trees ... then when you grow up and have your own family ... you know that these trees are useful you shouldn't cut them ... if you start a shamba ... you have to keep those types of trees in your field so that ... you can use them any time when you need it ...

Research on implemented Environmental Education

A great number of texts on environmental education in African countries have been presented at conferences, meetings and in-service training courses, often on curriculum issues (e.g. Mucunguzi 1995, Abedayo & Olawepo 1997) or interpretation of the concept of environmental education (Bak 1995) but research reports are very few. Below I present relevant research in Tanzania, South Africa and some Western countries.

Research in Tanzania

In Tanzania very little research has been done on environmental education. Ladi Nshubernuki (1986) conducted a minor study on conservation attitudes of 130 school children in the Kondoa district. The area was seriously eroded and a rehabilitation project for soil erosion control, Hifadhi Ardhi Dodoma (HADO), had been in place since 1973. Nshubernuki randomly chose four primary schools from three different areas based on the ratings of intensity of erosion—severe, moderate or little erosion. In each school ten pupils were randomly chosen for interviews. The main results of these interviews, according to Nshubernuki, showed that pupils were generally aware of the HADO project and there were no differences between the schools in the three areas of erodibility. Only 21 out of 130 pupils appreciated the importance of the project. Pupils did not seem to have clear ideas of the rudiments of soil conservation. They did, however, resent the erosion and wanted the project to continue. There were no differences in the teaching techniques of the three areas. Nshubernuki concluded that the pupils were not aware of the connection between erosion intensity and fuelwood shortage, despite the fact that women and children spent more than three hours per day collecting fuelwood. Participation in soil conservation measures on the part of the schools was high but it is possible that participation was stereotyped with no explanation as to why the measures were taken.

Studies on such issues as pupils' and teachers' perceptions of afforestation have been conducted (Chonjo 1992). The research team administered a questionnaire to 666 pupils in 49 primary schools in six regions (and also interviewed a few of them) to find out about their understanding of what the environment is, qualities of good environment, use of trees and what could be done to rehabilitate their surroundings. Primary school teachers were also interviewed on basically the same issues. A large number of schools had seedling nurseries but these were not used to educate the pupils on afforestation. They served as centres for distribution to the villages. The result of the research is not quite clear but the findings indicate that most teaching was done through lectures without connecting theory to practical implementations. Furthermore, the teachers had not thought about their own role in improving the environment.

Christian da Silva conducted an interesting study on traditional environmental knowledge and environmental education in secondary schools (1996). He interviewed students and elders in the local area around the school and compared their answers. He concluded that regarding two of the schools, the elders in the local area were much more informed about environmental changes than the students. In the third school, where the students came from the nearby local communities, there was more consensus between the students and the elders, although the latter were still much more knowledgeable. According to da Silva this was a sign that the school did not relate the teaching to what was happening in the local environment, since if it had done so, the pupils would have been more well-informed. In this third school some knowledge was probably received through education from the family. In the first and second schools, where the students came from far away and thus lived in the school boarding houses, such education in the family was limited.

Research in South Africa

The Republic of South Africa is the only sub-Saharan country that, to some extent, has a research tradition (see e.g. Hurry 1980 and 1992) in environmental education but the research is still limited to solving day-to-day environmental problems (Loubser & Ferreira 1992). The Murray & Roberts Chair of Environmental Education at the Department of Education at Rhodes University was set up in the beginning of the 90s, partly to develop research capacity. Eureta Janse van Rensburg was the first beneficiary of the chair and concentrated her research on identifying research priorities in environmental education. Inspired by the social critical theory her research (1995) identified three orientations:

– Research for management to restore order to nature and society.
– Research to resolve practitioners' and communities' problems.
– Research for radical reconstruction.

Van Rensburg outlined research priorities from a reflective perspective to open up possibilities for transformative knowledge emerging from versions of education as a process of social change.

Development of curriculum material has been done through participatory reconstructive action research (O'Donoghue & Taylor 1988 and O'Donoghue & McNaught 1991) which instigated a support service (Share-Net) that has been a model in the development of environmental education in Southern Africa. Robert James Taylor (1997) reviewed the development of Share-Net, an informal resource materials network, which is located within the developing environmental education activities of the Wildlife and Environment Society of South Africa. In his study he described the process of change from top-down decisions to collaborative work in the course of the development.

How teacher students conceptualise environment and environmental education was researched by Alistair S. Robertson (1995). He also focused on their conceptualisation of the relationship between humans and other forms of life and the natural world. Robertson questioned the assumption that students were ignorant of environment issues when registering for environmental education sessions during their teacher education programme. The study was conducted at Rhodes University in South Africa with single semi-structured interviews of 13 students and a focused group interview of nine.

The students' conceptualisation of 'environment' (actually, environment was equated with 'surroundings') was categorised in five different ways of thinking:

> The first conceptualisation framed environment in largely social terms, where interpersonal behaviour in social settings was the main focus of interest in one's surrounding. The second conceptualisation was based upon explicit references to political factors in the South African social environment, with attention given to economic and power inequities among different racial groups and relationships between economic impoverishment and lack of access to natural resources. In the third conceptualisation, attention was focused more directly on the natural world, and on human effects on bio-physical features. The fourth conceptualisation portrayed environment in terms of systems theory, as an aggregation or assemblage of conceptually separable parts joined in regular interaction or interdependence.

Finally, the fifth conceptualisation portrayed a way of thinking of environmental features which had been experienced directly as coming to constitute a part of one's sense of self. (ibid. pp. 117).

The three first categories corresponded to categories used by several South African authors to describe elements of the environment (they also had a fourth one, economic, but it was not conceptualised here). The two last were findings of Robertson's study. The political category is not surprising, considering the South African context. The last category, environment as part of one's self, is unexpected since it is mostly related to concepts of environment in Nordic countries or certain Asian societies.

Research in Western countries

Environmental education, according to the international definition, focused early on both cognitive[8], affective[9] and psychomotor[10] domain. Louis A. Iozzi (1989a) noted that in his summary of research on environmental education during 1971–1982 he found that almost 60 percent of the studies dealt with the affective domain followed by the cognitive domain (about 40 percent). Closer inspection revealed that the result was disappointing. Most of the conducted research was essentially descriptive and many of the studies were poorly designed, because they lacked appropriate controls, utilised faulty or inadequate instruments or employed inappropriate and rigorous statistical procedures.

From the research findings Iozzi identified eight major ideas related to environmental education and the affective domain. Environmental education was effective in producing environmental values but only if programmes and methods were designed specifically; the relationship between environmental knowledge and positive environmental attitudes and values was unclear; positive environmental attitudes and values once acquired appeared to be long lasting; development of environmental attitudes and values should begin as early as possible, even before pre-primary school and be regularly enforced through the school years; the relationship between environmental attitudes and age, socio-economic status, place of residence and gender was conflicting and inconclusive; outdoor teaching was an effective method; various teaching methods also seemed to be effective; and the media were powerful sources of influence. Iozzi (1989b) further stated that environmental education must be included in more than just science and social science programmes.

The research focus which Iozzi explored was typical for the decades of 1950–1990. Environmental education struggled with definitions, curriculum and teaching methodology. Masters and doctoral theses between 1976 and 1982 (Hanselman & Yuen 1978; Kogut 1982) examined by the National Association for Environmental Education, Troy, Ohio (altogether 113) were organised into

---

[8] See Bloom, 1956.
[9] See Krathwohl et al., 1964.
[10] See Simpson, 1966.

six categories: 1) site analysis: descriptions and development plans for areas to be used for environmental education; 2) parks and camps: users/interpreters characteristics; 3) media communications: examination of effectiveness of various media; 4) pupil-centred studies: research on attitude change, instructional effectiveness and learning characteristics; 5) teacher-centred studies: research on training, attitudes, teacher behaviour; and 6) resources and administration: research on environmental education policy, administration and philosophy.

Research paradigms

The nature, meaning and significance of environmental education research has been critiqued by Ian Robottom and Paul Hart (1993) who are well known researchers within this field. They claimed that education in general has applied the research methodologies of other disciplines rather than developed its own. The dominant methodological framework for behaviour and social sciences has been empiricism and positivism, an opinion that is supported by Leeming, Dwyer, Porter and Cobern (1993).

The North American Association for Environmental Education signalled in 1990 the opening of the environmental education field to the possibility of alternative approaches to research. Their 1990 conference discussed and analysed the issue of research paradigms in environmental education (Mrazek 1993, Disinger & Roth 1992). Quantitative methods were confronted by qualitative (Marcinkowski 1993), positivist paradigm with interpretative and critically reflective inquiry (Cantrell 1993, Hart 1993, Wals 1993, Gough 1993).

Robottom argued for making environmental education research more educational:

> ... environmental education researchers do not ... seem to be very educational lot ... recourse tends to be made to applied science fields like psychometrics, behaviour analysis, natural resources, human ecology and statistics (Robottom 1993, p. 138).

Alistair Robertson (1994) likewise claimed that the theoretical foundation for research was mostly lacking and the references to educational literature were few. The emphasis is often on the 'environment' in environmental education and behaviourist researchers ignore conceptual or cognitive activity. Robertson argued for a constructivist theory of knowledge, which has not been focus for research in environmental education. One example of such approach was presented by Marilyn Lisowski and John F. Disinger (1991).

Robottom and Hart (1993) concluded that it was an appropriate time for the research community in both science and environmental education to work towards a meta-research agenda for research about the political theories of the different approaches to research. Robottom had argued earlier (1992) that the purposes of environmental education were socially transformative and that the dominant (North American) approach to research in the field was behaviouristic and deterministic. Robottom was one of several Australian environmental educators (Fien 1992, Gough N. 1993, Greenall Gough 1993, Hart 1993, Gough A. 1997) who were advocating socially critical theory based on a dialectical view of knowledge where school and society reflect one another. School is seen as an instrument in overcoming social inequities and preparing students for participation in social, political and economic activities with an emphasis on socially, morally and politically justifiable conflict resolution.

The nature and tradition of environmental education research has been explored in terms of an individualist ideology without taking into account the historical, social and political context within which the environmental actions of individual and groups gain meaning and significance (Robottom and Hart 1995).

Criticism of the empirical-analytical methodology has been challenged by Sharon Connel (1997). In some cases, she felt, the criticism was unjustified. She argued that it was done to promote an antagonistic view of this methodology in educational research and that it may distract researchers from considering more enlightening, complementary and co-operative dialogues about research methodologies in environmental education.

Kim Walker (1997) was critical to the social critical theory and argued that it did not take account of an implementation theory since it denied the teachers' practical knowledge. If environmental education is to lead to an improvement, a more adequate theory is required. Walker argued for a problem-based methodology, e.g. a methodology where learning is based on questions or problems to which one tries to find answers through texts, field studies, experiments, etc.

Implemented research

A substantial number of studies have been done. The North American Association for Environmental Education (NAAEE) presents 211 abstracts of research reports published in 38 periodicals between 1981 and 1990 and 611 dissertation abstracts from 1971–1980. Recent graduate works, mainly from North America and Australia, in 1996 and 1997 list about 110 Masters theses and a few doctoral theses on the subject of the environment, of which 27 are related to educators.

Now, what kind of research have been done in environmental education during the last decade? In order to structure an overview of recent research in environmental education, I have chosen an approach that is used by some Australian and South African researchers (for example Robottom & Hart 1993, Gough 1997, van Rensburg 1995). I have thus used Jürgen Habermas' (1972) identification of three basic cognitive interests in rationality: technical, practical and emancipatory. Technical interest is related to the social labour process since it needs to have means to achieve control of materials and components. Technical interest is part of empirical-analytical science which generally adopts a positivist philosophy. Practical interest is related to social interaction for understanding and the hermeneutic sciences. The third interest, an emancipatory interest, is comprised within critical science. These three interests make up different types of approaches towards knowledge and how knowledge is generated and organised in our society. Knowledge is something which people construct together .

I have chosen these three different interests since I think they correspond well with aims for environmental education according to John Huckle (1993) and with which I sympathise. Huckle is considered by Annette Gough (1997 a) to be one of the first (in the early 80s) to point out the relationship between environmental education and environmental ideologies. In order to relate research approaches to each other, I have combined, in Table 1, technical interest with education for environmental management and control, and practical interest with education for environmental awareness and interpretation.The emancipatory interest has been linked with education for sustainability, although the latter concept is not agreed upon. The core contradiction, according to John Huckle (1996), is between a weak and a strong mode. Weak sustainability is compatible with free markets, individual property rights, a minimum of state control and egocentric values. Here, the value of nature is seen in relationship to the value people derive from its use. Strong sustainability is related to social ownership of the means and conditions of production, democratically planned development and homocentric values. In this perspective, the value of nature is seen as an integral part of society which should be planned and cared for in the interest of present and future human well-being. Prices, taxes, licences, laws, public expenditure, education and land-use planning systems would all be used to ensure that environmental performance targets are met (Huckle, 1996).

The three columns are related to Robottom's well known and widely used distinction of emphasis within environmental education: education about (shown in the first column), through or in (second column) and for (third column) the environment (Robottom, 1987, 1992).

There have been several other attempts to categorise environmental education and research. Hart (1993), for example, describes different emphases in action research:

> British action research tends to emphasise interpretative inquiry ... the Australians tend to be more critical, more politically aware ... American versions had tended to be more technical (ibid. pp. 111).

After reading all the issues of *The Journal of Environmental Education* since 1990, searching for relevant doctoral theses, I have chosen works of the period that are related to teachers and teaching. I have studied the texts, focusing on the aims and the research methods that were used (for examples see Appendix 1). I have compiled an overview in the table below. As can be seen, all three interests and educational categories are represented.

The first column (technical interest or education for management and control), could actually have been longer, since I found eighteen articles that fitted

Table 1: *Categorisation of environmental education research based on Jürgen Habermas' division of knowledge interests and John Huckle's division of environmental education focus*[a]

Technical interest	Practical interest	Emancipatory interest
A basic orientation towards controlling and managing the environment through rule-following action based upon empirically grounded laws. Congruent with the *empirical-analytical sciences*.	A fundamental interest in understanding the environment through interaction based upon a consensual interpretation of meaning. Congruent with the *hermeneutic* concept of application (promoting knowledge and action which is a subjective process).	A fundamental interest in emancipation and empowerment to engage in autonomous action arising out of authentic, *critical* insights into the social construction of human society (through processes of self-reflection).
Key word: *causal explanation*.	Key word: *understanding*.	Key word: *reflection*.
Education for *management and control*.	Education for *environmental awareness and interpretation*.	Education for *sustainability*.
Authors Brody 1990–91, Pomerantz 1990, Lisowski & Disinger 1991, Sutherland & Ham 1991, Spork 1992, Arcury & Christianson 1993, Ramsey 1993, Boerschig & de Young 1993, Lane, Wilkie, Champeu & Sivik 1994, Smith-Sebast & Fortner 1994, Boyes, Chambers & Stannisstreet 1995, Cottrell & Graefe 1997	*Authors* Palmer 1993, Simmons 1993, Faulconer 1993, Hillcoat, Forge, Fien & Baker 1995, Helldén 1995, Robertson 1995, Östman 1995, Earl Todt 1995, Gough 1997, Alerby 1998	*Authors* O'Donoghue & McNaught 1991, Fien 1992, Greenall Gough & Robottom 1993, van Rensburg 1995, Fien & Rawling 1996, Wals & Alblas 1997, Taylor 1997, Axelsson 1997, Payne 1997

[a] Sources: all references are based on material in English and Swedish, found in the library database DISA of Uppsala University, LIBRIS of the Swedish libraries, the database ERIC and The Journal of Environmental Education (North America) as well as contacts with the Rhodes University, South Africa. There are unknown sources in Asia and South America as well as in Eastern Europe which makes my overview incomplete, not to mention sources in other languages.

within my delimitation. Those chosen show a variety of issues. North American researchers are very numerous, which is not surprising since that region is also where the journal is published. Research issues were the outcome of teaching, definitions of variables and the development of instruments of assessment.

Ten research reports (including five doctoral theses) fit the second column, practical interest or education for environmental awareness and interpretation. The dimension of understanding was a dominant research theme.

Nine research reports (including four doctoral theses) fit the third column (emancipatory interest or education for sustainability), a theme favoured by several Australian researchers, represented here by Anette Greenall Gough, Ian Robottom, John Fien and Richard Rawling. O'Donoghue, van Rensburg and Taylor are South African researchers who have been influenced by the

Australians. It is notable that African researchers are not represented in the first two columns and that only one North American is found who fits into the third column. Reflection and action research are most common. All articles and theses that I found to fit into columns two and three are included.

Aims and objectives of the study

I became interested in the issue of environmental education while I was working in Eastern Africa with soil and water conservation training for agricultural and forestry personnel. In some programmes developed by ministries of agriculture or forestry, there was also school involvement. It included the training of teachers and provision of teaching material such as booklets, tools or planting material. I became aware that the impact of land degradation in these countries mainly depends on agricultural practices.

Land degradation is the main environmental problem in East Africa and in many other poor countries. It is characterised by loss of biological diversity and productivity. Rehabilitation is possible if there is still some soil on the land. It is, however, a slow process. Tanzania suffers from grave environmental problems. About 33 percent of the country's land surface has been affected by desertification, especially in the central and northern parts. The rate of removal of forest cover and bush land was estimated to be 300 000 to 400 000 hectares annually. Poor agricultural practices resulted in loss of soil fertility and soil erosion which led to declining productivity. Land tenure issues, inadequate rainfall, rapid population growth and poverty were major causes of land degradation (National Environmental Management Council 1994).

Another thing that evoked my curiosity was the depreciation of teachers and schools in Tanzania. I asked about the existence of environmental education and got answers such as: 'nothing much is being done' and 'teachers are ignorant' from officials at high levels. I also met 'general' complaints about the low standards of schools.

Although I considered comparing several countries, I finally decided to concentrate my efforts on only one in East Africa, namely Tanzania. The government of Tanzania, one of the least developed countries of the world, was interested at an early stage in environmental issues and this interest influenced the curriculum development work of primary and secondary schools. They inherited a colonial school system and set about to change it to suit the new independent state.

I am interested in the formal educational system and its role in developing environmental awareness and knowledge. Environmental education is an issue of concern for most countries and Tanzania is no exception. It is infused in the curriculum at both the primary and secondary school levels. Therefore it will be necessary to analyse the curriculum from this perspective. I will also try to get a bearing of pupils' understanding of environmental issues. Of importance is how teachers view environmental education and I will make an attempt to find out.

In my work I wish to explore the conditions of implementation of environmental education within the formal educational system in Tanzania. By studying the development of environmental education since the1960s through the educational and political policies, I hope to make the influencing factors for the formulation and realisation of the curriculum clear. Are the frame factors in Tanzania of the same kinds as in Sweden and other Western countries? If not, what other factors are important?

What possibilities do teachers have for realising the curriculum? How do they understand environmental education? Is the outcome of environmental education dependent on teachers' understanding and attitudes towards the issues? Does understanding vary among the teachers? Do teachers have the necessary methodological repertoire? Are there other factors that influence the outcome and if so, what are they?

The aim of this study is to describe and analyse the difference between the formulated and the realised curriculum of environmental education in Tanzanian formal education. By exploring the development of the curriculum, the frame factors, teachers' perspectives and understanding of environmental education, and relating this to the frame factor theory approach, I hope to generate understanding of the conditions of the teachers' implementation of environmental education. In this way, I hope to contribute to a more realistic picture of realisation of curriculum in the least developed countries, while testing common Western research methods in an African context at the same time.

Limitations of the study

Language and cultural background in communication are important. When the partners involved don't share either of them, it is a setback. This is the condition in my case since my mother tongue is Swedish. The study was carried out in Tanzania with some 120 different mother tongues and two official languages (Swahili and English). Of course this is of importance for the outcome, especially in the interviews. One advantage, though, is that I have lived about seven years in Southern and Eastern Africa, including Tanzania.

Another restricting factor has been the access to documents, research reports and curricula in Tanzania. These materials have not been easily available due to several conditions. Literature written by foreign authors and published outside Tanzania has generally been more easily available.

I will use research methods that are common in Sweden and Western countries. Are these methods feasible in a very different cultural, political, economic and geographical context?

The language barriers will cause reliability weaknesses. Since I have been using multiple sources of evidence, the construct validity[11] is better than the external validity[12]. In the latter case the use of Western research tools in an African context could be doubtful. Also the choice of research approach, a single case study, implies restrictions as to how the findings can be generalised.

The structure of the study

In the first chapter environmental education, the issue in focus for the study, has been introduced as well as the context in which it appears, Tanzania. Chapter 2 describes the theoretical and methodological point of departure. The realisation of the study and the empirical procedure is given in chapter 3. In chapter 4 there is a presentation of the educational reforms with a focus on post-independence and of the frame factors in the educational system. The development of an expectation on environmental education in Tanzania is depicted in chapter 5. The conditions of the lives and work of the teachers in Tanzania are introduced in chapter 6 while my observations of lessons in classrooms are recounted in chapter 7. The two latter chapters are both introductions to chapters 8 and 9 which consist of the results of my studies on teachers' and pupils' understanding of environmental education. Finally, I make conclusions and discuss the implications of the findings in chapter 10.

Diagram 1 describes the planning of my work, from the stating of the phenomena in focus to the reflections over the outcome. Another way of describing the logic of the process, inspired by Rune Wigbald (1997), is that I have started with descriptions, continued with analysis of the results to get a more holistic understanding of the phenomena in focus and finished with reflections over points that enrich the knowledge of the same (i.e. the phenomena).

---

[11] Construct validity in a case study is increased when it is necessary to select the specific types of changes that are to be studied in relation to the objective of the study. Tactics to increase the construct validity include the use of multiple sources of evidence, establishing a chain of evidence during the data collection and/or having the draft case study report reviewed by key informants (Yin 1994).
[12] External validity deals with the problem of knowing whether the study's findings are generalisable beyond the immediate case study. Case studies rely on analytical generalisation whereby the researcher is striving to generalise a particular set of results to some broader theory (Yin 1994).

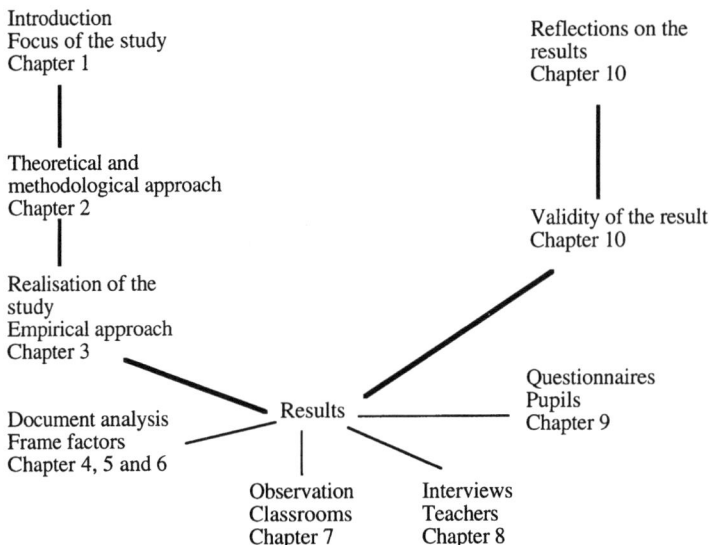

Diagram 1. The outline of the planning of the thesis.

CHAPTER 2
Theoretical and Methodological Points of Departure

Introduction

In this study, I am asking 'how' and 'why' questions about environmental education. The study focuses on teachers' thinking and teachers' situations in the context of the historical, political, economical and educational system in Tanzania. Teachers are, as a matter of routine, often blamed for the outcome of education. But to what extent is that true? To reveal a possible answer, it is necessary to see what other variables are of interest and how the inter-play affects the result. I will use multiple sources in the data collection in a triangulation fashion. In accordance with the criteria expressed by Robert K. Yin, my study has an explorative single case study approach because my research questions explore (what, how, why and not how many or how much) a contemporary phenomena (and not historical) within its real-life context; the relevant behaviour can not be manipulated; it relies on multiple sources (among them interviews and direct observations); and the study is conducted only once (Yin, 1994, pp. 4–9, 13, 40–41). It can also be called an intrinsic case study in accordance with Robert E. Stake because I am mainly interested in a better understanding of the conditions for realising environmental education and not in theory building (Stake 1998, pp. 88).

Through literature and document studies I will explore historical, economical, political and educational policies which have had an influence on education in general and environmental education specifically. By analysing the syllabi and their environmental education components, I will map out the planned environmental content. I will examine Tanzanian primary and secondary school teachers' conceptions and experiences of environmental education. Through interviews with teachers I concentrate on teachers' thinking and reasoning around the definition of, rationale for, and ways of learning environmental education. Through the interviews I hope to gather qualitatively different categories of understanding of environmental education. Furthermore, I will collect information, through questionnaires, in a quantitative base-line study on the occurrence of environmental education in schools, time allocation, resources, pre- or in-servicetraining of teachers and perceived problems. The base-line data will provide basic information about the working conditions of teachers and indicates differences, if any, between primary and secondary school teachers as well as between rural and urban areas. I will collect information about pupils' and students' understanding of environmental education through a questionnaire. The questionnaire will be the same for primary and secondary school although it is in Swahili for the former and in English for the latter. By entering schools and classrooms, I will observe the context of teaching as well as the teaching process.

The researcher

To what extent do the pre-conceptions of the researcher influence the result? This is not easy to answer but one part of the answer could be a brief presentation of the researcher herself. During my pre-school and early school years, I grow up in rural areas in northern Sweden. I have felt that to be a great asset for my work and research in Africa.

My professional background is dual; I am both a licensed psychologist and a teacher of psychology and education. My work experience as a psychologist and a secondary school teacher is short while my experience as a teacher trainer is long, almost 30 years. During 1982–1983 I worked with adult education in agriculture in Mozambique. I also taught for one year at a teacher training college in Kenya and made visits to students during their teaching practice in schools. This particular college, Kenya Science Teachers' College, was advanced, from a regional point of view, in the field of environmental studies. Later, I had the opportunity, in 1986, to participate and implement workshops and training for professionals within soil and water conservation. Soil erosion is one of the most common environmental problems in Eastern Africa. This work also included curriculum development. In Tanzania, during 1991–1993, I participated and lectured in workshops for teachers concerning environmental education and co-arranged a regional workshop in Kenya. I have studied syllabi for the Kenyan as well as Tanzanian school system. After 1993 I have worked, during shorter periods, in Ethiopia, Namibia and Botswana with environmental education issues. I consider myself to have sufficient knowledge of environmental education in relation to the purpose of my research, even if I am not an expert.

At the time of the interviews, I had lived and worked for four years in Mozambique and Kenya and one or two years in Tanzania. Hopefully, I had learnt how to approach people in a courteous way and with respect for authorities and elder colleagues. I was conscious of the necessity to demonstrate that I was not a governmental official on inspection duty but a non-threatening researcher who was grateful for co-operation. This was easier in the interviews with the secondary school teachers. The contact with the primary school teachers was mediated through an educational officer or my assistant and it was difficult for me to judge the emotional climate between them. The topic, however, was not of a provocative nature. I was at one point trained in interviewing people, although it had been quite some time since I professionally practised this particular field.

I will now present the theoretical approaches used in my study. My main approach has been the frame factor theory approach. I supplemented it with a study of teacher thinking using the phenomenographic research approach when analysing interviews with teachers.

The Frame Factor Theory Approach

The frame factor theory approach concentrated originally on physical frames (Dahllöf 1967) with time as an important frame factor. In the later development of the theory, frames of historical background were analysed, as well as the relation between social production and social reproduction (Lundgren 1984) and the theory has developed into a curriculum theory.

Factors that affect the work of the teacher are various political and administrative decisions. This influence on the learning outcome of the teaching process was developed into a curriculum theory by Urban Dahllöf (1971)—the frame factor theory-approach, later expanded by Ulf Lundgren (1972, 1981, 1984a, 1984b).

The learning outcome is assumed to be a product of the teaching process. Urban Dahlöf re-analysed the material of an earlier study using two different groups of pupils, lower secondary school and comprehensive school. Among other things, he analysed the time factor, i.e. how much time had been spent on different topics. He found that for every pedagogical process there are frame factors that will limit the outcome. The frame consisted of physical and time restrictions. His next question was, what kind of processes can occur? What organisational factors affect the teaching process? In its simplest form, it can be illustrated thus:

Frame factors → Teaching Process → Learning Outcome.

It is a straightforward, one-way chain of causes and effects.

The frames that are found within an educational organisation both limit and facilitate different processes and results. The frames are the external boundaries for the system of formal education and have an impact on school laws, curriculum development and physical structures (such as classrooms, school buildings) as well as the organisation of the school day (such as time tables, class sizes, age grouping).

Lundgren expanded the model to include three systems which are linked together; the *formal rule* system (school laws and school legislation), the *frame system* (the administrative apparatus), and the *goal system* (curriculum) (see Diagram 2).

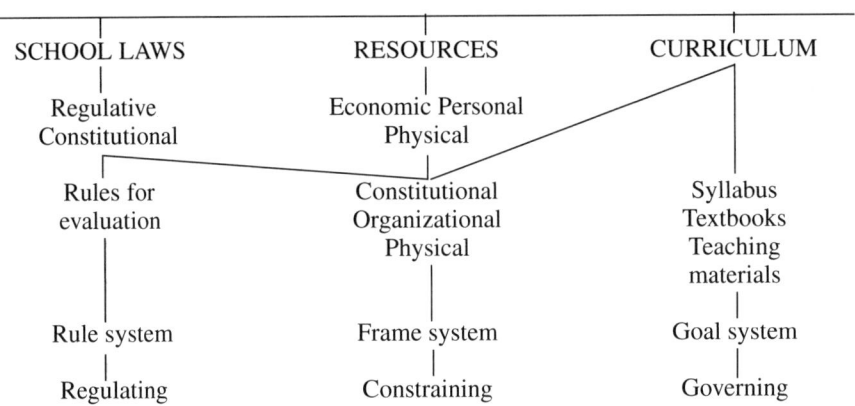

Diagram 2. Model of the frame factor theory approach. Ulf P. Lundgren (1972, pp. 94).

The *rule system* is about regulating and controlling the school. It regulates the duties of the teacher. There are rules concerning employment of teachers and demands on competence. There are also rules for evaluation, i.e. the examination, and control of the educational system, for example the school inspectorate.

Lundgren (1981) defined *frames* as factors that are products of decisions about the resources and organisation of teaching. He distinguished three different levels; the teaching unit (level I), the school unit (level II) and the educational system as a unit (level III). The decisions on level III will constrain decisions on level II, which will be frames for decisions on level I. Lundgren assumed that the concepts of frames could be grouped as constitutional, organisational and physical. Again, the different factors in the frame system have a constraining effect.

The *goal system* is comprised of concrete consequences of the curriculum. The curriculum can contain nation-wide syllabi with clear directions on content, time allocations and methodological directions in addition to general goals and objectives. In other cases the curriculum can serve as a guide and leave considerable autonomy to teachers and students. Then other means of controlling the content must be established, i.e. through examinations. Textbooks and teaching materials are included in the goal system. The purpose of the goal system is to steer.

The frame factor theory approach is related to education initiated, funded and steered by a government. In the classroom the activities are governed by the curriculum, and regulated and constrained by administrative and physical frames. It was developed during a period when education was ruled by central governmental authorities in Sweden, i.e. during the 1960s and 1970s, and is thus typical for that period of time. It reflects a top-down perspective in the educational system.

The frame factor theory approach has been used as a theoretical base for a number of researches on the teaching process (Lundgren 1972, Gustafsson 1977), evaluation (Franke-Wikberg & Lundgren 1980, Dahllöf 1991, Gustafsson 1994) and educational planning (Lindensjö & Lundgren 1986) to mention only a few.

Classroom teaching reflects the society and the reproduction processes in the society. Education is used as a political tool and will have an impact on the content of the curriculum and on the knowledge that is going to be learnt and later used in each particular society. How is the curriculum formulated and what is the outcome of its intentions?

The formulation and realisation of curriculum

In any society where production has been separated from reproduction, a representation problem will occur. Ulf Lundgren (1984b), whose work is important to this study, defined the concepts of production and reproduction in the following way:

> 1. Production processes, i.e., the creation of the necessities for social life and the creation of knowledge from which production can develop.
> 2. Reproduction processes, i.e., the re-creation and reproduction of knowledge from one generation to the next; the reproduction of knowledge and skills for production but also the reproduction of the conditions for production (Lundgren 1984b, pp. 10).

These two concepts are interrelated in the social and cultural context, as well as the conditions for social context and patterns of thinking. Social reproduction involves processes which constitute the reproduction of culture, knowledge and skills. Along with family life, education and schooling transmit culture. The representation problem concerns whether the production processes can be reproduced and is therefore the object for the educational discourse according to Lundgren.

The communication between production and reproduction will, in terms of the school, depend on texts, i.e. a curriculum. Reproduction can be differentiated into two aspects, the *context of formulation* (developing the curriculum) and the *context of realisation* (teaching in schools). The formulation process mirrors the educational ideals and intentions in the particular society and is related to the specifics of culture, politics and economics. Realisation depends on the conditions for teaching, i.e. economical, administrative and professional resources. The two processes are of course interrelated.

The goal system is thus separated into the context of formulation and the context of realisation (Lundgren 1984b, Lindensjö & Lundgren 1986). The context of formulation includes both political and administrative actors. The curriculum is used to implement political intentions and the policies formulated and decided upon by politicians. Furthermore, other actors are involved in the formulation process. On the political level, pressure groups such as organisations with specific interests (parents and teachers, for example), international organisations or political parties in opposition to the ruling party will make their voices heard in an attempt to have an impact on the aims and content of the curriculum. The aims concern not only reproduction of knowledge, skills and values but also desirable changes in society. The politicians are dependent on the administrators in the actual formulation of aims, objectives and content of the curriculum and syllabi. This is normally carried out on a central administrative level but interpreted for implementation at local levels.

Regarding the context of realisation there might be an additional level of interpretation. Besides the curriculum and syllabus, administrators write guidelines which are the interpretation of the political decisions. Curriculum, syllabus and guidelines are the base for the field implementation which is the work of the teachers in the school and the classroom. The last level is crucial for a successful implementation and is, among other factors, dependent on the professionalism and the competence (i.e. the quality and capacity for successful teaching) of the teachers.

What determines and limits the teacher's realisation of the curriculum?

The work of the teacher is determined by the circumstances in which it is being executed (the institution in a societal connection). The teacher who works within an educational system is thus influenced by what he or she thinks should be done, a perception of what is possible to do and the factors that constrain the realisation of these ambitions. The capability to manage such a situation is not something that is built into the system as such but is an effect of the development of professional competence, organisation of work, and control of what is going on, as well as of resources (Lindblad 1994).

Teachers' thinking and reasoning must be seen in a social and historical context (Carlgren & Lindblad 1991). The teacher's intention is steered by general motives but also by a judgement on the part of the society regarding the role of the teacher. The perception of the teaching role is related to the division of labour in the society—what is a teacher expected to do? This is determined on one hand by the duties formulated by administrators and on the other hand by the expectations of community members, i.e. the society. The ability of teachers to perform their duties restricts and determines the execution of their work. Teacher training has an effect on this ability but another factor is their earlier experiences of being a student and thereby having teachers as role models, which may be of equal importance. Furthermore, the social position of teachers plays a role in the execution of their work. Another restricting factor is the frames of teaching, as expressed by Lundgren and others.

Field investigation approaches

I have used three approaches for my field investigation. I am interested in teachers' conceptions of environmental education. Thus 'teacher thinking' research is a valuable source. A phenomenographic approach seems reasonable, to find how teachers are thinking about and experiencing environmental education. In this manner, the choice of interviewing follows as the method for collecting data. My approaches are presented below.

Teachers' thinking and reasoning

Teacher thinking research is comparatively young and there is an ongoing debate about its' purpose. This is shown, for instance, in the series of books derived from the conferences of the International Study Association on Teacher Thinking (ISATT) which was founded in 1984. The book, based on the contributions to the 1995 meeting, offered the following description of teacher thinking:

> 'Teacher thinking' is understood as encompassing several perspectives: teachers' thoughts, conceptions, practical theories, 'voice' etc.; teachers' intentions, thought processes and cognitions, personal practical knowledge; teachers' thinking as an aspect of professional actions; teachers' thinking and action as influenced by contextual factors in their structural, cultural and social environment (Kompf, Bond, Dworet and Boak 1996, pp. 2).

Teacher thinking research embraces a wide variety of issues and theoretical concepts, from the earliest work on the teacher as a decision-maker to trying to understand and interpret the ways in which teachers think and act in the classroom. Some of the concepts that are focused on are teachers' understandings, teacher constructs, decision-making strategies, beliefs, practical knowledge, personal intentions, teachers' cognition, teachers' cognitive activities, teachers' perspectives, teacher as a reflective practitioner, subjective theories and dilemmas (Pope 1993).

'Teacher thinking' has mainly been related to teachers as educators but ISATT has lately been discussing a change to 'teachers and teaching' which would also include the interests of teachers (Carlgren, Handal and Vaage 1994). Another issue discussed is whether research should be 'about' teacher knowledge or if it also should include research on what this knowledge is as well as acts of teaching.

The research tradition can be grouped into three major forms: positivist (striving for principles or generalisations that will facilitate prediction and control), phenomenological (understanding of particular individuals' perspectives), and critical (emancipation and sensitising of people through critical analysis), according to James Calderhead (1993). Maureen Pope (1993) based her grouping on Jürgen Habermas' categories; the positivist, the interpretative and the critical. The research methodologies consequently show a wide variety in quantitative and qualitative studies with an increasing interest in autobiographic and ethnographic approaches (Pope 1993, Hansen Nelson 1993, Kelchtermans 1993 and 1994, Day 1993, Knowles 1993). For my study, I have chosen the phenomenological form.

Mary Lynn Hamilton pointed out that although research has been done on individual teachers' beliefs, very little has been focused on group or cultural connections. She argued that an understanding of teachers' actions and beliefs must be done in connection with the cultural context (Hamilton 1993). She defined cultural model as a tacit, unspoken and taken-for-granted aspect of the world. The culture of the school, which shapes teachers' understanding of their actions, is linked to a larger social context. According to Hamilton, exploration of cultural models contributes to the understanding of teachers' decision making and the motives behind certain beliefs.

Ingrid Carlgren and Sverker Lindblad stressed the interaction of social and historical context in teachers' thinking and actions. They consider teachers' conceptions of the context in their professional world as important links in the complex interplay between internal and external determinants on teaching (Carlgren and Lindblad 1991).

The impact of the social context on knowledge, as inherent in cultural, physical and material, social, historical and personal systems, as opposed to the idea that knowledge is only acquired and applied by the individual, was also discussed by Robert Yinger and Martha Hendricks-Lee (1993). They put forward two categories of working knowledge of schools; *technical orientation or intelligence* which emphasises technical problem-solving based on specialised scientific knowledge and *ecological intelligence* which emphasises that intelligence is embedded in social, cultural and practical exchanges as well as in individuals. The life in the classroom is constituted by the lives outside the classroom and the cultural, physical, social, historical and personal systems which exist.

The teacher as a reflective practitioner is a field of great interest. In teacher education the concepts of reflective teaching, action research, research-based and inquiry-oriented have been common during the last decade (Zeichner 1994). The teacher is not seen as a passive actor in a top-down educational system but as a bearer of knowledge and theories about teaching. This wealth of knowledge has been called 'knowledge-in-action.' Ingrid Carlgren emphasises another concept, also coined by Schön—reflection-in-action—which includes not only the carrying out of teaching but also its design (Carlgren 1996).

My research will focus on teachers as bearers of knowledge and not on teachers in action.

Phenomenography—a research approach

There is a difference between what a subject matter, phenomenon, concept or principle is and how a person understands the subject matter, phenomena, concept or principle. The first aspect, what something is, is called the first-order perspective. The second aspect, how people understand what it is, is called the second-order perspective. People's understanding of various phenomena and the like differ qualitatively in a limited number of ways. Ference Marton exemplified this in his study on teenager students' physical explanations of sight, i.e. the fact that we can see an object in front of us:

> A. The link between eyes and object is 'taken for granted'; it is not problemised; 'you simple see' (the necessity of light may be pointed out and an explanation of what happens inside the system may be given).
> B. There is a picture going from the object to the eyes. When it reaches the eyes, we see.
> C. There are beams coming from the eyes. When they hit the object, we see.
> D. There are beams going back and forth between the eyes and the object. The eyes send out beams which hit the object, return and tell the eyes about it.
> E. The object reflects light, and when it hits the eyes we can see the object (Marton, 1990, pp. 144).

The students' explanations illustrate a research method for surveying the different ways in which people experience, understand, perceive and conceptualise various aspects of their surrounding world. This qualitative research method was developed by a research group at the Department of Education, Gothenburg University, during the 1970s (Marton, Dahlgren, Svensson, Säljö 1977) and was later coined phenomenography (Marton 1981). The aim is to try to understand differences in peoples' ways of thinking and understanding various aspects in life.

In phenomenographic research a starting point is that people have different understandings of reality. Different understandings are explained as different people having different experiences due to their different relations to the world around them. People make different interpretations and reach different knowledge about various aspects and objects. The researcher tries to describe these differences and variations in understandings (Alexandersson 1994).

The major characteristics of phenomenography, according to Hazel Francis, are an attempt to capture conceptualisations which are reflections of the individual's experience of the learning phenomenon and aims to categorise conceptions of learning and to explore relations amongst them (Francis 1996, pp. 36).

A broader description was given by John A. Bowden. Phenomenography is used to study a range of issues, including approaches to learning, teaching and understanding of scientific phenomena learned in school or of general issues unrelated to the educational system. He made a distinction between research methods and theory of learning—outcomes of phenomenographic research can be dealt with in a broad framework which has its base in a characteristic theory of learning. But outcomes can be used in quite a different framework as well. The relation between the individuals' conceptions and the categories of description is problematic—they are often used interchangeably. Bowden favoured a definition which states that individuals' conceptions are presented in form of categories of descriptions and that the basic idea is to identify and describe individuals' conceptions as faithfully as possible. This indicates a distinction between conceptions and categories (Bowden 1996, pp. 49).

Biörn Hasselgren's answer to, What is phenomenography?, was that it is a qualitative analysis of transcribed semi-structured interviews or conversations which have been conducted together with the research subjects by the researchers themselves (Hasselgren 1996, pp. 68).

There are two aspects of ways of experiencing: what and how. The what-aspect is concentrated on the object of the thought process, being physical or mental to its nature. Statements are made about the world, about phenomena and about situations. The how-aspect is the demarcation of the thought process. This is the (underlying) ways of experiencing the world, the phenomena or the situation of which we usually are not aware of (Marton 1996).

Contextualisation and de-contextualisation are two other important concepts. Decontextualisation means that ways of experiencing the world are disconnected from their context, as expressed (described) in the interview. Contextualisation implies that content, form and context are analysed in relations to the ways of experiencing (Uljens 1989).

Marton explained that the nature of phenomenographic research is *non-dualistic*. Subject and object are not separated since how the subject experiences the object constitutes a relation between them. There are not two worlds but a real objective and a subjective world consisting of mental images and comprising only one world, a real existing world that people experience and understand in different ways. Experiencing such a world involves a relation between an object and a subject. The experiencing is as much an aspect of the object as an aspect of the subject. 'How the subject experiences the object' is synonymous with 'how the object reveals itself to the subject' (Marton 1992, pp. 30). It is said that the object is not identical with how it is experienced but that the object encompasses the different ways in which it can be experienced. The different ways of experiencing are related to each other in a logical way since they are different ways of experiencing the same object (Marton 1992, pp. 31). One way of experiencing is only one of several different aspects that taken together constitute what is experienced.

First- and second-order perspectives of ways of experiencing the life-world is a central concept in phenomenography. Statements about the world, phenomena and situations are first-order perspectives while statements about the ways people experience the world phenomena and about situations are second-order perspective.

From a first-order perspective we find phenomena that can be demarcated to some extent. They can be experienced several times by an individual without changing, for example a stone, a scientific text etc. (Uljens 1989). Within a second-order perspective some phenomena cannot be fully described by the researcher. When we are investigating second-order perspectives of any phenomena, we are concentrating on a variation of conceptions of that phenomenon. Marton explained that we are talking about the thing as experienced and we are looking for qualitatively different ways of experiencing the actual phenomenon regardless of whether the differences are within or between individuals (individual or collective level).

As stated above, the researcher cannot demarcate in advance the second-order perspective. What the interviewees say (the what-aspect) about a phenomenon demarcates the way they experience it (the how-aspect). The implication of this is that the answers in the interviews give both a background for comprehension against which the ways of experiencing should be analysed and expressions for qualitatively different ways of experiencing (Uljens 1989, pp. 33).

The researcher interpreting the material is a bearer of a specific cultural context and a personal history. The interpretation will thus be done based on a background that is different from the background of the interviews. This problem could be solved to some extent, according to Uljens, if the researcher and the interviewee share the cultural context as well as the language. Then there might be a higher probability that they are talking about the same phenomena, which is vital for the validity aspect.

This quote by Marton can be seen as a summary of the definition of phenomenography:

> In phenomenography individuals are seen as the bearers of different ways of experiencing various phenomena, and even as the bearers of fragments of different ways of experiencing various phenomena. The description is a description of variation, a description on the collective level. Moreover, it is a stripped description where the structure and essential meaning of the different ways of experiencing the phenomena is left, while the specific flavour, the scent and colour of the life-world is gone. Phenomenography is simply an attempt to capture critical differences in how we experience the world and how we learn to experience the world. Nothing more and nothing less (Marton 1996, pp. 187).

In this study I will use the phenomenographic approach for exploring teachers' different ways of experiencing environmental education. Thus, environmental education will be the what-aspect and how teachers think about the issue will be the how-aspect.

Interviews as a research method

An interview is a conversation between people, a specialised form of communication for a specific purpose on some agreed subject matter (Anderson 1997). The use of the interview as a research method within the social sciences has a relatively short history. It has been a common method within anthropology and sociology but normally the positivistic approaches used in natural sciences have been used as models. Steinar Kvale (1997) made an attempt to summarise the main aspects or comprehensive form of the qualitative research interview. The objective of such interviews, he said, is to obtain descriptions of the world of life of the respondent in order to be able to interpret the meaning of the described phenomena. The topic of the qualitative interview is the world of life of the respondent and his/her relation to it. The interview tries to interpret the meaning of central themes in the respondent's world. The interviewer registers and interprets the meaning of what is said and how it is said. Descriptions of specific situations and actions are sought after, not general opinions. The interviewer shows an openness towards new and unexpected phenomena instead of having ready-made categories and models for interpretation. The pronouncements of the respondent can sometimes have various meanings and reflect contradictions of the world in which he or she lives. Different interviewers can cause a person to respond differently to questions depending on shifting sensitivity for or knowledge about the topic of the interview. The knowledge that emanates from the interview is a result of inter-human interplay (ibid. pp. 35).

The interview is thus an inter-view where information and data are constructed rather than found. This interactive view of interviews implies that the role of the interviewer is critical. The interviewer takes part in the construction of the outcome of the interview or, to put it differently, the outcome is created during the interview.

In Tanzania the accessibility of documents, records and reports is awkward. Some things are not documented and/or registered and access is limited, not to mention, time-consuming. The result is that at times information is best gathered by approaching people and listening to what they have to say. I thus consider that in my case interviews are the best way of collecting peoples' ways of experiencing a phenomenon.

CHAPTER 3
Realisation of the study

Introduction

My fieldwork included study and analysis of curriculum and questions in national examinations. A questionnaire has been answered by 1,410 pupils. I have interviewed 75 teachers and analysed them from a phenomenographic approach (Marton 1981, 1990, 1992, 1996). This approach implies that the collective aspects of opinions and reflections are de-contextualised. I have tried to supplement the interviews with visits to schools and classes, in order to be able to relate to the context in which the interviews were performed. When approaching the school and the classroom, there are a number of aspects to consider. Apart from the selection process, there is also the question of how to gain access as well as how to be accepted. Sara Delamont (1992) stresses, among other things, the importance of reflexivity, meaning that research includes interactions and inter-relationship with the respondents.

Empirical procedure

The educational system in Tanzania can be understood only in relation to its historical background. I felt it was necessary to map out the economic and political development of the country, especially after independence in 1961. Educational policies were another important frame factor to be studied as well as regulating and governing factors. This information could be found in documents, for example reports and official statistics, and literature such as books of history, doctoral theses, UNESCO publications and others.

To find out what I wanted to know about teachers' ways of experiencing environmental education, I needed to interview some of them. I also needed to study their work places, e.g. the schools and their surroundings. To get a glimpse of pupils' and students' knowledge of environmental education issues, I asked a number of questions using a questionnaire. The teachers and the students came from the same school, with both primary and secondary level.

The results of the interviews were analysed using a phenomenograpic approach while the results of the questionnaire was analysed according to quantitative methods.

In this chapter I present the empirical procedure: how schools and teachers were selected and how questions were posed and interviews implemented. I also present the problems I faced during the field work and doubts about the reliability of official statistic data. Finally I describe how I have processed the data from the interviews.

Collection of field data

The data was collected from January 1992 to May 1993. I visited one region at a time and called on primary and secondary schools as well as teacher training colleges.

The beginning of the 1990s was a time when the political, economical and educational policies were all in a transition period. The one-party state was breaking up, a market-oriented economy was developing fast and the educational system was being questioned. The Minister of Education had appointed a task force to re-examine the education system in order to sort out the current strengths and weaknesses and report their findings in 1993.

During these years the financial strains were felt in the schools. The Ministry of Education and Culture had increasing difficulties in fulfilling its obligations to teachers and schools. The food situation in boarding schools and colleges was aggravated. Besides that, the country suffered from energy shortages and electricity was rationed. For rural schools, this had very little impact, but for urban, as well as boarding schools and colleges, it meant that they had to collect and use their own wood fuel.

The implications of this for my research is difficult to discern. The economical crisis had started in the beginning of the 1980s and had had a visible effect on the school system since then. In my opinion, the time for my collection of field data occurred during a time when the educational system and the situation of the teachers were almost at their peak (that is, bottom) of decline.

Procedure

How the schools were chosen

The Faculty of Education at the University of Dar es Salaam trained teachers for secondary schools. For their teaching practice they were using most of the schools in the country. One person—a male professor at the time—was in charge of planning teaching practice. That meant that he had to visit most of the schools every year. I went to him and explained that I wanted a suggestion of at least one urban and one rural secondary school which were used for teaching practice in the regions I was interested in. My only restriction was

Table 2: *Schools visited for data collection during 1992–1993*

Region and districts	Primary School rural/urban	Secondary School rural/urban
Arusha		
District A	Primary One (rural), Primary Two (urban)	Secondary Three (urban)
District B	None	Secondary Four (rural)
District C	None	Secondary Five (rural)
Dar es Salaam		
District A	Primary Six (industrial setting), Primary Seven (industrial setting)	Secondary Twelve (urban), Secondary Thirteen (rural)
District B	Primary Eight (urban), Primary Nine (rural setting)	Secondary Fourteen (urban)
District C	Primary Ten (urban), Primary Eleven (urban)	None
Kilimanjaro		
District A	Primary Fifteen (rural setting), Primary Sixteen (rural)	Secondary Seventeen (urban)
District B	None	Secondary Eighteen (rural)
Morogoro		
District A	Primary Nineteen (urban)	Secondary Twenty (urban), Secondary Twenty-one (urban)

that they should be fairly easy to reach in terms of road conditions. I did not want the best ranked schools in terms of examination results. The chosen secondary schools are listed in Table 2.

In 1990, the results of the national exams in English showed that there were another 93 secondary schools with lower results than Secondary Five and 37 schools with better results than Secondary Twenty-one. This is out of a total of 298 schools. Grade A pass was awarded 1 mark, grade B pass 2 marks and so on, down to 5 marks. A low mean indicated good grades for the students. As can be seen in Table 3, the results varied and from that point of view fitted my criteria. The number of students failing the test is also presented.

I applied to the Ministry of Education for permission to visit these schools. At the same time I also asked for permission to visit a number of urban and rural primary schools in the same districts as the secondary. (Since my choice was focused on the secondary schools, I did not know which primary schools I was to visit until I came to the district office. I did not collect examination results for them.)

There was quite a bureaucratic procedure before I could be visiting the schools. I had a general research clearance from the Tanzania Commission for Science and Technology and a specific clearance from the Ministry of Education in Dar es Salaam. The ministry sent information letters to the Regional Development Director (a position directly under the Regional Commissioner).

Table 3: *Mean marking values in national form IV English national examination in 1990 (marking range 1–5 with 1 as the 'best' score)*

School	Region	Mean score	Percent of failures
Secondary Twenty-one	Morogoro	3.39	20
Secondary Seventeen	Kilimanjaro	3.44	19
Secondary Eighteen	Kilimanjaro	3.48	20
Secondary Three	Arusha	3.50	11
Secondary Fourteen	Dar es Salaam	3.60	22
Secondary Twelve	Dar es Salaam	3.71	25
Secondary Twenty	Morogoro	3.74	23
Secondary Thirteen	Dar es Salaam	4.16	41
Secondary Four	Arusha	4.40	33
Secondary Five	Arusha	4.56	65

From the ministry, I also got introduction letters to the Regional Educational Officers and the heads of secondary schools as well as to the directors of the teacher training colleges, who are called principals in Tanzania.

When I first arrived in a region, I introduced myself to the Regional Development Director and got an introduction letter to the Regional Educational Officer. I went there and stated my business and got an introduction letter to the District Educational Officer. The District Educational Officers assisted me in the choice of urban and rural primary schools according to my criteria. Since all schools were ranked in terms of results of final exams, I wanted to visit those schools that had average results, i.e. not the schools with the best or lowest results. In some cases my wish in that respect was not granted but I was referred to schools with usually good results in the Standard VII exams. The District Education Officer allocated one or two of the staff to assist me. They travelled with me to the schools and also acted as interpreters (the teaching medium being Swahili). In the districts of the Dar es Salaam region, I employed an assistant who did all the interviews according to my instructions and in my presence.

How the interviewed teachers were chosen

I asked to meet and interview teachers in the following subjects: agriculture, domestic science/home economics[1], geography, chemistry/ physics/mathematics or science (at primary level). I chose the subjects according to my preconception of where environmental education components might be found, after I had studied the curricula. The head of the school informed the teachers and asked them to co-operate. I interviewed the teachers who were available on the actual day when I visited the school (see Table 4 and 5). Often they just left their classes for my sake although I tried as much as possible to find lesson-free time.

---

[1] In primary school the subject is called domestic science while in secondary school it is called home economics.

Table 4: *Distribution of the interviewed teachers, sex and subjects in primary schools*

Sex	Agriculture	Domestic science	Geography	Science	Total
M	1	0	4	4	9
F	8	9	5	7	29

Table 5: *Distribution of the interviewed teachers, sex and subjects in secondary schools*

Sex	Agriculture	Biology	Chemistry	Geography	Home economics	Physics	Total
M	3	5	3	5	0	2	18
F	0	6	1	7	5	0	19

At each school three to five teachers were interviewed. In the primary schools, interviews took place through an interpreter. In the secondary schools, I did the interviews myself and taped and later transcribed them. The interviews in Swahili were all transcribed and translated by the same person who conducted the interviews in the Dar es Salaam region. I interviewed 38 teachers in primary schools and 37 in secondary schools.

Data about teaching experience was not properly collected. The age of the teachers varied from c 23 up to 45 years. Their teaching experience varied from two to twenty-two years with a statistical mean of c 12 years.

How the questions were posed

I collected the data through interviews and questionnaires. The teachers were presented with a small number of open questions (see below) and their reflections were tape-recorded. Afterwards, in most cases, they were asked to fill in a questionnaire. The same questions were used for both primary and secondary school teachers but in different languages—Swahili in primary and English in secondary school.

The number of introductory questions in the interviews were four and they were presented to the teachers in written form, in Swahili for primary and in English for secondary school teachers. The teachers were thus able to start reflecting on the questions they felt were most easy for them and then answer with whatever came into their minds. Most of them started with the first question, especially the primary school teachers. The four questions were: What is environmental education? What should be the content? Why is environmental education important? How should it be learnt?

These questions were not related to any special text as in studies made by

Marton et al. (1977), or related to specific problems that students solved in front of the researcher as in studies made by Leif Lybeck, H. Strömdahl & A. Tullberg (1985), Dagmar Neuman (1987) or John A. Bowden (1996). Instead my questions belonged to the second large category in which people are able to reflect upon 'what is x' as in studies made by Larsson (1982, 1986).

It should be observed that a problem with the type of questions I have used is that they were not placed in a context. In a particular context, the teachers might have understood the topic differently or concentrated on different aspects of the topic. Or they might have no experience at all of environmental education.

Michael Uljens (1989) demonstrated this problem by using the example of a matchbox. The problem which the researcher poses to the interviewee is the box itself. The interviewees can watch the box from several different angles, viewing the box accordingly from different perspectives. A basic starting point for discussion is whether the interviewee has any way of experiencing the box at all (Uljens 1989, pp. 37). Roger Säljö (ibid. 1996, pp. 31–32) had similar critical points as well as Bowden (ibid. 1996, pp. 58) and Lindblad (1983, pp. 36). On the other hand, Marton (1996, pp. 175 ff.) argued that we cannot describe the world in independent terms, for the world is not independent of our descriptions or of us as describers. It is a world experienced by us and each human being has a unique experience. He claimed that knowledge is an internal relationship between the person and the world and that the interesting thing is how the relationship between the two changes. Uljens (1989, pp. 27) asserted that this question is a problem that has not yet been solved and he maintained that it is shared by all qualitative research methodologies. The main problem is, of course, a question of validity.

Pertinent to my research, however, is the fact that during 1990–1993, which was a crucial time for this research, there were a number of national environment campaigns organised by the Ministry of Agriculture. One was 'Plant a tree, cut a tree', another 'Stop burning forests', a third 'Modern farming' and a fourth 'Conserve water resources'. The campaigns were propagated through radio programmes, posters set up around the country (at health stations, schools, regional and district offices etc.) and by agricultural advisers at regional, district and local levels. The campaigns had the farmer and his family as a focus. Since so many of the teachers had extra economic activities and to an overwhelming extent these were related to farming practices, it was very likely that they were reached by the messages. During 1992 there was a very popular radio programme, 'Hafadhi ya Mazingira', which was a dramatisation about a person who indiscriminately cut down the forest, and the programme took up the consequences and kinds of problems that followed. The programme was created by the National Environmental Management Council and had an environmental education purpose. A large majority of the population has access to radios and the radio programmes normally have a good number of listeners. (Some of the interviewed teachers referred to this programme.) In addition, Wort (1998) has pointed out that many primary school teachers had their teacher training through distance education which also used radio broadcasting for transmitting education (ibid. pp. 84).

The National Environmental Management Council and some of the non-governmental organisations (NGOs) did have competitions for pupils, such as essay writing or drawing of pictures on environmental issues. The competitions were administrated by the teachers. It did not reach all schools of course, but it did reach some. The Danish International Development Agency (Danida) had competitions between schools in their School Maintenance Programme (repairs of roofs, electrical fittings, sewage etc.) for secondary schools. Prizes were based on which school had made the best environmental improvement or conservation of its compound. In these competitions, the teachers were involved as well and the prizes were attractive (competitions were a common means of motivating schools to take action on different issues; these could be improvements of the surroundings or essay writing on specific environmental topics etc.). In some schools I was shown what they were attempting to do in order to win the competition.

I also observed that the daily newspapers had articles on environmental education issues, at least once a week. But the editions were small and reached only a fraction of the urban population. The secondary schools, which I visited for this research, normally had access to one or two daily newspapers which were kept in their staff rooms. In the primary schools I did not see any newspapers.

I would therefore argue that the research questions were not totally decontextualised. The concept of environment and environmental conservation was probably rather well established in the minds of the radio listeners. The secondary school teachers had more opportunities to absorb environmental education approaches or discussions as compared to primary school teachers.

How the interviews were performed

The interview is a crucial point in qualitative research and the role of the interviewer has been analysed by, for example, Kvale (1997). He put forward a number of requirements for an interviewer (ibid., pp. 138–139), which I will use as the basis for comments on my own qualifications as an interviewer as well as on the implementation of the interviews (see Chapter 2).

The teachers were interviewed one by one in the secondary schools and in groups (but answering one by one) in primary schools, where an interpreter was also present. I asked for permission before taping the interview. It was always granted. We looked for and found a place to sit together, where there was as little interference as possible from other people. It was not always quiet, comfortable or 'cosy' but at least other people not involved in the interviews were not present.

I presented the purpose of the interview, what kind of questions that would be asked, and at the end I always asked if there was anything else the interviewees wanted to touch on or develop. The interviewees were informed that they could talk freely around the four questions that were given and that they could start with whichever one they wanted. My participation was mostly limited to 'uh-humming' supportively when it was necessary. I also elaborated on a question or asked for clarification at times.

I think that in most cases I managed to let the interviewees express their viewpoints and avoid being the one who directed the interview. I also discussed this approach with my assistant for the primary school interviews in Dar es Salaam. However, due to language difficulties, my control over how the educational officers approached the primary school teachers in the other regions was very limited. The attitude from the school leaders could be considered a problematic influence at times. For example, on some occasions when the head teacher summoned the primary school teachers to the interviews, the head teacher was saying to me in front of the teachers, that 'you won't get any answers from them—they don't know anything about it.' In secondary schools I seldom met this attitude, but then the comments about the teachers' knowledge was made only when I was alone. I was always conscious of the need for empathy and can only hope that I was able to show it.

The interviewer should, however, still have control over what is said in order to attain the purpose of the interview. This was facilitated through the fact that the questions I wanted the teachers to reflect upon were written in English or Swahili. Each teacher got his/her own copy which was lying on the table in front of them or, if no tables were available, on their knees. I believe that the content of the interviews was steered by the teachers in the secondary schools themselves. This is reflected by the fact that the responses of the teachers showed variety.

In the primary schools, the necessity to work through an interpreter made the flow of speech and interactions less free. The teachers tended to concentrate mostly on answering the questions and hence, seldom discussed or presented their own private ideas. Outside Dar es Salaam I was normally assisted by a District Educational Officer. In the Dar es Salaam region, I had a university student at the Faculty of Education as my assistant. She was, to some extent, trained in interviewing since she had participated in other educational studies. I discussed the purpose of my study with her and we analysed the interview situation after each interview. In Dar es Salaam primary schools, the answers were much more restricted than in the secondary schools.

Checking the reliability of the answers during the interview, *remembering* what was said by whom, for example, making short summaries, and *interpreting* statements made by the interviewee are aspects or requirements of the interviews which I tried to carry through. After the initial interviews I also started to ask what kind of environmental changes the teacher had experienced during the last ten years. I got interesting answers which indicated that the teachers generally were very aware of environmental problems in their home area.

After the interviews the teachers were asked to fill in a questionnaire (in a few cases it was done before). The reason for this was that I wanted to secure certain factual information which I did not collect earlier because I did not want these facts to govern the interviews.

My impression is that my accent of English was easily understood by the interviewees (Scandinavian accents of English are generally well understood by East Africans, since especially the Swedish sounds are very similar to Swahili).

Problems encountered during field work

In Tanzania two different languages are used in primary and secondary education. Most often neither of them is the first language of the pupils. There are about 120 different languages in the country. Swahili as a mother tongue is generally spoken along the coast and in the urban areas. In primary schools, one could expect Swahili to be fairly established in Standard VII, although findings from the previous years indicated that much needed to be done to improve the conditions. Due to the lack of textbooks in the schools, especially at primary level, pupils had few opportunities to improve their language competence. When they (the selected few) reached the secondary level, their performance in English was often so low that remedial training was necessary. The majority was still not fluent by Form IV (see for example Table 3).

The questions in the questionnaire were short, and seemed simple and clear to me. Before I used them, I had asked four primary school teachers to read and assess if the questions could be easily understood by pupils. Their opinion was that the language of the questions was not difficult to understand. My presumption was, that if the questions were accepted as suitable for Standard VII, they would also be understood by Form IV students. I pilot-tested the questionnaire in the Morogoro region. I did, however, make slight changes in the formulation of a few of the questions.

When I visited the school directors, I always presented a copy of the intended general (four) interview questions. This was simply to declare my intention. To my knowledge, the questions were not used to prepare anyone for the interviews.

None of the participating teachers were specifically prepared in advance to answer the questions, since I wanted their immediate comments and reflections. Primary school teachers sometimes asked for ten minutes to prepare themselves, which was granted. I was searching for a variation of conceptions of environmental education and it is not possible to ask a person directly about his or her conceptions (Carlgren 1990). Instead I informed them that I wanted to discuss environmental education, as part of a research project. In a few cases I did permit teachers to prepare themselves during a couple of days, when they insisted, but the result was that I was given a 'lecture' or written statement, which I had to disregard because the conditions were not comparable with the other interviews.

The teachers in primary schools were trained in Swahili and their knowledge of English varied. Since many lacked sufficient confidence, they hesitated to speak English although in most cases they understood English. After a while on some occasions, it was possible for me to participate in the interviews without help from the interpreter. In a few cases, I was able to conduct the entire interview in English. Most of the primary school teachers, however, expressed their views in Swahili. Their comments were taped and later transcribed and translated into English. Generally, their comments were short and concise. Very few associated freely but kept a rather strict line of thoughts. I very much felt the language barrier when I worked through an interpreter. It was difficult to follow up an answer or viewpoint, although I was always present. However, later, when I employed an assistant (who was instructed to follow up answers or reactions) who conducted the entire interviews on her own, I noticed, that the comments from the teachers were not essentially more extensive than when I acted through an interpreter.

In secondary schools teachers are supposed to teach in English but not all of them were confident in the use of this language. However, as far as I could see, the teachers I interviewed showed no restrictions or hesitations in expressing their opinions in the interviews. I can sympathise with the communication issues because English is also my second language and I have done most of my practise of it in Kenya and Tanzania. Alas, I cannot claim to speak grammatically correct English and my accent is not British but rather East African. Although I have experience of teaching students in English and have held a number of workshops in English for teachers and instructors in Eastern Africa, I cannot claim that my understanding of concepts was always correct. I would, however, argue that this is the case in many communication situations.

The language problem at all school levels is well known in Tanzania and whether or not to use Swahili as an instruction medium throughout the formal educational system has been the subject of debate. This led to the strengthening of English in 1984. In her study, Birgit Brock-Utne (1993) asked if the use of English had political and economical links. Because of the economic crises, the former colonial language gained a more powerful position which was also due to its link to the capitalist system. She referred, among other things, to a statement of Zaline Makini Roy-Campbell which points to the interests of strengthening the English language in the former British colonies (ibid. pp. 43). It was also claimed that English language teaching was a good business for publishers in Britain. Furthermore, she claimed that the use of English was an effective barrier to learning science and technology and to restoring the heritage culture (see also Buchert 1994 and Wort 1998 on the language and learning issue).

According to my experience, use of the English language causes serious problems in most secondary schools. During the first year, it is necessary to have remedial classes in English but that is not enough. I have heard teachers using both English and a fast translation into Swahili while I have been visiting schools, not on single occasions but regularly. I have witnessed how difficult it is for the teachers, too; they must teach in English but prefer to communicate between themselves in Swahili. During a span of about five years, I saw students' incomplete and erroneous English and their misinterpretations of a topic in written 'tests' in Form III. It is hard to maintain an English-speaking environment in secondary schools although it is agreed that this is necessary if the students are to be able to develop their language competence. There are, of course, exceptions, especially in the schools that have the best examination results in the country.

Statistical data—to what extent are they true?
In my data collection, I will use statistical data from relevant ministries and other sources. How credible are they?

The reliability of statistics can be discussed in general terms. Numerical data can give a false sense of precision. The situation in Africa has been discussed in detail by Joel Samoff (1991) who exemplified using the situation in Tanzania. Due to the emphasis on education after independence and the involvement of many donor agencies, Tanzania had an extensive source of information.

> Many of the problems with Tanzanian education data are precisely those encountered elsewhere. Carelessly or purposefully, head teachers miscount their students. Their reports do not arrive in the district education office. The figures for boys and girls may be reversed. Many head teachers do, while others do not, include repeaters in their counts. Some students are, inadvertently or intentionally, listed twice. More or less carefully constructed guesses fill in for missing information. This process is then repeated at the regional level. Since recording figures gain credibility, errors propagate. These problems are compounded by difficulties of communication and transport, and by the hostility of the tropical climate to the storage of paper. All of this is commonplace, the sort of challenges all field researchers must face. Some data problems, however, are specific to the Tanzanian situation. (Samoff 1991, pp. 670–671).

What Samoff meant was that there was an official as well as an unofficial system. In some areas there were nearly twice as many children in primary school as the official records reported. Schools run by for example local churches had been established due to the demand. Although this was known to the educational officers, they did not want to report such data since all primary schools were supposed to be run by the government. Samoff estimated that the official school population reported in the Kilimanjaro region amounted to only 50–60 percent of its actual size in late 1960s. The same phenomenon was occurring concerning secondary schools during the 1990s.

Samoff looked into the expenditures of education. He found that different and contradicting conclusions were drawn by different external agencies, such as UNESCO, Sida or the World Bank, although the same statistical raw data were used. This was a serious situation since the extent of grants, loans and aid programmes was based on these conclusions. A striking example was taken from the different estimates of recurrent expenditures in education. Samoff showed that the discrepancies between lowest and highest values on recurrent expenditures among different agencies between 1965 and 1981 varied between 2 and 10 percent, with about 5 percent more common than below (Samoff 1991, pp. 681). It should be noted that, as stated above, the same statistical raw data was used. This indicates that statistical data from ministries, for example, might be considered more reliable than interpretations from different aid agencies. However, no statistical raw data reports the actual situation as it is, so the level of reliability is still doubtful.

In the next chapters I will refer to statistical data, most of it compiled by the Ministry of Education and Culture in Tanzania. Although I am aware of the problem of reliability, I am left with no alternative.

Data processing

Transcription of the interviews

My interviews were taped with the help of a portable tape recorder of good quality, using batteries as energy source and with an additional microphone. Not all primary schools have access to electricity, and if they did it was used for lightning only—there are no sockets in the classrooms. Although most secondary schools were electrified, the lack of sockets was common. Besides, during the years when I conducted the interviews, there was a rationing of electricity in Tanzania. The recording conditions were not the best considering the environmental circumstances, but the sound quality was, nonetheless, quite good. We always made a 'trial run' at the beginning of the interview to check if everything was working. Besides, many of the teachers had never heard themselves recorded. This became part of the introductory preliminaries and it helped to release possible tensions before the interview. The transcriptions of the interviews in the secondary schools were done by myself and those in the primary schools were done by my university student assistant, who also translated them into English.

Transcription of interviews and the related considerations have been discussed by several researchers. Kvale (1997) emphasised that the written version is a construction of oral communication. One has to translate an oral language with its special rules and constructions into a written language with other rules and constructions. The transcription is an interpretation made by the transcriber, which will have an impact on reliability. Is everything transcribed or was something excluded or shortened? Kvale points out problems such as: When is a sentence completed? Body language and emphasis is lost. For example, how do you reflect cultural ways of expressing oneself? When should a silence be considered a pause? How do you transcribe a tense voice, giggling or nervous laughter (ibid. 1997 pp. 151)? He suggested that there might not be any solutions to such questions. The validity of the transcription is even more difficult. The oral interview is conducted in a context which cannot be re-created in written form. In the interview we have access to the implications of what is said but in the written transcription, the meaning is hidden. Transcripts are decontextualised conversations between two people; they are abstract in the same ways as topographic maps. Some aspects are there, others are omitted (Kvale 1997 pp. 152). But through transcription we get data in a form that makes an analysis possible.

In the secondary school interviews, I decided to try to transcribe everything that could be heard on the tape. Change of speaker (the interviewer or the interviewee) was indicated by a new line and a hyphen. A pause was indicated by 3–4 dots (but not related to time). Repetitions were taken down. Inarticulate sounds were indicated by uhhm, ehhh, yahh, ahhh (with the 'h's indicating the Tanzanian tendency to draw out the sound). If it was not possible to discriminate what was said, I indicated this by ...xxxxxx... In the primary schools interviews, my assistant had a more difficult situation. The interviews made in Swahili were also to be translated into English. In the process the sentences became more similar to written language than to oral language.

What have I lost by transcribing the interviews? The transcription is built on interpretations which are incomplete.

The advantage of transcription is that I obtained an overview of the material which facilitated my analyses. For my particular case, with 75 interviews, this has undoubtedly been of help. Organisation and categorisation of the content were facilitated.

Ways of experiencing and ways of finding categories of descriptions

When using the phenomenographic research approach, the phenomenon in focus will reveal itself to the researcher during the process of research, according to Marton (1992 pp. 28). By investigating a phenomenon we will get information about it. These statements are not always true for the research outcome, but as Marton claimed this is the case when using phenomenography and he referred to the research done over two decades.

Of course there are some methodological problems involved. One of the problems that faces researchers when using decontextualised interviews on a specific topic is, as has been mentioned earlier, the question of whether the different interviewees are describing the same phenomena or not. Lindblad (1983) has suggested one approach that might improve the situation—an analysis made in two steps. The first step is to examine what the interviewees are talking about and referring to. This is referred to as description of domains. The second step is to scrutinise the thinking and reflections of the interviewees regarding the actual phenomena. This is referred to as comparisons of statements within each domain.

Uljens (1989) considered this approach as a procedure with a pattern consisting of 'starting in the whole—division into pieces—going back to the whole.' An interviewee can be found to be within several domains on the same occasion. Through this procedure it is possible to get categories of descriptions for the ways interviewees experience what exists for each single domain. As a part of step two, the categories of descriptions are integrated. The interviewees are distributed according to the categories of descriptions. The concordance between the logical considerations of the relations between the categories and the empirical relations between the categories constitute a value of validity (ibid. pp. 36).

When my interviews were transcribed, I tried to apply the approach of an analysis in two steps. First, I read the interviews several times. I marked with colours all statements about what, cut them out and tried to match them with each other in different groups of statements. I did the same thing again, this time working with the word processing programme. I collected all the what-statements and gathered them in a special document. I re-read all the interviews and the what-collection and looked for similarities and discrepancies and tried to create categories. I compared the categories I obtained by manual categorisation and the one I got through the computer work. I did this several times and on different occasions. I worked with the separate data from the primary and secondary school teachers.

I have also used a second approach for the creation of categories of description—a computer programme. The use of computers in qualitative research has been discussed by, among others, Anders Bruhn and Odd Lindberg (1996). They make a primarily positive evaluation of computer programmes as tools for formalising the qualitative research. The computer makes it easier to account for all the steps of the analysis in the research work. The authors also stated that the use of computer programmes improves creativity. There are three types of programmes: word retrievers, code and retrieve programmes and lastly theory builders. This is an area that is developing rapidly.

I have used the programme NUD*IST (Non-numerical Unstructured Data Indexing Searching and Theory-building), which is mainly used by social scientists but is also being applied to health, legal and market research. The programme is designed to store, code, retrieve and analyse texts, video tapes etc. (see Diagram 3). It was developed by Tom and Lyn Richards at La Trobe University, Melbourne, Australia. It has been categorised by Eben A. Weitzman and Matthew B. Miles (1995) as a Code-Based-Theory-Building programme.

The texts are divided into segments and stored under a certain name, a code. The codes form a base for a (not necessarily) hierarchical system or an index system (see Diagram 4). This system can be pruned or re-arranged. The programme also maintains a document system (the original data, transcribed interviews or articles for example) and it is possible to explore data from either the index or the document system. Each first-level code is the root of an unlim-

NUD•IST processes.

Non-Numerical Unstructured Data

Inputs (left box):
research questions
prior theory
emerging ideas
categories of people, sites
hypotheses for testing

Inputs (right box):
interviews, documents, diaries, photos, maps, videos, stories, open ended responses...

Indexing

Index System
Tree-structured Index system of categories called nodes.
Nodes: titles, definitions for memos, references to text units in documents.
Can be investigated in many ways, structure rearranged and contents changed at any time.

Documents
Can be on line or off line.
Header: information about file.
On line documents can be divided into sections with sub-headers.
Numbered text units (user defined chunks). Can be indexed at any nodes.

Searching

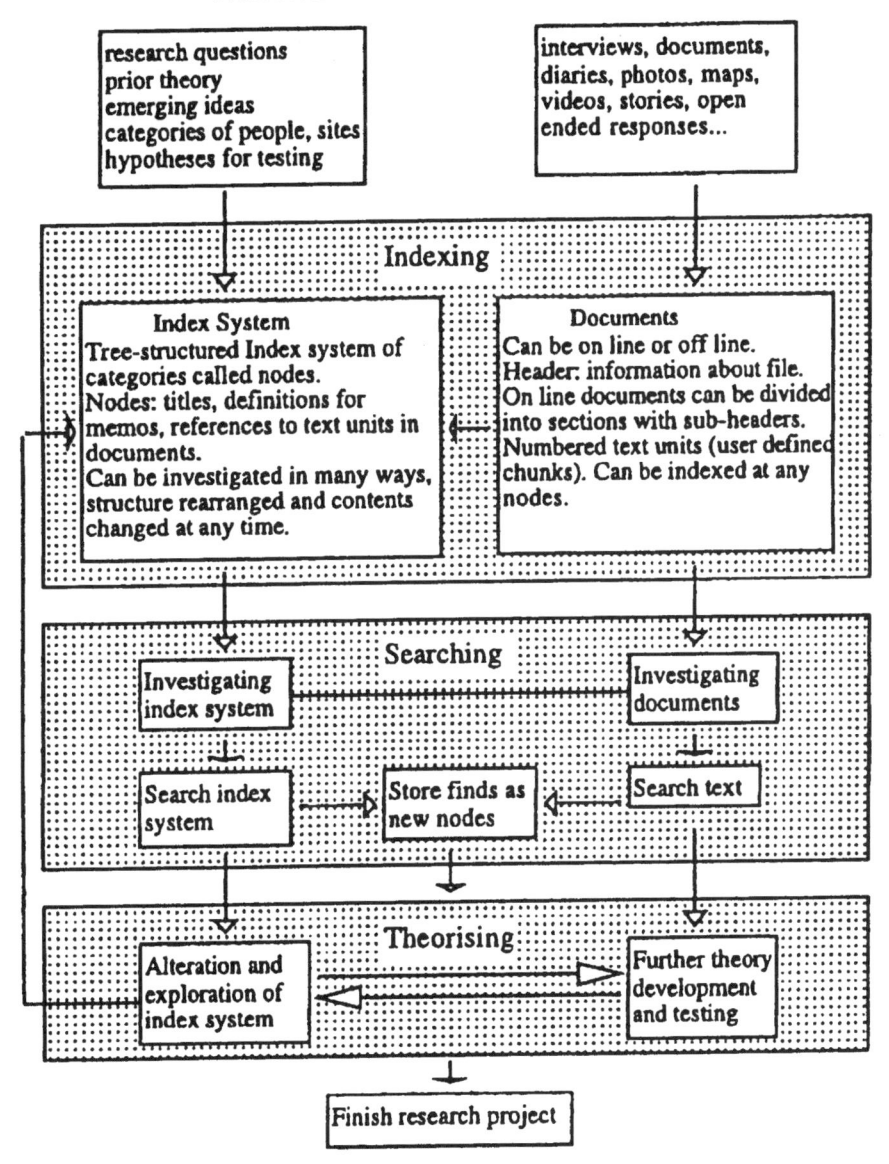

Investigating index system — Investigating documents
Search index system → Store finds as new nodes ← Search text

Theorising

Alteration and exploration of index system ⇄ Further theory development and testing

→ Finish research project

Diagram 3. The NUD*IST process. Source: NUD*IST user guide, 1994.

ited tree of subcodes and the codes are referred to as nodes. Each branch of the tree represents a category.

The nodes are described as containers for thoughts about the data and the results of questions posed about it. Nodes can be disconnected (e.g. to record a

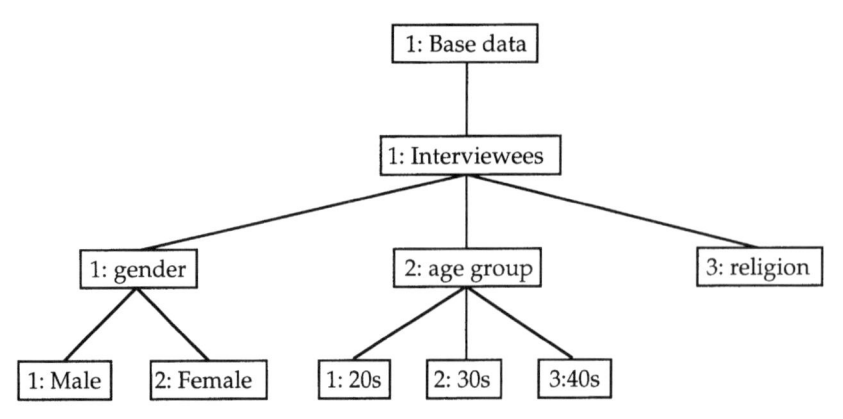

```
                    ┌─────────────┐
                    │ 1: Base data│
                    └──────┬──────┘
                           │
                  ┌────────┴────────┐
                  │ 1: Interviewees │
                  └────────┬────────┘
         ┌─────────────────┼─────────────────┐
   ┌─────┴─────┐     ┌─────┴──────┐    ┌─────┴─────┐
   │ 1: gender │     │2: age group│    │3: religion│
   └─────┬─────┘     └─────┬──────┘    └───────────┘
      ┌──┴──┐        ┌─────┼─────┐
 ┌────┴─┐┌──┴────┐┌──┴──┐┌─┴───┐┌┴────┐
 │1:Male││2:Female││1:20s││2:30s││3:40s│
 └──────┘└───────┘└─────┘└─────┘└─────┘
```

Diagram 4. A simple example of how the index system is constructed as an upside-down tree. Source: NUD*IST user guide 1994.

hunch about the data for later investigation), or they can be organised into a hierarchical structure reflecting the analysis. This structure can be created and refined as the researcher develops an understanding of the data (Weitzman and Miles 1995).

I have used the NUD*IST programme for only the secondary school interviews. I started to do it also with the interviews of the primary school teachers, but discovered that it did not change my original categorisation and decided not to spend more time on this work. One advantage with using this programme compared with manual work, is that it is easier and faster to find a single statement again.

CHAPTER 4
Education in Tanzania

Introduction

The educational system must be seen in a historical perspective. For Tanzania various rulers have had an impact on how the school system was organised, what the aims of the curriculum were, and for whom the education was intended. It is also of interest to look at the economic conditions and the educational policies over time, as there were changes especially after independence. Concerning the educational aims, I will focus especially on the foundations of environmental education. My findings about the chosen perspectives are presented in a chronological order.

The historical overview provides a background to an exploration of the frame factors of the educational system, as defined in the frame factor theory approach. These are the governing (goal system and curriculum), the regulating (school inspectorate and national exams) and the constraining factors (financial, structural adjustment and physical frames—see Chapter 2).

Historical background

Early history

By the East African coast, parts of which were referred to by the Romans as Azania, traders brought their experiences from Oman and India and a mercantile civilisation flourished between 700 and 1498 AC (Atieno Odhiambo, Ouso & Williams 1988, pp. 15–16, Mokhtar 1990, pp. 309–312, Iliffe 1997, pp. 76–79). When Vasco da Gama rounded Cape Horn in 1497 on his way to India, he brought with him a new era of foreign control of the east coast—commercial, religious and political (Atieno Odhiambo, Ouso & Williams 1988, pp. 82–89). The slave trade found a centre off the coast on the island of Zanzibar. By 1839 between forty and forty-five thousand slaves were annually sold at the slave market in Zanzibar (Atieno Odhiambo, Ouso & Williams 1988, pp. 96).

Colonial rule

Germany occupied parts of East Africa in the 1880s and German East Africa (today mainland Tanzania) was established at the Berlin meeting of 1884–85 (Adu Boahen 1990 pp. 15–16, Atieno Odhiambo, Ouso & Williams 1988, pp. 116). This was an agreement between colonial powers without any respect for the tribes living in the areas. Germany and Britain divided East Africa between themselves. Zanzibar was declared a British Protectorate in 1890. The Sultan retained his control over the island but all external matters were passed to Britain. Britain was given the mandate over German East Africa by the League of Nations in 1920 after defeating Germany in World War I. The area was renamed Tanganyika (Atieno Odhiambo, Ouso & Williams 1988, pp. 142, Adu Boahen 1990, pp. 141, Iliffe 1979, pp. 432).

A closer union between Uganda, Tanganyika and Kenya was developed in the years between the First and Second World Wars and an East African High Commission was formed in 1948. A wide range of governing functions were shared. They included railways and harbours, post and telegraph offices, customs and excise, and an army and a navy (Atieno Odhiambo, Ouso & Williams 1988, pp. 161–62).

Independence

The African soldiers learnt a great deal from participating in the Second World War (Atieno Odhiambo, Ouso & Williams 1988, pp. 163, Iliffe 1997, pp. 306-308). Their experiences stimulated the independence struggles and on 9 December 1961 Tanganyika became independent. In the beginning of 1964 the Sultan of Zanzibar was overthrown and on 22 April the new United Republic of Tanzania, consisting of mainland Tanzania and Zanzibar, was proclaimed. The first elected president was Julius K. Nyerere who was also the founder of the Tanganyika African National Union (TANU) in 1954 (Atieno Odhiambo, Ouso & Williams 1988, pp. 163–169, Iliffe 1979, pp. 436–37, 567–76). An East African Community emerged from the East African High Commission in 1967, with its headquarters in Arusha, Tanzania. However, the union failed in 1971 due to economical and political differences.

In 1977 TANU and the Afro-Shirazi Party in Zanzibar joined to form the Chama Cha Mapinduzi[1] (CCM), a party that aimed to build socialism on the basis of self-reliance (Othman 1995, pp. 175). In October 1978 Tanzania was invaded by Ugandan troops led by Idi Amin. The cost of the war, which Tanzania had to bear alone, contributed to the decline of the state budget and the development of serious economic difficulties in the late 1970s. Falling prices on main export goods and rising prices on imported products, such as fuel, caused economic imbalances which affected the social development programmes in the country (Svendsen 1995, pp. 115–121).

The Third World Guide (Instituto del Tercer Mundo 1992) describes the

---

[1] 'Party of Revolution'.

development of the 80s as a decade when corruption within the public sector and pressure from the International Monetary Fund (IMF) increased. Nyerere fought corruption and resisted IMF pressures for almost three years, while introducing a series of austerity measures to keep the economic situation under control. On 5 November 1985, after 24 years as head of state, President Julius Nyerere passed power on to Ali Hassan Mwinyi. In 1986, an economic recovery plan went into effect. It was designed by Ali Hassan Mwinyi's government, following IMF and World Bank guidelines.

In May 1992, the United Republic of Tanzania became a multi-party state and by the end of the year more than 20 parties were registered. The first election for the parliament was held in 1995 (personal observation).

Development of the educational system

The United Republic of Tanzania consists of mainland Tanzania and Zanzibar. Both have their own educational system. Whenever Tanzania is mentioned here in an educational context, it indicates mainland Tanzania only.

Pre-independence
During the pre-independence period indigenous education was community related, and carefully chosen persons from home and society took educational responsibilities. Attitudes and rules of behaviour were transmitted from one generation to another. Education took place at certain ages and was given by relatives to the child. In those days, education was geared towards preparing children to take their place in society—a socialisation of rules for a collective life.

Before colonialisation the only alternative were the Koranic schools which were affiliated to the mosques (Furley & Watson 1978, pp. 45). One of the first schools was established at the Kilwa mosque. Kilwa had a Muslim ruler as early as the year 1200 (Iliffe 1979, pp. 36). Western education was introduced by the missionaries who came with the European traders, of whom the first were the Portuguese.

During the German rule most of the schools were mission schools at a primary level, with up to three years of schooling. The Germans were not interested in promoting African education at all and the governmental schools were few. During the German colonial period from the 1890s to the end of the First World War, the formal education system focused on the production of middle level administrative personnel (Furley & Watson 1978, pp. 50–63, Buchert 1994, pp. 15–17).

When Britain took over Tanganyika in 1919 many schools had closed during the First World War and the teachers were dispersed. Britain's aim of education for Africans was to promote the system of 'indirect rule' by educating Africans to supply the central administration with personnel, like the Germans did. In the first middle school (high school), the pupils were often sons of the headmen or kings. In 1925 it was estimated that 15–20 percent of the children at school age actually attended some sort of school (Furley & Watson 1978, pp. 135–37).

An important source of input came from the Trustees of the Phelps-Stokes Fund (U.S.) which initiated the Educational Commission of East Africa in the early 1920s. Besides receiving aid from the Phelps-Stokes Fund, the Commission was also funded by the British Colonial Office and the Church Missionary Society. The Commission consisted of U.S., English, Scottish and West African citizens. They travelled in both West, South and East Africa in 1920–21 and 1923. In commenting on the activities of the Commission Thomas Jesse Jones (1925) wrote:

> Probably the most important single task of the Commission to East Africa was to try to find the types of education best fitted to meet the twofold needs of the Negro masses and of the Negro leaders of Africa in the near future. In general, the members of the Commission are convinced that all education must be of a character to draw out the powers of the Native African and to fit him to meet the specific problems and needs of the individual and community life. In this connection, they have been profoundly impressed by the ideals of education developed by General Armstrong at the Hampton Institute in Virginia, immediately after the Civil War. He saw that book learning of the old type was entirely inadequate: that the plow, the anvil, the hammer, the broom, the frying pan and the needle must all be used to supplement the customary instruction. In other words, that education must be vitally related to the needs of the people as they took up their work as freemen on the plantations and in the towns of the South (pp. xvii).

In other words, the members of the Commission were impressed by the education curriculum for former slaves in the southern states of the United States and this had an impact on the curriculum and educational system they proposed, which was largely accepted and adopted by the British colonial authorities in then Tanganyika. The educational system became segregated with different policies, resources and structures for Africans, Asians and Europeans. The policy for the Africans was that of 'adaptation' to a rural life and cash crop production (Furley & Watson 1978, pp. 138–39).

The African Education Ordinance of 1928 was the first national charter for education in Tanganyika. All schools were registered and put under governmental supervision. A school that was approved for standards received a grant-in-aid of up to two-thirds of the salaries paid to its African teachers and up to £300 for the European staff (Furley & Watson 1978, pp. 140). The main purpose was to encourage the mission schools—which out-numbered the few governmental by far—to provide elementary education and not religious instruction only.

The education system that slowly began to be developed between 1920 and 1930 consisted of small, often unassisted mission schools, bush or village schools and six governmental central or intermediate schools with a four-year long primary education (Furley & Watson 1978, pp. 140–42, 224). These central schools were largely schools for the kings' sons up to the mid-1930s. After

1926, a third type of school developed: the Native Authority schools. This gave the chiefs freedom to build a school for their own people. The funding was private but the syllabus was governmental. All were day schools and closely related to the surrounding rural community. This 'tribal' education was important. They all kept gardens and, in Kilimanjaro, even coffee plantations. The schools became cultural centres in the villages (Furley & Watson 1978, pp. 142–43, Buchert 1994, pp. 7–9).

It was not until 1934 that junior secondary schools for Africans were opened. In the beginning, the output was very small and by 1939 it was suggested that full secondary education be extended. But then World War II came and put a halt to things. Meanwhile, the very few students who qualified and had economic support, went to Makerere University in Uganda or to Southern Rhodesia for secondary schooling (Furley & Watson 1978, pp. 140). Since Tanganyika had no institution of higher education, students had to study in Uganda, Kenya or Britain. Before independence, only two white-collar jobs were available for Africans: as a teacher or an office worker. Consequently, these became high status professions which guaranteed a middle class life. At the time for independence, out of about 2,100 posts requiring university education, only 147 were held by Africans (ibid. pp. 378).

Independence

At independence, Tanzania set off to reorganise the economy, develop access to social services to even out inequalities, develop patterns of distribution and redistribution oriented toward collective consumption, and to initiate participatory politics. The transition process also had to meet basic human needs and supply an improved standard of living as well as reduce the power of the largest private producers but integrate all private producers into a national economy (Samoff 1990). Samoff pointed out that 'this must occur in a setting where the production system is highly dependent on the world economy, the proletariat is undeveloped, and the peasantry remains semiautonomous' (ibid. pp. 211).

In 1961, less than 10 percent of the children were attending school (Buchert 1994, pp. 68). In 1962, the population was 12 million and less than 500,000 pupils were in primary school. In 1978, the Education Act made primary education compulsory for seven years resulting in an increase in the number of pupils in primary schools to about 3.2 million. How was this rise possible?

The First Three Year Plan (1961–1964) called for the abolition of the segregated educational system and the integration of European, Asian and African schools. The Educational Act of 1962 aimed at changing the racially based school system into a unified national and governmental system. The fees for secondary schools were abolished in 1964 but there were no major changes in the inherited Western-style education (Lugalla 1993). The First Five-Year plan (1964–1969) included the New Science and Modern Mathematics Programmes (influenced by the English Nuffield Programmes) as well as the Education for Self-Reliance.

Soon after the Arusha Declaration on Socialism and Self-Reliance in 1967, President Nyerere issued his paper on Education for Self-Reliance (ESR). This paper has been the basis of all major educational changes in the country (Ministry of Education 1984a) and expresses all the hopes of what should be realised through education in the transition of the society. Here the concept of self-reliance projects was also introduced in order to prepare the pupils for a productive life in the (mainly agricultural) community, using the approach of 'learning by doing'. Later the schools were expected to contribute to their own economy with 25 percent of the costs through their self-reliance projects.

In the Second Five Year Plan (1969–74) it was a requirement of each primary school to operate as an adult education centre. The primary school teacher also taught adult literacy courses despite his or her very limited training. The school developed into a community centre where a lot of activities took place, since it 'belonged' to the village.

In 1974 the politicians decided on Universal Primary Education (UPE) which was to be implemented immediately, i.e. by 1977. The number of primary school teachers was at the time 28,000 but 90,000 were needed, according to TANU, if the target, which was for all pupils to have a school within walking distance, was to be reached. No consultation had been made with the administrative structure, the Ministry of Education, so to solve the problem, the village councils became involved. The ruling party (TANU) was well structured and easily mobilised. The ten-cell system had been introduced in 1965 and had developed into an effective network. Each village council chose 25 reliable young people to become teachers. One tutor from a teacher training institute came to the village. During two years 'teacher training' took place, in the beginning outdoors or at the village office. The village tried to support the training as much as possible. The students were Standard VII (grade 7) primary school leavers and for quite some time this was the educational background for most primary school teachers in Tanzania.

Mrs Mema (see introduction) called this training 'crash courses' for as far as she remembers, the students had only nine months to learn the same content as in the two year courses. She also considered these teachers to be better qualified than those who had taken the ordinary two year course.

However, in 1977 with about 90,000 teachers, 3.2 million pupils were able to attend primary schools, most of which were built by the villages. This meant that there was at least one primary school in each village (Johansson 1989, Johansson, personal communication 1994). In 1985 the teaching staff had increased to 92,586 and in 1989 to 98,392 (Ministry of Education 1990b). The average number of teachers per school was nine.

UNESCO developed a literacy programme in the beginning of the 1960s and Tanzania was one of the chosen countries. At the same time as participants were taught to read and write in Swahili, knowledge and vocational skills were transmitted. Swahili had been chosen as the national language when the country became independent and the literacy campaign strengthened the unity of the nation. Training teams for adult education were schooled on the regional and district level. In the beginning, youth in all higher education were mobilised and in the afternoons they went to the villages to teach in addition to their own studies. Later this was taken over mainly by the primary school teachers. Literacy, for at least 70 or 80 percent of the population, was considered a necessary prerequisite for economical and industrial development. The relation was, however, complex and might not be valid for an economy dominated by the agricultural sector (Fägerlind & Saha 1983).

In the early years of independence, a massive stake was thus invested in education as a tool for the social transition of Tanzania—a 'revolution by education' (Samoff 1990, pp. 210).

Education in the least developed countries
Education in the least developed countries encountered severe problems during the education expansion of the 1980s. They were not alone; also the developed countries were affected by economic recession but the latter did not have the same debt burden. The situation for the least developed countries was aggravated by an increase in oil prices and a decline in prices for export.

As a result of the recession in education, a World Conference on Education for All was organised in Jomtien, Thailand in 1990, by UNESCO, UNICEF, UNDP and the World Bank, to forge a global consensus on the importance of basic education. Three major dimensions of the economic, social and cultural lives of all people were formulated: the interplay between 'culture,' broadly defined, and the education process; the impact of unprecedented scientific and technological development and quality of life and education for sustainable education (UNESCO, 1991).

Education is dependent on its social, economic, political and cultural context as well as being regarded as a tool for social transformation. After independence in 1961, the government of Tanzania, for example, saw education as the most important tool for changing the society into a socialist state, independent of foreign aid. The leader of Tanzania by that time, Julius K. Nyerere, strongly pointed to the role of education in achieving the aims of political, cultural and economic development as well as the development of the 'new man'.

Martin Carnoy and Joel Samoff (1990) described the expectations on education for achieving social transformation thus:

> Education is seen in such societies as a route to all things. It is expected to be the primary vehicle for developing and training skills to ensure that the next generation in the society is adequately prepared for the specific tasks that the society expects of it. It is expected to be the place where appropriate ideas, values, and world views will be developed so that from the process of schooling there emerges a new person—not simply someone with skills, but also someone with understanding of his or her role in the world and what is important for that society (ibid. pp. 7).

During the 1990s, economical and political changes have also resulted in education policy changes. The IMF, the World Bank and aid agencies, all with a dominating role, have had a poverty focus including emphasis on social sector development and support to basic education in Tanzania (Buchert 1997). This is a reflection of the level of aid dependency in the least developed countries, which increased during the late 1980s and 1990s (Sida 1996a).

Context of formulation of educational polices
German rule ended after the First World War and the British took over. During the colonial rule, the male Africans were assumed to work either in large cash crop farms or plantations owned by white settlers or in the colonial administration at the lower levels. The society was to a large extent dependent on agricultural products, so the education of Africans was aimed at fulfilling their roles in the agriculture-based villages. The *adaptation philosophy* relied heavily on the transfer of Western values to the Africans. The aims of education at the time was much influenced by the Phelps-Stokes Education Commission to East Africa as mentioned before. Odora (1992) has called attention to the effect of the Commission's proposal:

> Women were taught to sew and knit, be good mates for changed men, help in the cleansing of native life, and to be obedient ... it would not be an exaggeration to say that in the context of the Phelps Stokes Commission, Thomas Jesse Jones and the Tuskegee spirit ... successfully sold to Africa, through willing customers in the British colonialist and the Christian missionary, an affirmation of the caste system of education, which they then used to displace, dislocate, denigrate and obliterate the complex and varied indigenous cultures that African people have had, and upon which their development was based (Odora 1992, pp. 79).

After the Second World War, the *modernisation philosophy*, which later superseded the adaptation philosophy, included a segregated educational system with mass-education for the Africans and elite education for Asians and Europeans. The modern sector was to be developed (Buchert 1994).

In 1961 Tanganyika received its independence and a new *manpower development* focused on the much needed expansion of secondary schools. It was important to develop manpower for the republic when taking over from the European administration. An African philosophy, Education for Self-Reliance, was seen as a consequence of the declaration of a socialist one-party state.

In 1967 the strategy of socialism and the above-mentioned *Education for Self-Reliance* was introduced and this was one of the very few genuine efforts to break away from the colonial education philosophies (Odora 1992). Now concentration was on primary schools and after some years on universal primary education for all.

The next important change was in 1984, when pressure from IMF and the World Bank on Tanzania with regard to the structural adjustment programme required the country to change from a socialist to a market-oriented economy.

The structural adjustment, together with political liberalisation from the mid-1980s on had a visible impact on the education system (Odora Hoppers 1998). With the Cost Recovery Programme of 1984, cost-sharing was introduced to primary schools. The Economic Recovery Programme of 1986 and the Enhanced Structural Adjustment Programme forced further cuts in state expenditures. According to Holger Daun (1996) the countries which had a centralised and socialistic government and which opted for self-reliance, welfare and gender equality, were the ones that had changed their educational system the most due to structural adjustment programmes. The change in the enrolment in primary schools between 1980 and 1988 was less in adjusting countries than in non-adjusting countries in Africa (ibid. pp. 30).

The educational focus shifted to *manpower development* again. In consistency with his political ideals, Julius K. Nyerere resigned from his post as president. In 1986 the new government accepted the Structural Adjustment Programme.

The steering factors are political and economical powers and the related educational policies. From the end of the First World War, the formulated educational polices had the following phases (Buchert 1994):

– Adaptation philosophy	1917–1945
– Modernisation philosophy	1945–c 1965
– Manpower development philosophy, I	1961–1967
– Education for Self-reliance philosophy	1967–1990/95
– Manpower development philosophy, II	1991–

During the 1980s many developing countries became marginalised in the world economy. Daun (1996) points out that in the globalisation of the economy a new category of countries has emerged; the Fourth World, which are losers. Tanzania was considered to belong to this group.

Current educational system and policy

The current educational system is constructed as follows:

- 7 years in primary school (Standard I–VII). Enrolment: 3,603,488 pupils (Ministry of Education and Culture BEST 1994)
- 4 years in public and private secondary school (Form I–IV) leading to an 'O'-level certification. Enrolment: 175,903 students (Ministry of Education and Culture BEST 1993)
- 2 years in secondary school leading to an 'A'-level certification. Enrolment: 11,794 students (Ministry of Education and Culture BEST 1993)
- 3–5 years at tertiary level. In 33 teacher training colleges 6,767 students for grade B and A, and in 11 colleges 3,131 students were enrolled for diploma level (Ministry of Education and Culture BEST 1992b).

Education for Self-Reliance

It is necessary to look more in detail at the Arusha Declaration and the Education for Self-Reliance. The Arusha Declaration was the foundation for the strong link between the school and the society. The idea, however, was nothing new. Even in the 1952 syllabus for middle schools in the then British Colonial Tanganyika, integration between theory and practice as well as between the school and the local community were emphasised.

> It was hoped that the combination of practical work and community studies would stand the pupils in good stead as adult members of their communities, whilst the clear recognition implied in these changes that the primary education would be terminal for the majority of the pupils would help to reduce the selection focus of schooling and minimise feelings of frustration and failure among those not selected for further education. With agricultural skills they would serve as the means whereby improved farming practices might be more widely used. (Thompson 1981, pp. 117).

The ultimate aim in 1952, however, was different from the aims after independence. It was in a speech in March 1967, two months after the Arusha declaration, that Julius K. Nyerere focused on Education for Self-Reliance (Nyerere 1967a). He discussed the aims of education in Tanzania and suggested that the educational system should adapt to these aims. He recapitulated that his political aim was to create a society built on socialism where the citizens would be equal, where resources would be shared and where everybody would be working and nobody would be exploiting. This philosophy was built on traditional village life. He stressed that Tanzania was an agricultural society and should so remain for a long time and that the standard of living in the villages must be raised. The education system, he said, must encourage students to work for these aims and prepare them for an active role. The values that are to be transmitted must accentuate equality and co-operation as well as professional knowledge to be used in the villages. The education system must also develop critical thinking, capacity to learn from others, and self esteem as a member in a working society and not as a consumer.

Nyerere pointed out that the problem of the education system was the fact that it was alienated from society. The students did not take part in the daily life of the society; they were isolated. This was especially true for secondary schools, which were (and still are) predominantly boarding schools, while it applied to a lesser extent to the primary schools. Students tended to believe that knowledge was what is learnt from books—they did not appreciate the experiences of the ordinary man or of the elders. The society reinforced this view by valuing formal education and training more than experiences when employing people.

This problem can be rectified by the content of the syllabi, by the school organisation and by the age of entry to school. Cultural identity was strengthened by the use of Swahili as the national language and medium of teaching in primary schools. Thus the main objectives of the Education for Self-Reliance were:

— to change mental values and attitudes inherited from the colonialism.
— to transmit from one generation to the next accumulated wisdom and knowledge of the society, including the skills for self-reliance in a predominantly rural society.
— to include scientific and technological skills such as creativity, problem solving and the development of an enquiring mind appropriate to a society, constantly in change.
— to integrate theoretical knowledge with manual work and production.
— to prepare people for future membership in a socialist society that practises the concepts of equality, human dignity and value of work.
— to integrate school and community by making schools an integral part of the community that practices the concept of self-reliance.
— to promote a sense of belonging together and enhance the spirit of co-operation by making pupils value work, practice democratic rights but also become accountable in their responsibilities. (Nyerere 1967a, pp. 281–290).

The content of the syllabi needed to be geared towards the citizenship and preparation for a life in the village. The schools were seen as minisocieties which contributed to their own consumption. They were to be social and economical entities as well as educational. The pupils and students were expected to contribute to their own subsistence in school through a school farm, a work shop and by doing necessary work, such as cleaning and gardening, in the schools themselves. Nyerere (1967a) argued that social values were created by the family, the school and the society. Buchert (1994, pp. 95) pointed out that:

> Similar experiments were undertaken in other parts of the world at the time (e.g. China and Cuba), which may well have acted as an additional source of inspiration.

The emphasis on the role of education for social and economical development in socialist countries and its effect on the organisation and content of the curriculum was highlighted by Ingemar Fägerlind and Lawrence J. Saha (1983). They found there was no uniformity of opinions among the countries and even within the People's Republic of China there were different strategies.

The idea of education tied with production was not unique for Tanzania; similar thoughts were put in practice by a South African exile, Patrich van Rensburg, in Serowe in 1962 and in 1966 at Swaneng Hill School, in the former Bechuanaland, today's Botswana (van Rensburg 1974, Gustafsson 1987). The uniqueness of the Tanzanian project was its scope and breadth.

The strong emphasis on 'learning by doing' in the Education for Self-Reliance was undoubtedly an influence from the progressive ideas of John Dewey. But unlike Dewey, Nyerere also wanted to create a totally new content of the basic education and, as an ultimate goal, a new society. Nyerere did not accept the effect of formal education as it was at the time of independence, since it was encouraging an escape from the agricultural society as well as from the values and knowledge of the traditional (or tribal) education.

The idea of education as an investment, or 'investment in education,' was promoted by UNESCO through a number of international conferences, among them in Addis Ababa in 1961. The conference set a target of 1980 as the year when secondary school output should be 20 percent. Tanzania kept back the expansion of the primary schools in order to increase the number of the secondary schools. The 1974 Musoma Resolution (Tanganyika African National Union 1976), however, embarked upon the rapid development of universal primary education although resources were very limited. The emphasis of school development and school curricula, during the first period of independence had been on secondary and higher education in order to supply the need of manpower in a 'modern' society. After the Arusha declaration focus was on primary schools and mass education for an agricultural society.

There was also a village afforestation programme designed in the spirit of the Arusha Declaration to meet the demand of fuelwood supply. The 1969 Education Act established the implementation of Education for Self-Reliance. Primary schools and adult education came under the local authorities while secondary school, teacher training and higher education came under the Ministry of Education in the 1972 Decentralisation Policy.

The development of educational polices and its relationship to political development, i.e. to the ruling political party in Tanzania up until the middle of the 1980s, was clear and evident, as illustrated in the table in Appendix 2. The party had a strong governing role but the economy was constrained, which affected the intentions.

Educational policy of 1995

In 1990 a Task Force was set up, dominated by academics from the University of Dar es Salaam with the Dean of the Faculty of Education as chairman and Dr. J.C. Galabawa as Secretary General. They analysed the situation of the educational system in Tanzania and came up with extensive recommendations in 1993 (United Republic of Tanzania 1993).

In 1995 a new educational policy was approved by the cabinet of the Tanzanian government. The policy was never discussed by Parliament. The new policy was to substitute the Education for Self-Reliance policy from 1967. An amendment to the 1978 Education Act was approved later the same year. The amendments reflected some of the changes, especially those connected to the liberalisation of the education system, for example ownership of schools (Buchert 1997).

The formulation of the 1995 Tanzania Education and Training Policy (TETP) took consideration of the recommendations from the Task Force. The policy document (United Republic of Tanzania 1995) gave a historical background of the previous educational acts (1962, 1969, 1978) and other governmental actions related to the educational policies.

In the initial part, on education and training, it was stated that (as also emphasised by the Task Force in their report):

> Education makes man aware of his own potentials and responsibility to change and improve his own condition and that of his society, it embodies within it science and technology (pp.vii).

The relationship between education and development was commented on in the paragraph on education and development. The links to the Education for Self-Reliance policy was clear:

> The guiding philosophy of all development efforts in Tanzania is the achievement of self-reliance ... for Tanzania's development, the people will continue to depend mainly on themselves and their own resources and efforts, that is, their land, energies and readiness to work hard ... Tanzania aspires and is committed to continue following the people centred development and improvement strategy and in doing so, to concentrate on equitable and sustainable development ... (pp. viii).

The Task Force began their report with a scenario for development in the 21st century. The Tanzania Education and Training Policy adapted their view to a development in other sectors than agriculture, although it still was a base sector. Examples of other sectors were industry, commerce and trade, increased use of alternative and sustainable energy sources, efficient transport and communication systems and better conservation of the environment.

The Task Force's macro policy setting presented the consequences of the changed economical policies. It stressed the increased role of the private sector and the reduction of subsidies and the introduction of cost sharing in the education system. It spelled out the increased investment in infrastructure and social development sectors especially health and education. The Task Force did not include any economic suggestions, such as where to find the funding for all their recommendations.

There was a considerable shift from the policy emphasis from 1962 to the early 1980s which placed strong reliance on governmental control of economy and the public sector. The broad policies of education and training included enhancement of partnership in the provision of education, identification of critical priority areas such as the training of more and better teachers, broadening the financial base for education, streaming the management structure of education and increasing access to education by focusing on the equity issue.

The general aims and objectives of education and training in the 1995 policy were:

- to guide and promote the development and improvement of the personalities of the citizens of Tanzania, their human resources and effective utilisation of those resources in bringing about the individual and national development;
- to promote the acquisition and appreciation of culture, customs and traditions of the peoples of Tanzania;
- to promote the acquisition and appropriate use of literacy, social, scientific, vocational, technological, professional and other forms of knowledge, skills and understanding for the development and improvement of the condition of man and society;

- to develop and promote self-confidence and an inquiring mind, an understanding and respect for human dignity and human rights and a readiness to work hard for personal self-advancement and national improvement;
- to enable and to expand the scope of acquisition, improvement and upgrading of mental, practical, productive and other life skills needed to meet the changing needs of industry and the economy;
- to enable every citizen to understand the fundamentals of the National Constitution as well as the enshrined human and civic rights, obligations and responsibilities;
- to promote the love of work, self and wage employment and improved performance in the production and service sectors;
- to inculcate principles of the national ethic and integrity, national and international co-operation, peace and justice through the study, understanding and adherence to the provisions of the National Constitution and other international basic charters;
- to enable a rational use, management and conservation of the environment.

The general aims were not very different from earlier educational philosophies. Nyerere always emphasised the humanity dimension as well as hard work to promote development. What was new was the notion of environmental management and conservation. This was also stressed by the Task Force.

Other novelties were the ambition to include two year pre-primary education and the abolition of the thought of each level as a terminal education. In the specific aims for primary and secondary education it was stated that the objective was to prepare the child for the next level of education. By this, one of the most cherished thoughts of the Nyerere government was abolished.

The structure of the education remained as before 7-4-2-3, with the addition of two years of pre-primary education.

Buchert (1997) presented several doubts on the new educational policy. Her main point of criticism was whether the document reflected the predominate views of the Tanzanian government. The gender issue had been a key area for many agencies, and UNESCO, Sida[2], Danida, and the World Bank had pushed for local autonomy in primary schools.

Another question that she asked was if the policy had been adequately internalised. In the critique of the Education for Self-Reliance policy, one of the main obstacles to realisation forwarded by several researchers was that 'it was not fully understood' (Nkonoki 1978, Galabawa 1990, Mosha 1990, Buchert 1994, Ishumi and Maliyamkono, 1995).

Buchert interviewed officials:

> While some of the Government officials maintained that the privatisation was now a fact, that the Education and training policy reflected the reality as it had been developed within the secondary education sector, and that the Government had now realised that it cannot alone provide for the education, other officials and representatives of the international aid agencies and the academic environment, saw a determined World Bank hand behind it. As one interviewee put it: 'it has been stuffed down the throat of the Government by the IMF and the World Bank'.

---

[2]Swedish International Development Authority.

During 1994 and 1995, the World Bank held a number of education seminars in Africa and in Washington for key Tanzanian educators which had a direct and indirect impact on Government thinking on education (Buchert 1997, pp. 52).

The doubts that Buchert delivered were not encouraging for the implementation of the new policy considering the efforts that were made to launch the Education for Self-Reliance—still today, some of its main ideas are not fully accepted.

The frame factors in the Tanzanian educational system

This part of the study intends to give an overview of the frame factors[3] in the educational sector of Tanzania. Educational policy, including the curriculum, is in focus as *governing factors*. The Education Act of 1978, local governments, school inspectorate and national exams are presented and discussed as *regulating factors*. As *constraining factors* I have looked at the economic policies, financial allocations and factors affecting the teacher's job situation.

Governing factors

The problem of aid dependency

After decolonisation, foreign aid was seen as a tool for development and transformation of the developing countries. However, during the 70s and 80s, foreign aid created a state of dependency on external resources in certain countries, both for investment and for maintaining public and private consumption. Studies have shown that the dependency was not a result of excessive quantities of aid but of the manner in which aid funds had been given and utilised (Edgren 1996).

Roger Ridell pointed out that 'aid dependency should be understood as that process by which the continued provision of aid appears to be making no significant contribution to the achievement of self-sustaining development' (Ridell 1996, pp. 24). Rehman Sobhan also defined aid dependency as a structural problem deriving from the incapacity of the economy to react to 'external chocks,' for example rises in the price of oil or decline in export prices for commodities as a result of global recession (Sobhan 1996).

Foreign aid to the least developed countries thus became a problem in itself. Sobhan studied the aid dependency of Tanzania. Up to the mid 1980s Tanzania maintained a capacity to finance its developmental budget, even though it declined progressively from the 1970s onwards. From 1986, aid funds came to exceed total developmental expenditure (TDE), rising from 120 percent of the TDE in 1986, when the government accepted the first of the economic reform programmes designed by the World Bank, to 170 percent in 1993–94. Sobhan

---

[3] As defined by Ulf P. Lundgren, see Chapter 2.

Table 6: *The growth in external dependency of public expenditure in Tanzania 1961–1995 (in percent)*

Period	Aid grants/ TDE[a]	External finance/ TPE[b]	Recurrent deficit recurrent expenditure	Share of aid in recurrent budget
1961–65	1.3	5.94	–	–
1966–70	0.6	7.78	–	–
1971–75	20.28	14.26	–	–
1976–80	54.22	17.56	–	–
1981–85	78.54	12.92	–	–
1986–90	32.84	27.52	5.5	–
1990–91	56.50	34.82	15.2	19.2
1991–92	41.50	43.35	11.3	41.2
1992–93	70.60	40.02	40.4	20.1
1993–94	81.70	58.90	28.7	45.8
1994–95	–	–	28.3	–

[a] Total Developmental Expenditure.
[b] Total Public Expenditure.
Source: Mjema, World Bank, Minister of Finance, Semboja as compiled by Sobhan 1996, pp. 205–207.

claims that Tanzania's economy remained largely undiversified until very recently, which has left it more vulnerable to the current fluctuations than it was in the 1970s. Foreign aid, to a large extent, had become an import support, and it began to play a growing role in financing Tanzania's recurrent budget deficit. Consequently, the share of recurrent expenditure in the total expenditure, showed an increasing trend while the development expenditure declined. Further, disregarding this failure to expand the productive base left little scope for diversification of the economy.

Tanzania's aid relations can be divided into three phases. The first, after the Arusha declaration and the vision of self-reliance for Tanzania, was characterised by local ownership. The second, around 1980–86 when the economy of Tanzania was at its bottom with a GDP growth of an average of 0.7 percent and with a simultaneous decline in foreign aid between 1983–85, was seen as a period of confrontation between the government and the donors, including the World Bank. The third phase, after 1986, was dominated by the World Bank and other donors.

Even considering the uncertainty of statistics in Tanzania, the dependency of external finance of the total public expenditure has steadily grown after independence, as can be seen in Table 6. The figures from 1961–85 are based on annual averages.

The negative effects of the structural adjustment programmes and the aid dependency have aroused concern among researchers throughout Africa, as reported by Sobhan.

Aid dependency leads to lack of initiative and increases the tendency of passivity on the part of the recipient. The recipient will not bother to suggest new policies or projects because the donors will always insist on theirs. The World Bank and international donors, for example, were considered to be the driving force behind the Social Sector Strategy of 1995 and the Tanzania Education and Training Policy of 1995 (Buchert 1997).

Curriculum development
The governing factors concern the goal system. Lundgren (1972) concentrated initially on curriculum and teaching materials but later added the context of formulation and realisation (Lindensjö and Lundgren 1986). The context of formulation includes political, economical and educational policies.

Development of the *curriculum* was a task for the government but in 1964 the idea of a special institute was introduced at a University of East Africa conference in Mombasa 1964 (Kenya, Tanzania and Uganda were joined in the East African Union by that time). In Tanzania and Uganda Institutes of Education were founded to carry out curriculum development and teaching material production. The Institute of Education in Dar es Salaam established panels at the educational levels and subject levels as well as writers' workshops. The University of Dar es Salaam played an important role in the professional board.

The curriculum for the Tanzanian schools was prepared by the Institute of Curriculum Development (formerly the Institute of Education), renamed the Tanzania Institute of Education in 1995, and issued by the Ministry of Education and Culture (formerly the Ministry of National Education). Of the syllabi that were in use at the time of this study, some were issued in 1976 and some as late as the early 1990s.

The syllabi were developed by subject panels comprised of teachers from the field, ministry experts and specialists from the University of Dar es Salaam. Before a syllabus was issued, it was scrutinised by a board of members from the University of Dar es Salaam, the National Examinations Council and other institutions. In addition, the Institute of Curriculum Development (now Tanzania Institute of Education) was supposed to develop text books and teachers' guides.

The Institute was widely criticised for frequent curriculum changes—without being able to provide schools with the new syllabi—and slow manuscript production, mostly of poor quality. Mrs Mema (in the introduction) pointed out the decline of the quality of the textbooks that she had experienced during the decades. Nearly all publishing was done by governmental and parastatal[4] publishing houses, using donor-supplied paper. Lack of funds and expertise delayed publishing to between three and eight years. Once published, the books were distributed very slowly and easily went 'astray'. If, by chance,

---

[4] A parastatal is an enterprise owned by the government.

they reached a rural school, teachers had a tendency to lock the books up in cupboards. The system was a failure (World Bank 1995).

Hawes (1979) observed the dilemma of access to teaching resources when he compared curriculum with reality in several countries in Africa. The demands of the syllabi were based on urban situations very distant from rural reality. The curriculum showed no concern for the lack of resources in many schools (lack of teaching material, chairs and desks, class rooms, trained teachers etc.) or the composition of the target group (large classes, variation in ages in the same class, the use of the shift system which entails one stream having classes in the morning and another in the afternoon etc).

Regulating factors

The Tanzanian system of government consisted of three tiers. At the centre was the central government organised around a ministerial system. The second tier consisted of the central government regional administration reaching also district and lower levels. The third tier comprised local authorities such as the district and urban councils. Up until 1992, when Tanzania became a multi-party state, the ruling party Chama Cha Mapinduzi was included in the structure.

In the whole educational sector five ministries were involved, namely the Ministry of Education and Culture, the Ministry of Science, Technology and Higher Education, the Ministry of Labour and Youth, the Ministry of Regional Administration and Local Government and the Ministry of Community Development, Women and Children's Affairs. This fragmentation of institutions did not allow for re-allocation of resources according to priorities since each ministry was responsible for its own budget planning (World Bank 1995).

Primary school education was administrated by the local authorities at the district and village level under the Ministry of Regional Administration and Local Government. Secondary school education as well as teacher training was administrated by the central authorities, i.e. the Ministry of Education and Culture (see Diagram 5).

Nominally, the district governments owned the primary schools and were responsible for maintaining them as well as for paying teacher salaries, which were centrally established. The Ministry of Education and Culture provided teachers, set standards for physical facilities, set the curriculum, administrated national examinations, provided textbooks and posted ministry staff to manage the districts. The local governments, however, were almost totally dependent on central governmental funds and such funds (if they arrived) were earmarked for specific activities. Consequently, this left very small opportunity for things to be adapted to local priorities and needs.

The governmental secondary schools were administrated directly by the Ministry of Education and Culture and operating funds came straight from the

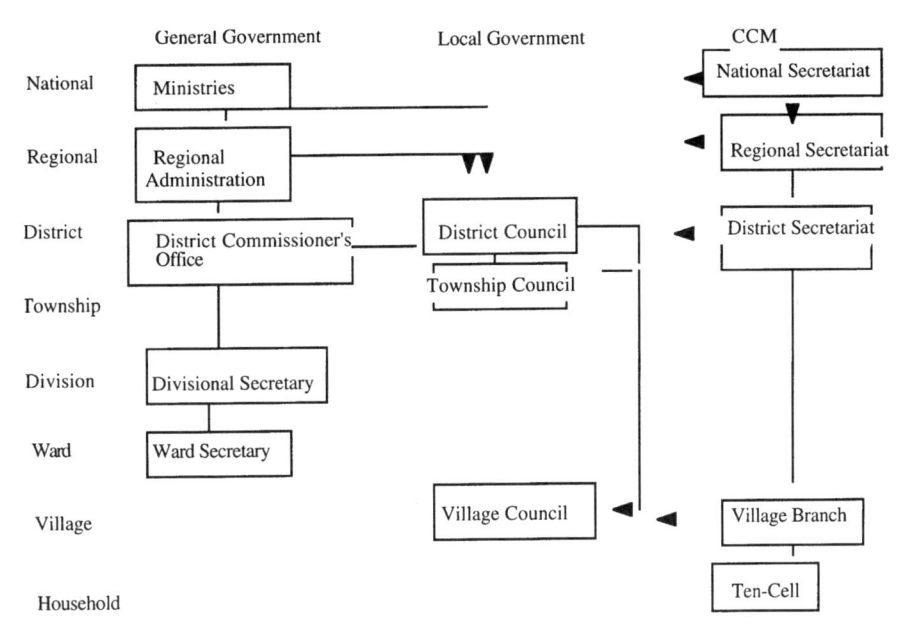

Diagram 5. Simplified structure of central and local government, including the CCM party.

central administration. The ministry was also responsible for ensuring quality in the private secondary schools.

The educational system as a unit had experienced a number of changes. The policy of Education for Self-Reliance was introduced in 1967, followed by the Universal Primary Education (UPE) policy in 1974. Together they led to large-scale increases in access to primary schools but reduced access to secondary and higher education. The UPE drive (1974–1984) ensured that primary schools were within walking distance from each household (World Bank 1995). From 1984, private secondary schools were once again allowed to operate and mushroomed to such a level that today they outnumber the governmental ones (260 to 177, source: Ministry of Education and Culture BEST 1994).

The general statute was the Educational Act of 1978, which empowered the Government to be the sole provider of educational services. The Act was amended in 1995 to make the new Tanzania Education Training and Education Policy possible.

The Local Government Act in 1982 re-established local governments in order to mobilise the communities. Committees were set up to make possible village participation in the management and administration of primary schools (Wort 1998). Primary education was nominally free with the exception of a TSh 200 (in 1995) UPE-fee to be paid by parents. This money was supposed to be collected at the local level. However, the local government managed to collect only about 30–40 percent of the UPE-fee (World Bank 1991, Temu 1995). Parents had other costs as well, such as school uniforms, teaching material and contributions to the construction of school buildings etc. It is possible that the collected money was not even used for educational purposes since the local government budget was inadequate (World Bank 1995).

School inspectorate

The central inspectorate is a department under the Commissioner of Education, Ministry of Education and Culture (MEC). The department was headed by a Chief Inspector. Mainland Tanzania was divided into seven zones headed collectively by a Zonal Chief Inspector. At this level the inspectors were responsible for secondary schools and teacher training colleges. At the district level school inspectors were responsible for primary schools and adult education. They reported to the zonal office (Ministry of Education 1982).

The aim of the school inspectorate was to develop and improve the educational conditions. They were supposed to evaluate all activities of the schools as well as advise teaching staff, head teachers/headmasters, the owners of the schools and the Commissioner at Ministry of Education and Culture. They had the legal rights to supervise the implementation and performance of the educational policy of the state.

The school inspector looked after the administration, i.e. the daily timetable, the use of various committees, division of labour and performance, discipline and communication. Another area was the curriculum—how the subjects were being taught, the storing and use of teaching aids, co-ordination of teaching, meetings of the subject departments, records of students performances, distribution of lessons, capability of teachers and existence of subject clubs. Of special interest was how the subjects were being taught. The inspector checked the number of subjects actually taught (which depends on the availability of competent teachers), scheme of work, lesson plans, standard of exercises and correction of pupils' work.

The school administration required that teachers prepared a scheme of work for the whole school year. This scheme was more detailed than the syllabus but followed the same structure, with topics, sub-topics, objectives etc. The scheme of work was to be presented to the heads of the schools in the beginning of the term and also to the school inspectors when they arrived. Lessons were planned based on the scheme of work. Visiting school inspectors assessed the ability of the school to carry out the curriculum mainly by studying the schemes of work (personally communicated to me[5]).

The inspector also studied the assessment and examination activities according to the National Examination Council directives and the number, qualification and distribution of labour among the staff. The next area was registra-

---

[5] Throughout the years from 1990 and onwards I have met school inspectors, heads of schools, teachers and other staff of the Ministry of Education and Culture during in-service training seminars, work shops and visits to schools. I have also stayed at teacher training colleges on 10–15 occasions for between two days up to three weeks at a time and have then had opportunities for informal discussions.

tion of students, attendance and transfer between schools. The physical state of the buildings, furniture and the like as well as of the school environment in terms of cleanliness, and the presence of trees, grass and flowers was also noted. Services available at the school such as water, electricity, telephone, transport, health and food were assessed. Finally self-reliance project plans and technology as well as financial control (of the projects) was scrutinised (Wizara ya Elimu 1986).

The report based on all this information was sent to the zonal senior school inspector, the district educational officer, the regional education officer and the head teacher of the school at the primary level. For the secondary schools and teacher training colleges the report was sent to the Commissioner of Education, the regional education officer, the headmaster/principal and the owner of the school.

The reports from the different school inspectors were the basis for quarterly reports which were sent to headquarters and zonal offices. Half-year reports were based on the quarterly reports and the yearly reports were based on the half-year reports.

In the yearly reports from the school inspectorate, covering all the schools that the inspectors managed to visit during the year, a number of quantitative data was collected. Generally the yearly report concentrated on matters that were physical and quantitative. If a subject was considered to be 'taught well,' the opinion was in most cases based on the study of schemes of work and lesson plans—not on classroom visits. Bearing in mind that much of the teaching consisted of transferring lesson notes to the students exercise book, it was not uncommon to see the scheme of works copied from teacher generation to teacher generation as well as the lesson plans (personal observation).

The school inspectors at district levels sometimes worked under harsh conditions. The restricted budget did not allow enough funds for transportation from head quarters to the different schools. The effect was that schools were rarely visited, as revealed in Box 1. A female district school inspector told me about the problem of logistics due to lack of financial funds. The only solution was to walk long distances and not everyone was prepared to do that.

What impact did the school inspectorate have on the education system? The World Bank, among others, criticised the managerial skills of the Ministry of Education and Culture (World Bank 1990). In their Staff Appraisal Report on educational planning, they brought up several critical points. They were of the opinion that the planning process consisted of merely collecting routine statistics and the preparation of annual budgets. The use of data information about educational performance was especially weak. No use was made of the results of the national examinations to modify or reorganise the curriculum and provide pedagogical support to the teachers (ibid. pp. 16). In short, the controlling and managerial functions of the educational systems were considered to be weak (UNESCO 1989, World Bank 1990, 1991, SIDA 1993).

> Female school inspector, Pwanni region.
> *The school farthest away is 130 km from the office ... it takes me several days to walk there ... we have no travel allowance ... I sleep two night in schools on my way ... in the classroom without windows and sometimes together with snakes ... food is given to me by the teacher in the village ... on the third day I arrive at the school for inspection ... the teacher and the pupils might not even be in the school but out working on the teacher's shamba ... I stay one day ... sleep in the school and then start walking back again ... a whole week is spent on one school only ... I can make this visit at most once a year ... I am the only one who is willing to do this ... my colleagues don't do it ..*

Box 1. A glimpse of the daily work of a district school inspector. Interview.

In the Social Sector Review 1995, the World Bank also reported this critique of the Tanzanian educational system:

> The school inspectorate system is well established in Tanzania but has very little impact on qualitative improvement of schooling. The major constraint can be traced to the issue of accountability. Inspectors have no professional responsibilities for the schools they supervise, apart from routine reports made to the Commissioner of Education (World Bank 1995, pp. 52).

I share the opinion of the World Bank in this matter. Owing to the fact that the bureaucratic system was very hierarchic and decision making was seldom delegated, as well as to the scarcity of resources, the development and improvement of the educational system was difficult to realise. There was no regularity in the implementation of inspection. My conclusion is that the role of the school inspectorate as a regulating factor was not strong.

National exams

Examinations in primary and secondary schools were prepared by the National Examinations Council of Tanzania, which was established in 1973. They were administered in particular locales and supervised by staff who were not the same as those who taught the students. The marking of the exams was also done centrally by specially appointed personnel, often from teacher training institutions.

In the primary school there were two examinations—at the end of Standard IV and VII. In Standard IV the objective was to identify slow learners, i.e. those who did not know how to read and write. In Standard VII there was a final exam in four subjects, English, Maths, Swahili and General knowledge. The language in the exams in primary school was Swahili, which was a second language for most of the pupils.

In the secondary school there were two examinations—in Form II and in Form IV. The latter was an examination at O-level. For those who were selected for Form V and Form VI education, there was a final exam at A-level in Form VI. The language used in secondary school was English.

The exam questions consisted, to a major extent, of multiple choice and matching character (objective questions) and papers (e.g. an open question of essay-type).

In 1975, a continuous assessment scheme was introduced which instructed the teachers in how to keep a record of students' daily academic performance, character attributes (e.g. commitment to duty, leadership quality, punctuality, care of property, co-operativeness, respect for others, cleanliness and quality of work done) and attitudes to work (participation in productive activities which range from agriculture, animal husbandry, commercial enterprises like canteens, shops etc.). These were to be assessed progressively. The continuous assessment formed 50 percent of the final national examination given at the end of the course. The other 50 percent were based on the results of the national examinations.

After Standard VII a School Leaving Certificate was awarded by the regional authorities. After Form IV, students received a Certificate of Secondary School Examination and after Form VI an Advanced Certificate of Secondary Education Examination.

Besides the number of drop outs, which varied between 20 and 30 percent of those who enrolled in Standard I, the result of the primary schooling was disappointing.

The quality of primary school academic performance is most unsatisfactory. Only 15 percent of the candidates, especially in urban areas, manage to score 50 percent in the Standard VII Examinations (United Republic of Tanzania 1993, pp. 6).

Of these about 15 percent continued to secondary school, which was the lowest ratio in the Sub-Saharan countries (in Kenya 50 percent of Standard VII pupils got into Form I, in Uganda 40 percent, in Zambia 40 percent and in Zimbabwe 70 percent, all in 1992). The remainder, 85 percent, had an uncertain future of no formal training. The rate of illiteracy was likely to increase as one of the unwanted effects.

The national examination further reduced the number of school leavers receiving a Certificate of Secondary School Examination (see Table 7). There was one exam in Form II which had to be taken before the students could continue. According to the statistics, the total rates of drop outs and failures in 1992 was 30 percent and in 1993, 37 percent of those enrolled (which already was a small number, as mentioned above).

Thus the examination system sorted out the vast majority of the children in primary school. Even those who continued to secondary school also experienced failures to a large extent. Joel Samoff pointed out that the term primary or secondary school 'leaver' indicates a failure—they are not graduates (Samoff 1990, pp. 253–254).

Table 7: *Secondary school form IV examination results in percentages by division 1989–1993 (public and private secondary schools)*

Division	I	II	III	IV	Failed	Total examined
1989	7.1	7.4	26.7	46.0	12.7	24 068
1990	7.7	8.8	20.9	42.2	20.4	27 677
1991	4.0	7.3	17.2	49.2	22.3	29 985
1992	3.4	5.5	18.7	53.4	18.9	31 522
1993	2.3	4.2	14.4	59.3	19.8	35 025

Source: Ministry of Education and Culture BEST 1994.

Constraining factors

The constraining factors are manifold. I will touch on two main factors, financial and physical frames.

Financial frames

The governmental *allocation to the educational system* decreased from 20 percent of the educational expenditures share of the total governmental budget in 1967 to about 4 percent during the decade of the 1990s.

There were apparent discrepancies in the different sources concerning the size of education sector support. It was claimed that the central Government expenditures as a share of GDP dropped from 4 percent in 1980 to an estimated 2.2 percent in 1992 (Buchert 1997). It was then lower than in other African countries where the education expenditures constituted up to 25 percent. Buchert, however, drew the conclusion that the IMF agreement in 1986 and the structural adjustment programmes, negatively affected the education sector but increased amounts had nonetheless been allocated in the 1990s. Education still remained a high priority sector in Tanzania.

Structural Adjustment Policies and Education

Since independence Tanzania has received external economical support. Nyerere's aim was to decrease dependency on foreign donors but at the time for introduction of Education for Self-Reliance the foreign share was 70 percent of the expenditures. Between 1968 and 1982 the share varied between 70 and 80 percent with a dip down to 50–60 percent during the budget years of 1969/70 and 1979/71 (Roy-Campbell 1991). Aid dependency has not decreased.

The economic crisis that developed during the late 70s and the 80s had a severe impact on the education sector. Central government budget allocation (recurrent) to the Ministry of Education in million shillings is shown in Table 8. The 'great leap' occurred after the Musoma resolution on Universal Primary Education. The number of enrolments in primary schools increased from about 1,969,000 pupils in 1974 to about 3,198,000 in 1979. It was a remark-

Table 8: *Budget allocation to the educational system (Tsh.mn.), enrolment in primary schools and primary school standard VII leavers 1967–1991*

Year	Total budget	Ministry of education allocation	Percent of total budget	Primary school share	Enrolment in primary schools	Standard VII leavers
1961	–	–	–	–	121,386	11,732
1967	–	–	20	–	–	–
1970	–	–	–	–	–	64,630
1974	–	–	–	–	1,228,886	–
1979	–	–	–	–	3,197,395	–
1980/81	14,895.0	1,737.7	11.7	–	–	357,816
1982/83	18,993.0	2,524.0	13.2	–	–	454,604
1983/84	21,460.9	2,502.6	11.7	–	–	649,560 (?)
1984/85	27,438.4	1,795.1	6.5	–	–	429,194
1986/87	53,300.6	4,227.1	7.9	–	3,159,726	–
1987/88	77,667.9	4,168.2	5.4	50.3	–	347,978
1988/89	118,672.0	5,659.3	4.8	–	–	267,744
1990/91	160,000.0	10,153.7	6.3	45.9	–	383,427
1991	–	–	–	–	3,507,384	–
1991/92	23,755.1	9,430.3	4.0	–	–	346,514
1992	–	–	–	–	3,603,488	–
1993	–	–	–	–	3,736,738	–

Source: Ministry of Education and Culture BEST 1994; the same BEST 1990; the same BEST 1994.

able effort considering that there existed neither school houses nor teachers in the beginning. Thereafter, however, the decline in the economy started:

> The decision to cut expenditure in education and other social services was a bitter pill for the government to swallow. From 1979 discussion emerged in government as to whether the economy was capable of maintaining social expenditures at the levels of the 1960s and 1970s, the IMF and others inside and outside Tanzania recognised that this was not practically feasible in the long term, but Nyerere remained confident that it was. Not until 1982–83 therefore were significant cuts registered.
> There were several reasons for Nyerere's resistance. One seems to have been a general optimism that the economic conditions would in any event improve in due course without change in policy direction. More significant was the intimate relation indicated between education on one hand and Ujamaa on the other. It was the transformations in the social sector which were the most successful elements of Ujamaa and probably the ones that earned Nyerere and TANU/CCM its breadth of support and degree of credibility both at home and amongst donors. Cut backs in the educational expenditure therefore represented not simply budgetary adjustments but also potential threat to government, party and presidential political reputations and ideological coherence (Lugalla 1993, pp. 196–197).

The Cost Recovery Programme introduced by the Government in 1984 after pressure from the IMF and the World Bank, included shifting part of the responsibility for primary school construction to the communities, introduction of school fees in primary schools (TShs 100 per year) and secondary school

(TShs 350 for day students and 2,000 for boarding students per year), purchase of textbooks and exercise books by the students and self-reliance projects at all levels. The results were not encouraging. The communities were not able to fulfil the expectations and collection of school fees has not been regular. The self-reliance projects—although introduced during Education for Self-reliance policy—contributed in average to only three percent of the recurrent costs of the secondary and technical schools. Control and accountability were lacking, together with a lack of initial capital (UNESCO 1989).

The emphasis of the Economic Recovery Programme of 1986, adopted after six years of conflict between Nyerere and IMF/World Bank officials, and the Enhanced Structural Adjustment Programme of 1989 was on the development of a market-driven society in which public and private initiatives would be blended and general cuts in the extent of state expenditure and economic activity would be undertaken (Buchert 1997).

> It seems that education's share of the GDP and the Total Government spending was negatively affected by the IMF agreement in 1986, but that some increased amounts haven been allocated in the 1990s. Primary education has continued to receive the highest priority. There are differences in opinions as to whether relative allocation for primary education has been declining during the 1980s (Samoff; Semboja, 1994:157), or has been increasing (Therkildsen, 1996). The most recent figures seem to indicate increased attention to secondary education, but substantial reduction in Government support for higher and technical education (Buchert 1997, pp. 17).

Mrs Mema (in the introduction) experienced the benefits of successful Education for Self-Reliance projects where she worked in the first half of the 1980s. But around 1987 she started to notice the decline of financial funds and its effect on schools. She also observed the decrease in the allocation of governmental funds to education.

After this change of policies, there were tendencies towards racial and religious controversies during the 90s. The quality of life of the majority of Tanzanians declined while the minority Asian community improved theirs tremendously. In 1993 there was a public outcry with claims for an independent Zanzibar state, when it was discovered by the general public that Zanzibar was a member of the Organisation of Islamic Conference (Kaiser 1996).

Twenty-four out of twenty-eight countries with a gross enrolment ratio in first level education of less than 90 percent in 1990, were situated in Sub-Saharan Africa. The other four countries lay in Latin America. The United Republic of Tanzania belonged to the twelve countries that had a lower gross enrolment in 1990 compared with 1980 (UNESCO 1993). Economic difficulties and population pressure were the main factors behind this.

Of the governmental input into primary schools, more than 80 percent was spent on salaries, one percent on staff training and only seven percent on materials and exam expenses. Nothing was spent on the operation and maintenance of schools since that was the concern of the local govern-

Table 9: *Distribution of expenditures in Education Sector Programmes, 1991/92 (shares in percent of total programme expenditures)*

Input to:	Government primary	Secondary total (all biases)	Teacher training
Total in Tsh	27,111 million Tsh	6,454 million Tsh	1,981 million Tsh
Personal emoluments	81	23	17
Travel & visits	2	8	7
Operation and maintenance	0	14	15
Staff training	1	0	14
Pupil transport	0	4	5
Student boarding/welfare	4	45	39
Materials/exam expenses	7	5	3
Hospital services	0	0	0
Other	5	1	0
Total in percent	100	100	100

Source: World Bank 1995.

ments. The large number of teachers in the primary school as well as underfunding was the explanation for the expenditure on personal emoluments rather than high teacher salaries, according to the World Bank (1995). In some regions the wage bill exceeded 90 percent of total allocations for primary schools.

For the secondary schools, 23 percent was spent on salaries. The largest expense (45 percent) was boarding and welfare costs. Since the schools were public, they contracted for operation and maintenance of buildings and premises. Nothing was spent on staff training and only 5 percent on material and exam (which was more per student than for primary schools). The proportions between costs in teacher training colleges was the same as for secondary schools with one exception, 14 percent was spent on staff training (see Table 9).

The extent to which local governments were able to have an impact on the local schools given their relation to the Ministry of Education and Culture and their own ministry, has been observed by the World Bank who commented accordingly:

> In primary and basic education, the roles and inter-relationships between Ministry of Education and Culture and the Prime Minister's Office/Local Government are unclear and frequently dysfunctional. Local Governments are charged with the delivery of educational services but are dependent almost totally on central level funds, which (when eventually transferred) come already earmarked, thus giving local authorities no opportunity to respond to local conditions and priorities (World Bank 1995, pp. 53).

The changes in the economic policy had obvious impacts on the educational system. Schools have experienced increased difficulties in implementing their tasks due to lack of funds. Tanzania fell from a top position of school enrol-

Table 10: *Shortage in percent of required number of equipment in primary schools in 1991*

Region[a]	Classrooms	Toilets	Desks	Tables	Chairs
Arusha	28	78	42	64	54
Dar es Salaam	24	35	29	30	15
Kilimanjaro	17	62	38	51	57
Morogoro	30	67	57	75	76

[a] The regions of Arusha, Dar es Salaam, Kilimanjaro and Morogoro were much better off than for example Lindi, Mtwara, Rukwa and Ruvuma.
Source: Ministry of Education and Culture BEST 1992b; the same BEST 1992c.

ment in Sub Sahara to a considerably lower position. Since the early 1980s, the World Bank has been actively trying to steer development in Tanzania. But Brock-Utne (1993), among others, has criticised their attempt to re-introduce a Western socio-economic and political structure. The World Bank has remained very critical of the conditions of the educational sector of Tanzania (as well as other social and economical sectors).

Physical frames

The conditions of the *physical surroundings* in the schools were pointed out in the reports from the School Inspectorate. As an example of the financial constraints, Table 10 shows the shortage in percent of required number.
The data in the table shows that:

- toilets are provided to a degree of only 22 percent of what is needed in the Arusha region.
- classrooms exist at only 76 percent in relation to the need in the Dar es Salaam region.
- 43 percent of the pupils were able to sit on their own chairs in the Kilimanjaro region.
- 25 percent of required tables could be observed in the classrooms in the Morogoro region.

On average 45 percent of the primary schools had no furniture in their classrooms. This meant that both teachers and pupils were working and studying in a learning environment where sitting on the floor affected the fine as well the gross motor ability of the pupils. The teacher was also, to some extent, restricted in the choice of activities. The school buildings in Tanzania were mainly constructed of mud with earth floors and corrugated iron sheets roofs on timber structures. Many of them were erected rapidly during the Universal Primary Education campaign.

In the schools there was an acute shortage of instructional material in all subjects, which was also pointed out in the reports from the school inspectorate. The recurrent cost per pupil in primary school was only 3,200 TShs while a boarding public secondary school pupil cost 160,000 TShs. In 1990/91 the slight sum of 300 TShs per student was all that was spent on instructional material (for comparison purposes, it can be added that the exchange rate in 1991 was 1 USD = 195 TShs) (Ministry of Education and Culture 1992b).

Another reflection regarding Table 10 is that it is not surprising to see that no funds were available for furniture and teaching materials. The local governments' financial situation was quite weak.

An important physical frame in the frame factor theory approach is time, which is defined as:

> the time needed by a student to master the content and, hence, achieve the goals ... the time needed is a consequence of the subject that is taught, and how this subject is transformed in the teaching situation (Lundgren 1981, p. 26).

According to my observations of teachers and students in schools, supported by my observations of the use of the work schemes, I would say that, generally, time is distributed according to the teacher's estimation and decision without regard to the backgrounds or needs of the individual pupils. Her decision is based on earlier experiences as well as on general assumptions of what can be learnt in the given time of the timetable and curriculum. This strategy is also based on a view of the nature of knowledge as well as on the roles of the teacher and the pupil in the teaching/learning process. Knowledge is seen as something that can be transferred from the teacher to the pupil and rarely from a constructivist perspective, where the pupil is active in the learning situation (searching for necessary knowledge according to needs, choosing individual learning strategies, working with group or individual projects, assessing own performance etc.). It is important to keep in mind the lack of textbooks and teaching material, which contribute to this situation. However, time is not enough. This can be seen among other things by results on examinations and by the fact that private tutoring is one of the side line activities of teachers, especially in secondary schools (see Table 15 in Chapter 6). If teachers, or financial funds, in a certain subject are not available, the subject is not taught. This happens especially in primary schools. In such a case, there is no time for teaching at all. Time allocation for teaching and learning, which was an important frame factor according to Urban Dahlöf (1967) can thus not be directly applied to the Tanzanian school setting.

The background of the pupils is another frame factor. Variation in age within a class is very common in Tanzania, especially in primary but also in secondary schools. In the indigenous education in many parts of sub-Saharan Africa, children were divided into age grades, age sets, and age groups. An age grade consisted of children with the same biological and/or socio-cultural age. An age set included all children in the same age grade within one or several villages. Within the set there were age groups (Daun 1992a). Mixing biological ages in the same class is thus not related to customs in the traditional informal education.

In primary school the gender equality is good, but there are fewer girls who continue to secondary schools. Gender-mixed schools at secondary level occur only in day schools but most secondary schools are boarding schools. The class sizes are big in urban primary schools and secondary schools at the first two levels (Form I and Form II). For 'class composition,' see Chapter 6, under the heading 'Teachers' working conditions.' The size of the classes differs from school to school and from subject to subject.

Summary of frame factors

Curriculum development was an important part of the *governing factors*. A special institute was created but it did not meet the expectations of providing schools with copies of syllabi or text books of good quality.

Of the different *regulating factors* the governmental acts and regulations, of course, had a strong steering effect on the number of pupils taken in at both primary and secondary schools. The work in the classroom was directly affected because the problem of housing facilities and number of classrooms was generally not solved beforehand. Classrooms built for 40 secondary school students were expected to accommodate 50 and in subsequent years 60 and sometimes over 70. This is based on personal observations over a number of years during the 1990s.

The possibility of the school inspectors to have an impact on the educational system was restricted when the contextual factors are taken into consideration. The school inspectorate system was well established but had very limited impact on quality improvement of schooling, according to the World Bank (1995).

National examinations were developed by the central authority with resource personnel from other governmental and ministerial departments. Their steering effect on the work in the classroom as well as on the work of the school inspectors was quite clear. During the last vacation before the last term in Standard VII in primary schools, it was not uncommon to have eight weeks extra teaching as a preparation for the final exams (personal observation). Much of the time during the last term was dedicated to repetition. The scarcity of schooling opportunities made the result of the exams very important for an educational career and this fact was well known in the society. It was, for example, one of the factors that contributed to the establishment of private secondary schools.

One of the *constraining factors* of schooling was the financial situation for the educational sector. The dependency of foreign aid prevailed and the situation was aggravated by the structural adjustment policies. More than 80 percent, sometimes 90 percent, of governmental input to primary schools was spent on salaries. The local governments which were responsible for maintenance and up-keep of school structures had financial problems and often did not have necessary funds to assist the schools. Secondary schools had to provide for boarding pupils and just as in primary schools, nothing was spent on staff training. Both types of schools had problems providing instructional materials—there was an acute shortage in all subjects. Classes were large and had a considerable age variation.

CHAPTER 5
Environment and Education

Introduction

In this chapter I will focus on the expectations on environmental education in Tanzania since 1967, when Education for Self-Reliance was introduced. I will make a brief historical overview by pointing to educational polices and their relation to environmental education up to 1995. I will also make a comparison between the Tanzanian policies and international key ideas as advocated by UNESCO and others. This section is a background to the main part of this chapter, which consists of a curriculum analysis. I will look into existing syllabi and the presence of environmental education components, for primary and secondary schools as well as for teacher training. The analysis is carried out by applying two curriculum emphasis approaches.

The expectations on environmental education

After independence, the necessity of environmental education was discussed in the parliament of Tanzania on several occasions. When summarising the official policy on environmental education, one can see that it has been an issue more or less since 1967, when it was formulated as a part of Education for Self-Reliance. It was clearly stated by the presidential commission in 1982 and was reported to the UNESCO conferences on education in both 1990 and 1992 as a matter of continuous concern in the educational system. In the new policy on education in Tanzania in 1995, one of the nine overall aims was 'to enable a rational use, management and conservation of the environment.'

The Arusha Declaration and Education for Self-Reliance
Some of the basic ideas for environmental education can be traced to the Arusha Declaration of 1967, a party document which marked a turning point in the political, economical, social and education policy in Tanzania. The full title is

'The Arusha Declaration: Socialism and Self-Reliance' (Nyerere 1967c). The principles of socialism were expressed in a number of statements, among them the following:

> Whereas TANU believes:
> ... That all citizens together possess all the natural resources of the country in trust for their descendants[1] (Nyerere 1967c, pp. 232).

The ideas for education were later explained in 'Education for Self-Reliance' (Nyerere 1967a). It was a policy document that started with an analysis of the education system in Tanganyika which was racially biased with segregated schools for Africans, Asians and Europeans. The result was an unequal educational system with very little provision for educational opportunities for Africans, given the 'European' content of the curriculum. These aspects were the first to be changed after independence. The content was Africanised and adapted to the social objectives and needs of Tanzania. In the Arusha Declaration it was pointed out that the base for development was agriculture. In Education for Self-Reliance (ESR) Nyerere said that

> ... Each school should have, as an integral part of it, a farm or workshop which provides the food eaten by the (school) community, and makes some contribution to the total national income ... The farm work and products should be integrated into the school life; thus the properties of fertilisers can be explained in the science classes, and their use and limitations experienced by the pupils as they see them in use. The possibilities of proper grazing practices, and of terracing and soil conservation methods can all be taught theoretically, at the same time as they are put into practice; the students will then understand what they are doing and why, and will be able to analyse any failures and consider possibilities for greater improvement ... The most important thing is that the school members should learn that it is their farm, and that their living standards depend on it ... any other activities now undertaken for pupils, especially in secondary schools, should be undertaken by the pupils themselves ... they have not learnt to take pride in having clean rooms and nice gardens, in the way they have learnt to take pride in a good essay or a good mathematics paper (ibid. pp. 283–286).

Especially secondary schools started with school farms. The produce contributed to the expenses of the high boarding costs. In implementing education for self-reliance tree planting became an important activity. School children got tree seedlings to bring back to their families to be planted. Today about 60 percent of all primary schools have tree nurseries (Bakobi 1993). But it was not easy to get the schools to understand the new policy, as Nyerere also had predicted. At a conference for secondary school head masters and mistresses he had to further explain the ideas and make it clear that he was not asking to reduce academic standards but to make the academic subjects relevant, for example, by using mathematical exercises arising from real problems (Nyerere 1967b).

---

[1] Compare this with the definition of sustainability that was coined by the Brundlandt report 1987.

The Presidential Commission on Education, 1982

In its document (Chapter 1), the Presidential Commission on Education of 1982 pointed out that the educational system in Tanzania had remained as it was in the late 1960s (Wizara ya Elimu 1984).

Once again it was stated that education should be related to the community and that it should be geared towards finding ways of improving the living conditions for all. It was clearly stated that the environment and the natural resources were to be used in a sustainable way. In addition, this was to be reflected in the curriculum of both primary and secondary schools.

Development during the 1990s

In August 1989 there was a discussion between the National Environment Management Council (NEMC) and Sida about intensification of environmental education, particularly in the curricula for primary and secondary schools. In the rationale, NEMC pointed to the necessity for human beings to have the knowledge, skills and attitudes which will enable them to understand and utilise the environment for sustainable development both for themselves and for future generations (Ndunguru 1989). Environmental degradation caused by human beings by shifting cultivation, indiscriminate cutting of trees, cultivation on steep slopes or close to water sources, indiscriminate burning of bushes (a major problem in Tanzania) which contributes to global warming, keeping of livestock beyond carrying capacity, use of explosives for fishing, and indiscriminate cutting of mangrove and removal of sea grasses were all identified as contributing to the environmental problems. While Tanzania had not reached the level of environmental problems experienced by the industrialised countries, there were nevertheless some signs that had started to appear here and there around the few industries in the country.

In its report to the UNESCO International Conference on Education, 42nd session 1990, the Ministry of Education (1990c) stated that efforts were being made to include environmental education in the school curriculum. The objective was to bring awareness to school population about the dangers pertaining to environmental pollution and destruction so as to create positive attitudes towards the environment. The statement was very general but what was surprising was the fact that the question of land degradation was not spelled out. It was vaguely formulated as 'misuse of environment'.

For the United Nations Conference on Environment and Development (UNCED) in July 1991, in Rio de Janeiro, Brazil, the government prepared a report on the current state in Tanzania. They emphasised that the establishment of institutions to specifically deal with environmental issues was quite a recent development in Tanzania. NEMC became operational in 1986 and the National Land Use Planning Commission in 1987. NEMC was expected to co-ordinate all environmental activities in the country. But it was only in 1991 that a Ministry of Tourism, Natural Resources and Environment was established. The

Division of Environment was supposed to carry out the function of seeing to it that environmental education brought about heightened awareness of environmental issues and programmes within the general public.

The report pointed out that Tanzania recognised the need for environmental education and for promoting public awareness.

> While the government is considering the introduction of systematic environmental educational programmes, this has happened only recently. There have been however, some initiatives to introduce environmental education into primary schools and training of trainers has started. However, it is essential that promotion of environmental education and awareness is undertaken as a two-way process, recognising that planners, decision makers and others at the top are just as ignorant of indigenous knowledge as those at the bottom might be of modern technical know-how which could help solve their problems. (United Republic of Tanzania 1991, pp. 14–15)

In 1992, at the 43rd session of the UNESCO International Conference on Education, the Tanzanians, reported on environmental education, saying that a programme for environmental education was being co-ordinated through the Family Life Education project initiated in 1987. (Ministry of Education and Culture 1992a).

A Task Force was appointed in 1990 to make a study and propose an appropriate educational system for the 21st century. Participants came from the Ministry of Education and Culture and the Ministry of Science and Technology and Higher Education. In their report they predicted that protecting the country's resources would need to dominate the education and training curricula for the 21st century (United Republic of Tanzania 1993, pp. 5). They recommended that the curriculum emphasise science, technology and the environment at all levels. All learners from pre-primary up to higher education must be exposed to basic principles of science and scientific application in order to solve technological, social and environmental problems. Basic education, including post-literacy programmes, should be community-based. Knowledge should focus as much as possible on real life situations in order to have practical meaning for the learner. Included in the curriculum should be relevant themes which should be integrated into wider disciplines, as well as improving the environment and technology. Social studies in institutions of higher learning should offer courses which reflect global politics and new meaning of such concepts as world peace, democracy and sustainable development.

In general, the Task Force of 1990 was very critical to what had been achieved within the educational system. Still, when they presented their recommendations, they did not differ much from the established educational philosophy although they formulated environmental education objectives very clearly. A proposal for a National Conservation Strategy for Sustainable Development was presented in January 1994.

In 1995, the Ministry of Education and Culture presented the Tanzania Education and Training Policy (TETP) (United Republic of Tanzania 1995). In the introduction, they stated that the recommendations from the Task Force had been taken into consideration. Nine general aims and objectives of education and training in Tanzania were listed, of which 'to enable a rational use, management and conservation of the environment' was the last.

Comparison of Education for Self-Reliance, Tanzania Education and Training Policy and international environmental education

The educational ideas of Nyerere as noted in Education for Self-Reliance document (Nyerere 1967a) were focused on the development of the rural society of Tanzania. It is interesting to note that many of his basic pedagogical thoughts corresponded well with some of the aims of environmental education expressed by various documents (for example in UNESCO 1978; the so-called Tbilisi Declaration which is considered a founding document, IUCN, UNEP, WWF 1980; Treaty on Environmental Education for Sustainable Societies and Global Responsibility 1992).

In the Tanzania Education and Training Policy some of the general aims corresponded with those of Education for Self-Reliance and internationally accepted aims for environmental education[2], see Appendix 3 for an overview.

All three of the policies aim at developing and transforming the society. Education for Self-Reliance specifies the type of society that is wanted—socialistic—while environmental education is value-based but does not identify the political values. Both Education for Self-Reliance and Tanzania Education and Training Policy mention human dignity. Education for Self-Reliance stresses the use of resources 'to the best advantages' while Tanzania Education and Training Policy and environmental education spells out sustainability. Close contact, involvement of the community and local power are common ground for all three. Self-reliance is a basic concept in Education for Self-Reliance and is still included in Tanzania Education and Training Policy while environmental education considers more general aims concerning economical and social realities.

When it comes to educational aims, all three favour critical thinking and enquiring minds. Education for Self-Reliance and environmental education want the pupils to be active in planning their studies, using different learning approaches (especially practical) and integrating knowledge, skills and attitudes. The same two policies also want to develop an understanding of the causes of environmental problems, in Education for Self-Reliance related to land degradation and for environmental education in a more general sense. Appreciation of traditional knowledge is important for all three policies.

In conclusion, the educational policies of Tanzania include approaches and values that correspond with internationally accepted aims for environmental education.

---

[2] Used by UNESCO, IUCN, and dominant actors.

Curriculum analysis

I will start by referring to an evaluation of the curriculum initiated by the then Ministry of Education in 1990. In November 1992, a Task Force on the Education for the 21st Century (United Republic of Tanzania 1993) presented their analysis of the educational situation in Tanzania.

Evaluation by the 1992 Task Force

The task force looked at the aims and goals of education in Tanzania. They found that in primary school the development of intellectual skills, citizenship, culture, environmental education and special needs for the talented were not clearly emphasised in the aims and objectives. In secondary school, science and technology were not always compulsory. At both levels there was a lack of systematic vocational education.

The primary school curriculum was comprised of thirteen subjects. In 1992 it was decided to reduce the number to seven, but the fewer subjects were still to include parts of the deleted subjects. The curriculum content was class-based instead of age-based. Since the classes had large variations in ages, there was a pedagogical problem of how to handle the situation. The primary school was expected to emphasise local-community based education with the understanding that it could not prepare the large majority of pupils, particularly those who do not go to further education, for a vocation.

At the secondary level, the Task Force stressed that the curriculum was mostly subject-centred. The content in such subjects as English, Geography and Science was repetitive since the curriculum was not a continuation of the primary school curriculum.

Regarding teaching, the Task Force argued that the methodology being used was not conducive to accomplishing the objectives, since the teachers prepared lesson-notes based on schemes of work and the most used teaching method was lecturing. In secondary schools teaching was also dominated by the lecture method.

Further, regarding the examination system, the Task Force stated that the quality of performance in the Standard VII examination was poor, with only 15 percent of the pupils managing to score half marks. Performance in the Form IV National Examination was not very satisfactory since well over 60 percent of the candidates either scored Division IV or failed.

The Education Act of 1978 had stressed three important components in education: the learner and the learning process, the community context and the cultural heritage. But the Task Force did not analyse the situation according to these overall aims.

The curriculum concept

There have been many attempts to define the concept of curriculum. A well-known definition is that a curriculum is organised around four fundamental questions concerning objectives, educational experiences for obtaining the objectives, organisation of these educational experiences and how to determine if the objectives have been attained (Tyler 1949). The 'Tyler Rationale' is considered to be the most influential paradigm of the twentieth century (Walker and Soltis 1986). A broader definition was given by Shirley Grundy (1987). In her opinion, the curriculum is not an abstract concept but a cultural construction. It is a way of organising a set of human educational practices. She argued that the conceptual approach to curriculum corresponds to at set of plans that will guide the teaching, while a cultural approach is concerned with the experiences people have of the existence of the curriculum (ibid. pp. 5–6).

The definition that will be used in this work is based on Ulf Lundgren (1984b). He identified two functions of education: qualification of labour and social reproduction. Social production and social reproduction are, by Lundgren, conceived as separated in most societies today. The interrelation between the two processes, Lundgren argued, depends on texts (or curricula). On this basis he defined curriculum as a selection of contents and goals for social reproduction, an organisation of knowledge and skills and an indication of what methods should be used in the teaching process. The principles behind the selection, organisation and methods constitute the curriculum code. This code is formed through the historical background and the presently existing cultural and materialistic conditions as well as political, administrative and pedagogical conceptions about education (Lundgren & Pettersson 1979). The curriculum code will thus vary depending on the context and the purpose with education. What is learnt and how it is learnt in the classroom, is related to how and why the curriculum was developed. This being so, it should be possible to detect the curriculum code by analysing what is written. I will do so by studying the curriculum emphases.

Curriculum emphases

I will analyse the curriculum according to two concept models. One was developed by Douglas A. Roberts as applied to science subjects and the other was proposed by Charles E. Roth and related to environmental literacy. Why did I chose these two? The first reason was that Roberts' curriculum emphasis had already been used by Leif Östman (1995) in relation to environmental issues and the outcomes could thus be compared. As for Roth, David W. Orr (1992) put forth that ecological literacy is one of the aims of education in the post-modern world, arguing that all education is environmental education (ibid. pp. 90). His opinions are similar to Roth's, who has divided environmental literacy into three stages or emphases, without any outspoken relation to curriculum. Neither of the men has any relation to African culture—they are North Americans—but relating my study to their theories is an attempt to study the Tanzanian curriculum from two different perspectives. This facilitates the interpretation of what basic ideas the curriculum really contains.

Roberts' curriculum emphases

Roberts developed his concept 'curriculum emphases' through a number of case histories. He argued that a curriculum emphasis is selective and expresses a value position (Roberts 1982). He also claimed that no curriculum emphasis is more right than any other. Each has theoretical possibilities like the others, and each provides an answer to students' questions related to why she or he should study science.

The curriculum emphases are organised into seven categories as follows:

> *1. Everyday Coping.* The objective is to comprehend objects and events of fairly obvious importance, for example knowing about familiar chemical processes in home, automobile and industry. The function of the telephone etc. The society needs 'autonomous, knowledgeable individuals who can do mechanical things well, who are entrepreneurial, and who look after themselves, are highly evaluated members of the social order' (Roberts 1988).

This emphasis is related to the daily activities of a citizen's life which she or he is expected to be able to manage. It is related to school subjects such as domestic science, natural science and agriculture.

> *2. Structure of Science.* The objective is to understand how science functions as an intellectual enterprise (attention is given to the relationship between evidence and theory, etc.). The view of society is that 'society needs elite, philosophically informed scientists who really understand how that conceptual system works' (Roberts 1988).

The process of explaining the content and verifying it or relating theory to practice is what this emphasis is about. It is the 'scientific mind' of a researcher.

> *3. Science, Technology and Decisions.* The objective is inter-relatedness among scientific explanations, technological planning and problem-solving and decision-making about practical matters of importance to the society. For example, what can be done about phosphates in laundry and dish washing detergents? 'Society needs to keep from destroying itself by developing in the general public (and the scientists as well) a sophisticated, operational view of the way decisions are made about science-based societal problems' (Roberts 1988).

This category shows the relationship between science and technological development in a society and its effect on people and society. For example, it requires paying attention during the teaching and learning process, planning and taking decisions in consideration of the environmental impact.

> *4. Scientific Skill Development.* This objective is to develop observing, measuring, experimenting, hypothesising etc. skills. Also means of scientific inquiry and scientific processes. 'Society needs people who approach problems with a successful arsenal of scientific tools' (Roberts 1988).

The teaching is focused on implanting skills for scientific approach to problems; i.e. an inquiry-oriented and/or problem-based approach.

5. Correct explanations. The objective is to learn something because it is correct. Emphasis is given to the ends of scientific inquiry. 'Society needs true believers in the meaning system most appropriate for natural objects and events' (Roberts 1988).

This involves learning the correct answer or explanation without discussing or questioning what is being taught, because there is no other explanation.

6. Self as Explainer. The objective is to deal with the character of science as a cultural institution and an expression of one of man's many capabilities. To be able to examine growth and change in scientific ideas as a function of human purpose and of the intellectual and cultural preoccupants of the particular settings in which the ideas were developed and refined. It makes the student understand the process of the explanation itself. 'Society needs members who have a liberal education—that is, who know where knowledge comes from' (Roberts 1988).

This emphasis places what is taught today in an historical context and gives consideration to how the theory has expounded from earlier theories. It reveals the relationship between human thinking and the political, economical and cultural development of the subject and the society.

7. Solid Foundation. The conditions for a student to learn something is that it fits into a structure that has been thought about and planned. It follows that secondary schools tell the primary school what they should teach as well as universities tell the secondary schools what they should teach. 'Society needs scientists' (Roberts 1988).

This indicates that a well-structured teaching method, where each step builds on earlier steps, is necessary. In short, it suggests that theory comes before application. Climbing a stairway could be a suitable metaphor for this kind of curriculum emphasis.

We could ask if this scheme is relevant for an analysis of a non-science curriculum developed in a different context. I believe it is, as it is general enough from a pedagogical point of view to do so. Every curriculum exposes some thought about knowledge and knowledge development, as well as the role of the learner in that process.

Roth's environmental literacy

Since I am interested in environmental education, the second perspective I used is called environmental literacy. A person with environmental literacy has the necessary knowledge to comprehend inter-relatedness, an attitude of caring and the practical competence for taking action. It implies a broad understanding of how people and societies relate to each other and to natural systems in a sustainable way. The environmental literacy concept is part of constructive post-modernism which involves a unity of science as well as ethical, aesthetic and religious intuitions, according to Orr (1992). It provides support for ecology, peace, feminism and other emancipatory movements.

Society has a tendency to use the term literacy as if it were binary—either you are literate or you are not. In reality, any type of literacy represents a continuum from zero ability to advanced skills.

Robert E. Roth described environmental literacy in the following way:

> It would appear that the degree of literacy can best be determined by observable behaviour. Environmental literacy must likewise be defined in terms of observable behaviour. That is, people should be able to demonstrate in some observable form what they have learned—their knowledge of key concepts, skills acquired, disposition towards issues, and the like. In addition, any literacy may be seen to involve degrees of proficiency. These are actually points along a continuum ranging from inability to sophisticated competency (Roth 1992, pp. 25).

Roth suggested three levels of environmental literacy on a continuum on which people tend to progress:

> *Nominal environmental literacy* indicates a person able to recognise many of the basic terms used in communicating about the environment and able to provide rough, unsophisticated working definitions of their meaning. Persons at the nominal level are developing an awareness and sensitivity towards the environment along with an attitude of respect for natural systems and concern for the nature and magnitude of human impacts on them. They also have a very rudimentary knowledge of how natural systems work and how human social systems interact with them.
>
> *Functional environmental literacy* indicates a person with a broader knowledge and understanding of the nature and of interactions between human social systems and other natural systems. They are aware and concerned about the negative interactions between these systems in terms of at least one or more issues and have developed the skills to analyse, synthesise and evaluate a selected problem/issue on the basis of sound evidence and personal values and ethics. They communicate their findings and feelings to others. On issues of particular concern to them they evidence a personal investment and motivation to work toward remediation using their knowledge of basic strategies for initiating and implementing social or technological change.
>
> *Operational environmental literacy* indicates a person beyond functional literacy in both the breadth and depth of understandings and skills who routinely evaluates the impact and consequences of actions; gathering and synthesising pertinent information, choosing among alternatives and advocating action positions and taking actions that work to sustain or enhance a healthy environment. Such people demonstrate a strong, ongoing sense of investment in and responsibility for preventing or remediating environmental degradation both personally and collectively and are likely to be acting at several levels from local to global in so doing. The characteristic habits of mind of the environmentally literate are well integrated (ibid. pp. 25–26).

Some examples of concepts that should be understood by environmentally literate citizens are: environment, ecology, ecosystems, system, food chain, food web, carrying capacity, interactions, land use management, sustainable development, climate, global warming, greenhouse effect, ozone layer, erosion, solid waste, toxic waste, desertification, endangered species, forestry, clear cutting, famine and natural heritage.

Roth pointed to the necessity to further develop the components of environmental literacy but argued that it derives its focus from four basic issues which distinguish environmental education from science education (Disinger & Roth 1992). These issues were: the inter-relationships between natural and social systems, the unity of mankind with nature, technology and the making of choices and developmental learning throughout the human life cycle.

The approach of environmental literacy is more general than Roberts' and has fewer categories. It is not developed on the basis of any particular branch of subjects as Roberts' is (science subjects) but has a multi-disciplinary base. The levels are very likely applicable to different cultures thanks to their general formulation.

Roberts' and Roth's emphases in the Education for Self-Reliance policy
While reading Nyerere's texts (speeches) on education and Education for Self-Reliance and considering the emphases, I find that the Roberts' category of Everyday coping stands out as important. Nyerere spoke of the sorts of things that every boy or girl ought to know to be able to live and contribute to the improvement of the society and to experiences of direct democracy. Science, technology and decisions could also be found; the output of good farmers who were able to think for themselves, to make judgements on all issues affecting them, to interpret decisions and plans and implement them in the light of the local circumstances. Scientific skill development was stressed; education should result in citizens who have an enquiring mind, have learnt basic principles of knowledge in agriculture and are able to adapt them to solve their own problems. Of the environmental literacy levels, the level of nominal could be detected; learning by doing terracing and other soil conservation measures after having been taught theoretically. The students would then understand what they were doing and why. The functional literacy level could be identified as an underlying notion of the whole educational aim.

Will the aspects above be reflected in the syllabi? The two curriculum emphases will be used as tools in the analysis of some selected syllabi. Before that, a brief description of the construction of them.

The planning of the syllabi

For the reader to understand the planning of the syllabi in primary and secondary schools of Tanzania, I will give examples of what they can look like. The approach to the syllabus is different in the 1970s' versions as compared with those after 1982.

In the example of the syllabus for agriculture in Form I[3] from 1976 (Ministry of National Education 1976) the syllabus is arranged in topics and comments. The latter are focused on advice to the teacher regarding what to stress

---
[3] Examples are taken from the secondary school since the primary school syllabi are written in Swahili.

as well as appropriate teaching method and what literature could be used. Through the comments the objective of the topic become more clear. The syllabi were based on the Arusha Declaration. The content was geared towards citizenship and preparation for a life in the village. An example of the structure and content of the syllabus :

Topics and Details	Notes
1 a) Agriculture as a science, a business and a cornerstone of civilisation	i) As a science, background subjects are: Chemistry, biology, geography, maths and physics. ii) As a business: Mention the economics of running a big farm. iii) As a cornerstone to civilisation: Mention Egyptian, Mesopotamian civilisations based on the fertile valleys of the Nile and the Euphrates-Tigres rivers—relate the development of Kilimanjaro, Mwanza and W. Lake regions based on coffee and cotton.
1 c) Role of schools in agricultural production	– The concept of self-reliance should be re-stressed. Pupils should be assigned productive projects, e.g. poultry-keeping for meat and eggs; growing of crops. – Use the Education for Self-Reliance Book by President J.K. Nyerere.

In the extract below from the 1989 syllabus in biology Form I (Ministry of Education 1989), the approach is different. The syllabus is arranged according to an educational technology approach. The learning process is mainly teacher centred. Some of the reference books are old, but we might still wonder if they were accessible to the teachers in view of the economic situation? My visits to the Institute of Curriculum Development library in Dar es Salaam in 1992–1993 revealed that the curriculum developers themselves did not have access to all literature. The probability that the teachers in schools would have a better situation is very unlikely.

Topic	Objectives	Suggested teaching/ learning strategies	Material/ apparatus	References
1.2 Objectives of studying biology	1. Discuss the importance of studying biology	Teacher to lead a discussion on the importance of studying biology		McLeroy, W.D. Swanson, C.P. Byffaloe, N.D. Galston, A.W. and Macey, R.A. 1968. Foundations of Biology. Prentice Hall, Inc. Englewood, Cliffs, New Jersey
	2. Value living things and the balance of nature	Teacher to lead a discussion on the role played by other organisms in the balance of nature, hence to the welfare of mankind.		Msaki, L.K. (1987) Simplified Biology for Secondary Schools. Book I. Diamond Distributors Ltd, DSM

With these two examples as a background, I will proceed to the analysis of the syllabi in primary and secondary school.

Analysis of syllabi for Primary Schools

The syllabi were those that were used in the schools in the Arusha, Dar es Salaam, Kilimanjaro and Morogoro regions which I visited in 1992–1993. They varied from 1969 to 1990. It was rare to find the latest version of the syllabus. Besides, not all teachers had copies of the syllabi. I had difficulties even to getting copies to borrow. The most natural place to find them, the Institute of Curriculum Development, did not have copies in their library or archive. Only through the kind assistance of educational officers at district and local levels did I manage to obtain copies. It happened that I brought a more recently developed syllabus to a school that I visited. As a consequence of these circumstances, different schools were using syllabi that were developed in different years.

I analysed the syllabi to see what components of environmental education could be found. The syllabi I have chosen for primary school are: agriculture, domestic science, geography and science. The reason for choosing these was that they were the subjects most likely to contain environmental education components. In primary school, biology was included in the science subject. I tried to identify all environmental components and they are listed in Appendix 4. As a working definition of environmental education I used the following from the US Environmental Education Act 1970 and also accepted in the Australia Environmental Education Act 1976 as cited in Gough (1997a, pp. 8):

> Environmental education is an integrated process which deals with man's relationship with his natural and man-made surroundings, including the relation of population growth, pollution, resource allocation and depletion, conservation, technology and urban and rural planning to the total human environment. Environmental education is a study of the factors influencing ecosystems, decaying cities and population pressures. Environmental education is intended to promote among citizens the awareness and understanding of the environment, our relationship to it and the concern and responsible action necessary to assure our survival and to improve the quality of life.

Identification of the environmental education components was not a problem (see Appendix 4), but I have also analysed the syllabi according to the two approaches presented in the beginning of this chapter, i.e. Roberts' curriculum emphasis and Roth's environmental literacy. I have studied the whole syllabus when trying to analyse them according to Roberts' categories while only the environmental components in the syllabus were classified according to Roth's levels of environmental literacy.

The categorisation of Roberts' emphasis took longer and required three readings before I could decide upon what category was the most appropriate. In late 1995 I met Douglas A. Roberts and had the opportunity to discuss my understanding of his categories by showing examples of syllabus text and examination questions. This discussion increased my confidence. The environmental literacy categorisation was less complicated, mainly depending on the lower number of possible categories and the more pronounced differences between them.

The result is presented below, subject by subject. In the analysis of the agriculture syllabus below, I present examples of how I classified topics into two curriculum emphases. The same approach has been used in all syllabi.

Agriculture

Agriculture is taught in Standard III–VII. The syllabus was issued in 1982 with a second printing in 1990 by the Ministry of National Education (Wizara ya Elimu ya Taifa 1982). It was organised with the following sub-titles: topics and content, objectives, teaching-learning method and references. The content was focused on soil science, animal husbandry and, from Standard IV, natural resources. Soil science started out with soil components and continued with types of soils, fertilisers, soil fertility and ended in Standard VII with soil erosion.

The goal of the subject referred to the Arusha Declaration and Education for Self-Reliance. It specified that the subject should give practical and theoretical knowledge to pupils and prepare for a life in the rural areas. The goal was also to produce more cash and food crops, to improve their quality and to teach respect for agriculture as the backbone of the economy. The subject was also expected to prepare pupils for further education.

The objective of the subject was to prepare and implement projects in the villages and help pupils to become good farmers. The pupils were to be able to make things with their hands and develop self-confidence and self-reliance. They were also expected to learn good agricultural techniques concerning soils, lands, economy, animal keeping and farm tools, as well as appreciate the role of co-operatives.

When looking at all the topics in the syllabus, the content was very much related to *Everyday coping* according to Roberts' categories of curriculum emphases. They aimed at helping the pupils to be able to implement basic farm activities. For example, the objectives for Animal Husbandry in Standard IV were (translated from Swahili):

> A pupil should be able to:
> 1. Realise the importance of keeping goats for food and income.
> 2. Keep a goat.
> 3. Recognise goats that are tamed in Tanzania.
> 4. Select the best method of keeping goats according to a. the environment
>   b. requirements.
> 5. Know various types of food required by goats.
> 6. Select the best breed.
> 7. Know source, symptoms and cure for various diseases.

The environmental literacy according to Roth was mostly *nominal*. There was a very practical focus to the content of the subject. In the syllabus the following could be found in Standard VI: 'know various methods used to fertilise soil and to maintain its fertility'; 'use these methods at home and school'; 'uses and how to put various types of fertiliser'. The use of natural and chemical manure was to be learnt, but I interpreted the words in the syllabus as if the aim was to recognise and be able to provide a rough working definition of the meaning. There is no mention of the concepts of cycles in nature, for example of nutrition or the effects of different kinds of fertilisers. Thus I have classified this aspect as belonging to nominal environmental literacy. To build fish ponds and keep bees were mentioned as ways to improve the nutrition of the family. What was missing was a discussion of the hazards of using fire when collecting honey. Forest fires were quite common in Tanzania as a result of wild honey collection. It was reasoned that if pupils were able to prepare a nursery and grow seedlings, then they would be able to plant a wood lot that could give wood fuel for their own consumption or for sale. These were all activities that did not exhaust the natural resources.

But in three cases in Standard VII the environmental education components were *functional*. For example, the pupils should select the best methods to keep goats. This requires a broader knowledge besides memorising basic concepts.

Domestic Science syllabus

The aim of this syllabus was to introduce domestic science education to pupils in a way that enabled them to understand the issues or topics in this area of science and to be able to follow all the changes which had occurred in the country. Issued in 1969 and reprinted in 1977, the syllabus also aimed to provide pupils with a political education (Wizara ya Elimu ya Taifa 1969).

The main aim, however, was to provide the pupils with a good foundation for their future life. For example, it sought to educate girls about their work as a housewife and that they should use all the skills and technology they could. Another aim was to provide an education based on people's preferences through the use of available material in the country.

The curriculum emphasis was on *Everyday coping*, since all components in the syllabus concerned practical activities in the daily caring of the house and family. The focus was on health education and preventing diseases spread by contamination of water and land/surroundings. The environmental literacy level was *nominal*. The teaching was concentrated more on instruction of healthy habits than discussion of causes and consequences in different contexts.

Geography

The goal of this subject was to facilitate the realisation of the Ujamaa philosophy and Education for Self-Reliance.

The pupils were expected to understand the problems of the area where they lived and learn how to solve them. They were to learn about the area in terms of what is produced, the physical structure, soils and all human activities. They were also to study how other societies in the world were solving their problems and learn from this. The teaching methods that were recommended went from the known to the unknown.

The syllabus referred to above was issued during the 70s (Wizara ya Elimu ya Taifa 1977?). The emphasis of the curriculum was on *Everyday coping*, using and conserving the environment in order to improve living conditions in the rural areas. The environmental literacy according to Roth was *nominal* with a more *functional* level in Standard VI and VII, i.e. in the last two years of schooling the geography content should be more contextual and applicable.

In the syllabus there was no mention of environmental pollution by industries or hazards of using chemicals in the agricultural sector (these environmental education related components are listed in Appendix 4). On the topic of national parks, which cover a considerable area of Tanzania, the focus was on the economic outcome, particularly from the tourist industry. There was nothing about conservation of endangered species, although poaching and co-existence with the local population were major problems.

Some schools were using the new syllabus, issued in 1990 (Ministry of Education 1990a). The main emphasis of the curriculum was on *Correct explanations*. The wording of many objectives in the syllabus started with 'lead pupils to ....' In Standard VII the verb 'discuss' is used, for example 'to discuss environmental destruction.' The meaning of 'discuss' is doubtful since in most cases it still refers to a teaching situation where the teacher gives the right answers to questions which are formulated by the teacher him/herself. The environmental literacy is at the *nominal* level. The pupils learn the basic concepts but do not get a broader understanding of the interaction between human and natural systems. Compared to the former syllabus, the topics of Game Reserves and National Parks as well as Forests were omitted. The number of environmental education components had thus decreased.

Science

Through science subjects pupils were expected to expand their curiosity and capability for research. They should be able to solve daily problems in their environment. They were to be able to make things with their own hands and develop self-confidence and become self-reliant. The school was expected to develop co-operation among the pupils, thus helping them to become less selfish. Also pupils were to be taught to be able to continue their development even after finishing primary education.

The science subject was comprised of topics on health science, agriculture and biology. The syllabus was issued in 1982 by the Ministry of National Education (Wizara ya Elimu ya Taifa 1982a). The emphasis of the curriculum was general *Everyday coping*, according to the Roberts' classification. This is different from Standard VII where curriculum focus was on *Scientific skills*.

The environmental literacy of the pupils up to Standard VI according to Roth's levels was *nominal*. The concentration was on cleanliness and soil erosion. In Standard VII the level was *functional*.

> 23. In one of his experiments, Hugo discovered that the type of soil in his farm was acidic. This enabled him to decide the following:
> a. Select a type of crop to grow
> b. Do terracing
> c. To mix soil by tilting it
> d. To leave this part of his farm for a while
> e. Use some chemicals that could change the soil.
>
> 24. Lions → Antelopes → Grass
> If antelopes move from this place, what will happen?
> a. There will be an increase in the number of lions
> b. Grasses will decrease in amount
> c. Grasses will conceal the lion
> d. An increase in grass
> e. Lions will eat grass.

Box 2. Standard VII exam questions with environmental components in the subject of science in the 1992 national examination.

Exam questions in Primary School with environmental education components

A school leaving certificate was awarded after successful completion of a final exam in Standard VII. This was necessary but not sufficient for selection to continuation to secondary school. The steering effect of exams was well known and therefore it was important to find out what the exam questions were about. The final examinations in Standard VII were standardised national exams prepared by the National Examinations Council.

In the 1992 examinations there were two questions related to environmental education. They were found in the science subject which had 20 multiple-choice questions with five answer alternatives. In the other subjects there were no questions related to environment at all. The subject Swahili had ten multiple-choice questions, history eight, civic seven, domestic science ten and English 17. In English there was also a short text with five multiple-choice questions on the content.

My conclusion is that there were almost no questions at all with an environmental content in the Standard VII exams (2/77).

How did the pupils understand the questions? What did the teacher teach about it and what did the pupil take down in her/his note book? Was it related to reality or was it a copy of the same simple diagrams that was drawn by the teacher on the blackboard? Did the pupil understand the concept of food web or was it just root learning? What were the 'correct' answers?

According to Roberts, the curriculum emphasis in Question 23 (Box 2) was *Everyday coping* and in Question 24 it was *Scientific skills reasoning*.

Table 11: *Summary of Roberts' curriculum emphases and Roth's environmental literacy levels in three subjects in primary school syllabi*

Subject	General aims	Curriculum emphases	Environmental literacy
Agriculture issued 1982 (reprinted in 1990)	Prepare for a rural life within an improved agricultural economy. Prepare for further education. Develop self-confidence and self-reliance.	Everyday coping	Nominal—functional
Domestic Science issued 1969 (reprinted in 1977)	Good foundation for future family life. Being able to use available material in the country.	Everyday coping	Nominal
Geography issued 1970s	Facilitate realisation of Ujamaa and self-reliance.	Everyday coping	Nominal—functional
Geography issued 1990	Learn how to solve problems in their local area.	Correct explanations	Nominal
Science issued 1982	Expand capability of curiosity and research. Be able to solve daily problems. Develop self-confidence, self-reliance and co-operative skills not only in school but continuously in life.	Everyday coping Scientific skills	Nominal—functional

Summary of analyses of curriculum for primary school

The curriculum emphases according to Roberts and the environmental literacy level according to Roth are summarised in Table 11. The analyses were carried out on the whole syllabus, not only on the environmental education components in the syllabi.

The environmental education components concentrated on soil science, soil conservation, and soil conservation methods. Soil erosion and soil conservation were repeated, probably overlapping, with agriculture in Standard VII, with science in Standard VI and with geography in Standard VII. Another focus in the agriculture syllabus was forest, as well as the keeping of fish and bee. In the science syllabus, information about hygiene and diseases as well as soil and soil erosion were present. In the last school year ecology was taught.

Nowhere were these components openly identified as environmental, except in the ecology topic.

The curriculum emphasis was on *Everyday coping*, related to daily activities in life in the syllabi issued 1982 or earlier. Only in Standard VII, in the science subject, was another emphasis found, namely *Scientific skills* (inquiry oriented or problem solving approach). The environmental literacy levels were *nominal* and at times *functional* in Standard VI and/or VII. The curriculum emphases fit well with the Ujamaa and Education for Self-Reliance philosophy.

In the later syllabus of geography from 1990, the emphasis is on *Correct answers* and the environmental literacy level *nominal*.

The emphases in the curriculum are mainly in accordance with the ideas of Education for Self-Reliance. The focus is on Everyday coping and what is less stressed is Scientific skills, i.e. the enquiring mind, problem solving competence and application of knowledge into practical situations.

The final examinations were very important and both the teachers and the pupils were mostly interested in the subject content that was likely to appear in the exams. In spite of the decisions and policies of environmental education, as have been referred to earlier, very little was reflected in the exams. Did the pupils leave Standard VII with an understanding of the environment so that they could use it in a sustainable way? It was very unlikely that the schools could produce this.

Analysis of syllabi for Secondary Schools

The syllabi from Secondary Schools that were analysed are those that were used in the schools in the same regions as the primary schools which I visited in 1992–1993. Secondary education from Form I to Form IV was divided into four biases[4]: agriculture, commerce, technical skills and home economics.

The curriculum design of the 1989 syllabi is oriented towards educational technology, with topics, objectives, suggested teaching/learning strategies, material/apparatus and references. In the 1976 syllabi, only topics were given, sometimes with 'notes' suggesting that students conduct practicals. Looking at the overall aims and objectives, the philosophical base of the curriculum was more towards realism than idealism.

In the educational policy, the learner and the learning process were considered to be important. In the design of the syllabi it was difficult to discover anything other than a teacher-dominated learning process with rather unchangeable roles. It is true that practical activities were promoted here and there, however they were not the basis for learning but they were attached as desirable activities.

I will analyse the syllabi in agriculture, home economics, geography and biology according to the two approaches presented at the beginning of this chapter, namely Roberts' curriculum emphasis and Roth's environmental literacy. The reason why I have chosen these subjects is the same as for the primary school syllabi, namely that environmental education components were most likely to be found here. I studied the whole syllabus when trying to fit it into Roberts' system. Further, I tried to identify all environmental components, and classify them according to Roth's levels of environmental literacy (see Appendix 5). I made the categorisation with the same considerations as for primary school syllabi as described above.

---
[4] 'Bias' in the Tanzanian school system is used to denote what would be called 'programme' or 'specialisation' in European schools.

Agriculture

The syllabus for agriculture, issued in 1976 (Ministry of National Education 1976a), stated that the aims and objectives of the agricultural subject were to ensure and develop domestic produce. The importance of the agricultural sector for Tanzania was emphasised. The current syllabus also highlighted the socialist economy and co-operative production. It was expected that secondary schools would be a good example for the surrounding community through their projects and production units—here we have the focus on education for self-reliance.

When studying the whole syllabus for agriculture, the curriculum emphasis according to the model developed by Roberts was on *Everyday coping.*

An example from Form II's Agro Mechanics and Techniques/Engineering:

> Elementary Plumbing. Cover various pipe fittings and valves; types of pipes (galvanised, steel, aluminium, rubber and plastic pipes). Repair of leaking pipes.

Another example from Livestock Science/Production in Form III stated:

> Selection of dairy cattle; the dairy herd records management of the dairy farm. Stress general principles involved in the management of a dairy farm, criteria of selecting dairy animals and types of dairy herd records.

The environmental education components in the agricultural subject were several as can be seen in Appendix 5. The syllabus suggested a number of practical activities. Those related to environmental education called for afforestation of the school compound; physical soil analysis; separation of soil humus; identification of various types of manure and fertilisers (specimen to be shown); run-off demonstration models established by pupils to illustrate erosion and loss of soil fertility; compost manure making and soil improvement; water and soil conservation reduction of run-off water, infiltration rate, sedimentation, capillarity, soil cover, contours, model of a conservation farm, meaning of land slope, soil loss; fertiliser use and soil conservation.

As for the kind of emphasis that was given to the environmental education components in the agriculture syllabus, I would chose the *nominal* but *functional* when it came to the practical applications, according to the categories developed by Roth concerning environmental literacy.

Home Economics

In the syllabus for home economics, particularly in schools with a so-called agricultural, commercial and technical bias (Ministry of National Education Applied Sciences 1976a), the aims and objectives were to foster a family and community member with certain attitudes, knowledge and skills. The family and the society co-operation was basic for unity and progress. The development of physical, mental and emotional health was one of the objectives in the syllabus.

Home economics was compulsory in Form I and II. In Form III and IV the pupils were allowed to chose between Textiles and Dressmaking or Nutrition and Cookery.

The curriculum emphasis according to Roberts was *Everyday coping*. The content of the syllabus with respect to its environmental components can be considered to be at a *nominal level* from an environmental literacy point of view (Roth 1992). The content was mainly focused on cleanliness and it was mostly a repetition of what was in the primary school syllabus (see Appendix 4).

Geography

The syllabus in geography was issued in 1976 (Ministry of National Education 1976b). The objective was to enable the learners to understand human communities and their occupations in different places and under different conditions. The objective was also to understand how these communities strive to raise their standards of living by utilising the resources found within their environments.

The subject was supposed to help students become aware of their country as their heritage and to develop awareness of the extent to which resources of their land can be developed to raise the standard of living of their people. It was also important that the students understand the social and geographical constraints in the developing process and try to find ways to overcome them. The students were also expected to develop methods of observation, measuring, recording and interpretation of geographical phenomena. By studying the geography of other countries it was hoped that the students would see the interaction between their country and other countries and how world problems were interrelated.

In the topics and sub-topics of the syllabus, the main impression was that it fits the definition of Roberts' *Correct explanations*.

The environmental components were few and only the soil conservation issues were certain to be taught as an effect of the relationship between human beings and the natural systems. The others were to be taught only as 'how to use the natural resources' without mentioning or discussing the effects. The level of environmental literacy was at a *nominal* level.

Biology

The biology subject had a syllabus that was developed by the Institute of Curriculum Development in 1989 (Ministry of Education 1989). The aims and objectives were much more concise than that of the syllabus issued in 1976.

The aim of the biology course was to enable students to understand principles and concepts and use the knowledge and skills so acquired in their everyday life in their community. The objective was to make them able to utilise their natural heritage (natural resources) and to raise their standard of living and free themselves from ignorance, poverty and diseases. Another objective

> 10. In forestry; weeding, thinning and selective cutting of trees are known as
> a. Taungya pruning
> b. Under cutting
> c. Canopy opening
> d. Tending
> 11. A place which is suitable for an apiary has all of the following characteristics EXCEPT
> a. Strong winds
> b. Water stream
> c. Flowering plants
> d. Warm weather
> 23. Briefly explain five cultural methods that may be used to control crop diseases.
> 29.
> a) What do you understand by the term crop rotation?
> b) List four advantages of crop rotation
> c) State any four factors which have to be considered when planning a rotation of crops.
> 32.
> a) Distinguish between organic manure and inorganic manure.
> b) Besides adding plant nutrients to the soil, in what other ways does organic manure improve the soil? Outline any four ways.

Box 3. Form IV exam questions in agriculture science related to environmental education in the 1992 national examination.

was to prepare the students for professional training in various institutions and for further studies in Form V and VI.

In terms of Roberts' terminology, the curriculum emphasis was *Everyday coping* and *Correct explanations.*

Environmental components were found mainly in Form IV but there were minor components earlier. Roth would classify the environmental literacy level as *nominal* and in some cases *functional*. The approach to biology followed a traditional orientation towards learning facts, with few relationships in and between systems being studied.

Exam questions in Secondary School with environmental education components

The reason why I looked into the exam questions was the same as said previously. The national examinations in Form IV were prepared by the National Examinations Council. For this treatise, the questions from the 1992 exams were scrutinised for their environmental education components. The questions in the exam papers were multiple choice. In each subject there was also an open-ended question where the student was asked to choose from among a few options. In physics there were 18 questions and one alternative to a practical with ten questions. In chemistry the number of questions were 39 and in the

> Growing crops on a soil with excessive levels of soluble salts will result in the wilting of the plants because of plasmolysis of root cells due to
> a. diffusion of water from the root cells to the surrounding soil solution
> b. diffusion of salts from surrounding soil solution into the root cells
> c. increased diffusion pressure of soil water
> d. changes in soil pH.

Box 4. Form IV exam questions in biology, related to environmental education in the 1992 national examination.

alternative practical ten. Biology had 20 questions and an essay-type question with a choice between three topics. In the biology alternative practical there were four questions. Geography had 11 questions and one section which consisted of ten multiple-choice questions. In agriculture there were 35 multiple-choice questions while cookery and nutrition (home economics) had 38 and an alternative practical with ten questions.

Questions with environmental components were found in agriculture (5/35) and biology (4/25) (see Box 3).

In Biology Paper 1, Section A (answered by all) there was one question related to soil, asking the student to mark one answer (see Box 4).

In Section C (students were asked to answer one question of three), two questions related to the environment were asked, as can be seen in Box 5.

In Biology Paper 2, which was an alternative to a 'practical' paper subject (a so-called 'theoretical practical'), there was one question related to soil science (see Box 6).

Questions 12 and 13 in biology, which were not answered by every student since there was an option between three questions, were those that were most 'environmental.' They were open-ended questions and gave the students an opportunity to develop their thoughts.

In geography there were no questions that can be said to be related to environmental education. Instead, the questions were on map reading and photograph interpretation, physical and mathematical geography in East Africa, the rest of Africa, North-western Europe, North America and Asia.

> 12. Give an account of the relationship that exists between producers, consumers and decomposers in an ecosystem stating the part played by each and the ways in which they are dependent on one another.
> 13. a) Explain how each of the following factors can bring about soil erosion.
>   i) Deforestation
>   ii) Overgrazing
>   iii) Cultivation.
>   b) How can soil erosion be prevented?

Box 5. Form IV exam questions in biology, related to environmental education in the 1992 national examination.

> 2. Three different soil samples, A, B, and C were each shaken up with water in a measuring jar and then left to settle. After some time the different size particles of soil settled in layers. The proportions of the various soil particles in the three samples of soil were determined and the results were shown in table 2 below.
>
> Table 2:
>
> | Soil Sample | % gravel | % sand | % silt | % clay |
> |---|---|---|---|---|
> | A | 70 | 20 | 5 | 5 |
> | B | 3 | 13 | 27 | 57 |
> | C | 20 | 25 | 35 | 20 |
>
> Percentage constituents of each soil samples A, B and C.
> a)
> i) What was the aim of the experiment?
> ii) From what type of soils were samples A, B and C taken? Give reasons.
> b)
> i) Draw a well labelled diagram to show the arrangement of the various layers in the measuring jar when soil sample C was being investigated.
> ii) Briefly explain how one can determine the proportion of each type of particle in a soil sample.

Box 6. Form IV exam questions in biology, related to environmental education in the 1992 national examination.

In the home economics exam, specifically in the cookery and nutrition portions, there were two papers and two (theoretical) 'practicals' but no questions related to environmental education. The questions were mostly on nutrition and meal dishes.

Summary of analyses of curriculum for secondary school

The syllabi in agriculture, biology, geography and home economics, for secondary schools in Tanzania were analysed with respect to the content emphases (see Table 12).

The dominating curriculum emphasis was *Everyday coping*, which was found in agriculture, home economics and biology. *Correct explanations* dominated the geography syllabus and could also to some extent be found in the biology syllabus.

The environmental literacy according to Roth could be found in all syllabi. For agriculture and biology the level was *functional*, especially in the practical parts.

The same conclusion as for the primary school curriculum can be drawn but with an additional comment, that the secondary school curriculum seems to lack the emphasis on Scientific skills development. *Correct explanations* appears almost as important as *Everyday coping*.

Table 12: *Summary of syllabi analyses according to Roberts' curriculum emphases and Roth's levels of environmental literacy*

Subject	General aims	Curriculum emphases	Environmental literacy
Agriculture issued in 1976	Develop domestic produce, especially in agriculture. Be a good example for the surrounding community through their Education for Self-Reliance projects.	Everyday coping	Nominal—functional
Home Economics issued in 1976	To foster good attitudes, knowledge and skills among family and community members. Family and society co-operation were seen as the basis for unity and progress, as well as the development of physical, mental and emotional health.	Everyday coping	Nominal
Geography issued in 1976	Be aware of their country as their heritage. Be able to understand human communities and raise their (and other people's) standard of living by using available resources.	Correct explanations	Nominal
Biology issued in 1989	Be able to understand and use principles, concepts, knowledge and skills in everyday life in their communities. Be able to use natural resources and raise their standard of living. Prepare for professional training.	Everyday coping. Correct explanations	Nominal—functional

The general impression of the secondary school syllabi is that there was a discrepancy between the aims and objectives of the syllabi and the presentation of topics and sub-topics. The aims were thematic and accentuated the society and the community context. In general, the topics and sub-topics had a traditionally subject-centred approach. This was, however, not the whole truth for agriculture, which stresses the production aspect, or for home economics which was centred around everyday activities in the family.

In the agriculture syllabus, there were many environmental components which were to be found to a less extent in home economics, geography and biology. But this was noticeable. In the final exams in 1992, there were five questions in agriculture with an environmental touch. In biology there were two which all students answered. There were no questions at all related to the environment in geography. This evidently reflected the syllabus orientation. However, it is important to consider the subject 'environmental' since it deals with the presence and use of natural resources.

A conclusion that can be made is that the official policies on the importance of environmental education in Tanzania had not been followed up by the national examination authorities but the situation was slightly better at secondary than at the primary school level.

Teacher training

Teacher training was done at teacher training colleges, presently around 40, spread over all regions of Tanzania. At that time only two different courses, one for primary school and one for secondary school were given.

The qualifications for teaching environmental education at the primary school training were low, since it was possible to enter teaching after seven years of primary schooling and after two years of college training in eleven different subjects. This kind of training was in theory to be phased out and was to be replaced by a training based on seven basic years plus four years in secondary school.

However, generally, the majority of primary school teachers had even lower professional preparation. During the years of the 'great leap' after the Musoma declaration for universal primary education, many teachers were 'crash course-trained' and many were still being up-graded through distance education. The up-grading was in knowledge (from primary to secondary school level) and not in professional skills.

The preparation of teachers for secondary schools was done at teacher training colleges and called Diploma courses. At the University of Dar es Salaam the training for the higher levels of secondary school was done at graduate level.

If we look at the curriculum for the diploma teachers, who were trained to teach at lower secondary levels, folk development colleges, colleges for national education and at teacher training institutions, we see that they studied two subjects in addition to the subject of education. The subject teachers in the colleges are supposed to teach methodology as well. Six weeks of teaching practice was included in the curricula.

The syllabi were developed in 1980 and followed a similar organisation as the one described above for secondary schools: topic, topic objectives, learning-teaching strategies and facilities, equipment and materials.

Some syllabi were written in Swahili (Education, for example) and others in English (for those subjects which were to be taught in English). This implies that some of the teaching at the teacher training colleges was done in Swahili, which would not be a help to these future teachers in developing their proficiency in English.

Education (Pedagogy)

The subject of Education (Pedagogy) encompassed educational philosophy, educational psychology, curriculum, research and evaluation, administration, guidance and counselling and finally adult education. Each of these were taught in two 40 minutes periods per week during four terms. In total, the number of lessons—more than 1000—was very high for education compared to other subjects..

The course goals are closely linked to the Ujamaa philosophy (Wizara ya Elimu ya Taifa 1980). Education was geared to solving the developmental problems of Tanzania and building a socialist society. It was expected that the student teachers would gain skills, knowledge and behaviour in accordance to the goals of education.

Teacher education was supposed to teach about the Tanzanian way of socialism. It was seen as lifelong education related to both growing up and acquiring of knowledge.

The training aimed to enable students to understand the pupil and his/her environment. The student was also expected to apply different methodologies to teaching and to observe professional requirements. The training also prepared student teachers for administrative duties and for research activities, curriculum development and evaluation. Lastly, the students were expected to play a role in the adult education programme after they graduated.

The educational philosophy contained the Arusha Declaration and its implication for the educational system, i.e. universal primary education and education for all as described earlier. The syllabus outlined the history from colonial times to independence. The syllabus was true to the political philosophy of the time. The other parts of education, educational psychology and so on, as indicated above, were traditional when it came to content and structure. They could have been written and taught in any country. The only difference was that the educational philosophy was clearly adapted to Tanzania.

Geography

The syllabus of geography (Ministry of National Education 1980) required a total of 640 periods during four terms. Of this, 384 periods were allocated to the subject and 256 to teaching methodology and practice. The objectives were few but clear:

a) consolidate and master his [the student teacher's] knowledge and skills in geography.
b) acquire and apply principles, methods and techniques of teaching geography in secondary schools (Form I–IV) and colleges of national education (grades C and A).
c) develop positive attitudes towards his social and physical environment.

The syllabus provided basic guidelines but they were not exhaustive. The teacher was expected to develop and improve his or her teaching and be innovative in his or her teaching methods.

The content areas included physical resources of East Africa, human resources of East Africa, Africa, other areas (China and Japan as case studies), practical geography, research methodology, the aims of teaching geography, the current geography syllabus for secondary schools, teaching techniques, teaching material and equipment, testing and evaluation.

The syllabus was more 'environmental' than what was actually being taught in primary and secondary schools (see Appendix 6). The emphases, according to Roberts' system, were on *Everyday coping, Correct explanations, Scientific skill* and *Science, technology and decision-making* (see Roberts' curriculum emphases above). The environmental literacy was at the *nominal, functional*, and in some cases, even the *operational* level.

The conclusion is that the syllabus in geography at the teacher training level was much more varied in various perspectives of knowledge and skills than the primary and secondary school syllabi. The same observation was made regarding the environmental literacy levels.

Conclusions

The general aims of the syllabi were intimately linked to the Education for Self-Reliance policy. My analyses of the syllabi indicate that the content was meant to preparing students for everyday life activities. The primary school syllabi included a number of environmental education components which also were related to daily life activities.

In the secondary schools the situation was not as clear-cut. If students attended a school that was agriculturally oriented, they had a possibility to develop a deeper understanding of soil conservation measures than was taught in primary school. They also had an opportunity to develop a better understanding of the cycles of nature. But most students took a secondary education course with other orientations. They studied geography, which most likely did not develop their environmental understanding. In biology the last topic in Form IV was ecology. It was poorly developed in the syllabus, and it is doubtful that the topic was really covered before the exams, due to time constraints.

The syllabi were dominated by the curriculum emphases *Everyday coping* and *nominal* and *functional* environmental literacy. But the intention of Education for Self-Reliance was also to develop Science, Technology and Decision and this emphasis was not seen in any of the syllabi. On the other hand, *Correct explanations* as a pedagogical approach was never mentioned by Nyerere, although quite frequently in the syllabi.

The content and nature of the examination questions did not encourage teachers and students to waste time on the environmental education components (except in agriculture). But as a general conclusion, the national examinations did not honour the official polices on environmental education by including such questions. The steering impact of exams on teaching was known as a negative force, but was accepted.

The role of Education for Self-Reliance as a transition tool

Since independence in 1961 Tanzania has made significant changes in the education system it inherited from the British colonial administration. The overall objective has been social change. The strong conviction that education plays a major role in transforming the society was expressed repeatedly by Julius Nyerere (Nyerere 1965, 1966, 1967a, b, c).

One of the basic ideologies behind the educational policies of post-independent Tanzania was the relationship between education and work. Gustafsson (1987) has identified two development perspectives: development as a uniform, upward-going process towards modernisation (dominant during the 1950s and 1960s) and development as a process aimed at reducing dependency on the industrialised capitalist countries. Tanzania under the leadership of Nyerere chose the latter strategy (Gustafsson 1987). The dominant educational polices have been Education for Self-Reliance and Universal Primary Education.

On the impact of Education for Self-Reliance

The foundation of the educational and curriculum development in Tanzania since independence has been the Arusha Declaration. Its impact has been called to question and criticised. Here I present some of the voices.

At the Tanganyika African National Union executive committee meeting held in Musoma in November 1974, an analysis was made of what the party had promised to do in 1967 and how it had lived up to these promises. The title of the paragraphs which described this implementation is very informative, it read, 'Where we got stuck.' The meeting pointed to the relatively short period of implementation and to the fact that the syllabi now reflected a Tanzanian perspective. But the influences from 'the international standards' were still frequent and the mentality of the people had not been liberated. The transformation of schools into economic productive units (self-reliance activities) had not been successful. The attitude towards education as a means of being able to leave the rural area and agricultural work had not been changed. Even in the government offices, an educational degree weighed heavier than other experiences. The meeting was in fact an attempt to discuss what could be done to change mental images of, and attitudes towards, the role of education and to outline a new strategy.

In an article in *The Tanzania Educational Journal* in 1978, S.R. Nkonoki assessed Education for Self-Reliance at a seminar held ten years after the Arusha Declaration. He gave an account of what had been done and achieved and he stressed the misinterpretation of the policy:

> In some Secondary Schools, students were made to cultivate many acres of land without being explained or helped to understand why they were being made to do so much manual work in the way it was prescribed ... This wrong approach in the implementation of the philosophy and policy of Education for Self-Reliance precipitated the undesirable attitude that this 'self-reliance' was equivalent to or in the final analysis, manual labour. In this way, a negative reinforcement took place and some students developed a strong dislike of physical labour in general and a resentment of farming in particular ... many times the students were not involved

in the planning of projects or in accounting for proceeds from self-reliance activities. As a result, some students began to feel that after all, the proceeds go to the headmaster's house and to the teachers. Who can blame some of these students who did later on resort to going to the vegetable garden or the chicken shelter at odd hours where they 'helped themselves' to whatever they could find there (Nkonoki 1978, pp. 9).

In addition to the lack of resources, other constraints in the implementation of Education for Self-Reliance that Nkonoki pointed to were poor relationships between students and teachers, staff authoritarianism and frequent transfers of heads of schools. Roy Carr-Hill in his review of research in primary schools (1984) pointed to the fact that Education for Self-Reliance was more than just integrating productive work with the classroom work. He found that research showed that the self-reliance activities were undertaken mechanically and there was little attempts to teach pupils the skills that were needed to carry them out.

H.J. Mosha (1990), professor of education (and later the chairman of the 1992 Task Force for the Tanzania education system for the 21st century), criticised the implementation of Education for Self-Reliance from the standpoint that the policy was not conceptually clear and the objectives were not thoroughly explained. He admitted that the educational philosophy had changed the attitude of students and workers towards manual work and managed (statistically) to bridge the inequality gap between the sexes at all levels. Also, commitment had been made to correct inequalities in regional, urban and rural access to secondary education through a quota system. Education for Self-Reliance paved the way for universal primary education and mass literacy. Mosha also stated that Education for Self-Reliance had facilitated the development of a united nation of self-confident and respecting citizens, who valued human dignity. Further, he pointed out that the education system had provided manpower to fill most low and middle-level positions and stimulated democratic processes at school. But Mosha went on to doubt whether in spite of this, Education for Self-Reliance policy was something more than a political platitude. He called upon leaders to be practitioners showing that the Arusha Declaration and Education for Self-Reliance were worthwhile, feasible and workable by being in the forefront in the implementation of them.

C.J. Galabawa (1990), professor of education and the present (1999) dean of faculty of education at the University of Dar es Salaam, identified two groups of debaters on the quality of Tanzania's education. One group, he said, looked at the face value of the objectives of Education for Self-Reliance. They argued that the objectives of Education for Self-Reliance were to transform the educational system from a capitalist to a socialist orientation to better serve a socialist society. Since the country was not yet (by 1980) socialistic and there were still capitalist tendencies in schools, then the educational system, they argued, was failing. The other group argued for a criterion of achievement based on examination results which were a disappointment. Galabawa questioned both groups' arguments, arguing that Education for Self-Reliance was misinterpreted and so was the concept of socialism. He noted that pupils in schools now came from quite different social backgrounds compared to the years prior to 1967, so the quality of schools could not be judged on the basis of academic quality alone. He referred to studies done in the United States which indicated that background variables and school quality inputs were the major determinants of academic achievement. Galabawa pointed to the concepts of 'primary education,' 'terminal education,' 'complete education' and 'basic education,' all of which had been intermixed and misinterpreted in the debate. He also pointed out following point:

> Among the elites and the academic excellence group, the Musoma Resolution policy was seen as an attempt by the society to equalise educational opportunity—the opportunity to allow the mature entrants to escape the limitations of their social group—and therefore it was opposed on the basis of its impact on academic efficiency. ... In reality, the above views represented an overt political-social pressure against the policy (Galabawa 1990, pp. 19).

Galabawa's conclusion on the implementation of educational policies (general expansion and extension of formal schooling, economic development, social change, efficiency and qualitative improvement of education) in Tanzania since 1961 was that some of the policy objectives were contradictory and constituted trade-offs and that not all policy objectives could be attained at the same time. In the short run, according to Galabawa, quantitative objectives were incompatible with efficiency ones. This implied that the rapid development of the expansion of access to primary school had a severe effect on the outcome in terms of the number of qualified teachers, physical facilities and pupils' learning.

On these issues, Lene Buchert argued:

> The strategy of Socialism and Self-Reliance, in some respects, led to a return to some of the emphases of the early British period. The key economic focus was, again, the rural sector. Attitudes were to reflect the interpreted African heritage rather than the Western one, and politically, the centralised system in the form of the one-party state was to combine with a decentralised administrative system. Education, again, became a mass education concept which was implemented in an integrated system and had about equal emphases on the general areas underlying economic, political and socio-cultural goals (Buchert 1994, pp. 169).

Donatus Komba and Elisha Temu (1995) looked into the experiences of education with a production dimension on Education for Self-Reliance. They claimed that research was still needed to assess the educational outcome in general educational institutions. The outcome for the society or surrounding community was also unclear. They claimed that the greater the number of educated citizens in a community the more it would lose human resources for development, since the educated would not return to village life. They found that if they deducted the cost of production from the gross revenue gained from Education for Self-Reliance activities, the average secondary school contributed 10 percent to the catering bill (costs for boarding pupils) in 1985.

A.G.M. Ishumi and T.L. Maliyamkono (1995) also argued that the effect of Education for Self-Reliance over the past 25 years remained unclear. On the positive side was the effect it had had on attitudes towards a socialist culture, although they voiced doubt as to whether the change was real. Nonetheless, they considered it an ideological success.

Ishumi and Maliyamkono pointed out that the main target for Education for Self-Reliance and Universal Primary Education was the children of peasant parents, who would in the future live in a rural society. The children of parents with high positions in the government bureaucracy and in the party did not go back to the villages. The over-representation of such children in private secondary schools and colleges within the country or without (Yugoslavia, Bulgaria, the UK, Kenya and elsewhere) was striking. These children were often neighbours of ordinary families in the villages. This double standard on the part of high-level officials contributed to the disillusion with the education system.

Summary

My conclusions are that it is important for students to understand what they are doing and why. They need to learn to be able to analyse failures and consider possibilities for improvement. They need to learn to prevent destruction of the environment, understand and practice soil conservation measures and conserve and protect the natural environment of the country for the succeeding generations. The role of education is to bring awareness to pupils and students about the dangers pertaining to environmental pollution and destruction so as to create positive attitudes towards the environment.

Poverty, ignorance, socio-cultural attitudes and lack of understanding on the impacts that human activities have on the environment are considered to be some of the contributing factors to the present environmental problems. The issue of incorporating indigenous knowledge into education programmes and awareness campaigns, together with acquiring and sharing more information on local difficulties and resource pressures, is so important that, according to my opinion, a special programme for local knowledge assimilation should be devised. These were some of the visions underlying objectives of an education programme, according to international ideas of environmental education.

Education for Self-Reliance aimed at preparing the majority of the population for their lives in villages in a rural economy. The ideals concerned a total change of the curricula and a break with the inherited Western educational ideas of content and form. The transformation from ideas to syllabi were not fully congruent. Many of the theories surrounding the active and critical role of the pupils in the learning process as well as in school life and integration with the surrounding community were never expressed in the syllabi. However, the syllabi were oriented toward daily life activities in many subjects, especially in agriculture and domestic science/home economics. This was more pronounced in the primary than in secondary school syllabi. But the syllabi assumed a traditional Western pattern of division into scheduled lessons in the classroom and so-called practicals outside classroom. The important planning part of the Education for Self-Reliance projects—decision-making and evaluation—were not integrated into the syllabi. Thus the school remained much as it used to be, although the content was Africanised in that, for example, history and geography were focused on Tanzania. Moreover, the examination system promoted 'the classroom lessons' rather than the application of knowledge or the collective or co-operative way of life, which was one of the main ideas behind Education for Self-Reliance.

As for the self-reliance projects, schools, in the early 80s contributed to, on average 16 percent to the costs of their operation. A few schools had produced as much as 90 percent of their catering bill (Ministry of Education 1984). Each school was required to meet 25 percent of their costs through self-reliance projects. However, the contribution declined over the years and by 1988 secondary and technical schools contributions were about three percent (UNESCO 1989).

The greatest impact of Education for Self-Reliance seemed to have been on an ideological level. Several reasons for the experienced difficulties had to do with misunderstandings of central ideas, lack of understanding from the teachers' point of view, lack of training, conflicting attitudes from the parties involved and lack of commitment from the party leaders etc. The policy was aimed at transforming Tanzania into a rural socialist society, but this was not accepted by the Western-influenced urban population.

CHAPTER 6
The conditions for teachers' lives and work

Introduction

In this section I will look into some of the factors that decide and limit the working conditions of teachers in Tanzania, such as qualification, teaching methodology (chosen because of its importance in the implementation of the educational policy of Education for Self-Reliance) and working conditions. The latter includes class composition, language, economy and parents' attitudes.

Teacher qualification

There are several categories of teachers when it comes to *teacher qualification* in Tanzania. Grade C and B teachers have primary school education plus teacher training. Grade C teachers were trained mainly as an answer to the rapidly developed Universal Primary Education which was seen as a 'crash-training.' This category is being phased out through in-service training. Since 1990, a phasing out of grade B teachers (certificate holders) has started with correspondence courses for up-grading these teachers' qualifications. The distance education and training of primary school teachers has been described and analysed by Michael Wort (1998).

Grade A teachers (certificate holders) have secondary school education and two years of teacher training. Diploma holders have upper secondary education as well as two years of teacher training. Lastly, there are the university trained teachers.

Table 13 shows the qualification backgrounds of teachers according to the statistics of 1993. About 80 percent (4 192/5 262) of the teachers in public secondary schools held a diploma then and about 17 percent (889/5 262) had an academic degree. In private secondary schools the situation was less attractive, considering that the teacher/student rate was 1/23 as compared to 1/16 in the public schools. Only about 50 percent (2 159/4 306) of the teachers were diploma holders, while university degree holders totalled about 17 percent 740/4306). The remainder of teachers had less qualification. In primary

Table 13: *Teaching staff in Tanzania by qualification, 1993*

Level	Graduates	Diploma	Grade 'A'	Others	Total
Public Secondary Schools	889	4 192	0	181	5 262
Private Secondary Schools	740	2 159	0	1 407	4 306
Teacher Training Colleges	241	697	216	17	1 171
Primary Schools	0	0	33 069	68 747* *Grade 'B'	101 816
Total	1 870	7 048	33 285	70 352	112 555

Source: Ministry of Education and Culture BEST 1994.

schools 32 percent had an A grade and about 68 percent a B grade certificate (while some were still C grade). Teachers in teacher training colleges were the best off when it came to qualifications; 21 percent held degrees, 55 percent held diploma A and 18 percent held certificates.

Teaching methodology

The aim of the Education for Self-Reliance educational policy was to use a teaching methodology that would develop scientific and technological skills such as creativity, problem solving, an inquiring mind, independent thinking, pupils' participation in the planning of projects, learning by doing, learning by experience, integrating theory with practice and promoting co-operation and practice of democratic rights.

The teaching methodology used in primary and secondary schools was, according to the analysis of the Task Force (United Republic of Tanzania 1993, pp. 27–28), mostly lecturing. My own classrooms observations support those findings (see Chapter 7). The teacher could not rely on textbooks or other kinds of teaching materials for the pupils' work. Since most teaching goes on in the classroom she or he was dependent on the blackboard for reproducing texts which the pupils then copied in their exercise books. One of the interviewed primary school teachers, on her first posting, summarised teacher's life in the following way: 'You make schemes of work, lesson plans and lesson notes. You teach that in your class and give the pupils questions. Then you have exercise books to correct. And all over again'.

The exercise books she was referring to contained the children's answers to the questions that the teacher had written on the blackboard.

This does not mean that there were no teachers using other teaching methods but that they were rare. Did the constraints of the school and the lives of the teachers during the last decades aggravate the situation? Or was it due to deficiencies in their professional training (pre-service or in-service)? Or were there other factors which in the end would affect and demotivate the teachers?

Mrs Mema (in the introduction) pointed to the lack of sufficient teaching practice. The 'old' teachers, trained before 1980, had teaching practice for six months in total, but in the beginning of the 1990s the teachers were lucky if they had one month.

During the late 1970s and the first half of the 1980s, the 'normal' teacher training colleges could not finance teaching block practice for their students. That meant that the teachers who were trained during this period had not entered a classroom before they came to their postings. Subsequent distance training (up-grading) of teachers was boosted during this period (Wort 1998).

The teachers' working conditions

In this section I will discuss the constraining factors which had an impact on the teachers' working situation. First, the composition of the classes (one of the organisational frames according to Lundgren 1972) will be explored, followed by an exploration of the teachers' salaries and sideline economical activities, language uses and finally the attitudes of the parents. These aspects were chosen because they are specific to the situation in Tanzania both compared to neighbouring countries and to Western countries.

Class composition
The vast majority of Tanzanian children start school later than the statutory age of 7 years and leave before completion of primary school. In 1992 the modal age for Standard I was 9 years. Only 32 percent of children between ages 7 and 9 were in school, 82 percent of those between age 10 and 14, while 36 percent of those between 15 and 19 were in school. Girls tended to start school slightly earlier than boys but they were less likely than boys to complete primary school. Children from lower-income households started at a later age than did better-off children and they also left earlier (World Bank 1995).

The pupils in Standard I were between 7 and 13 years, and in Standard VII they were between 13 and 17 years (Ministry of Education and Culture 1993). Consequently, many classes were multi-aged. The teachers were not trained for this situation.

Dropout rates were high for both girls and boys (see Table 14). In 1986, of the group of Standard VII leavers, only 79.3 percent of the boys and 77.5 percent of the girls were still in school as compared to the many that entered Standard I. For the total primary school group, the major dropout reason was truancy. For 12 percent of the drop-out girls in primary school, the reason for quitting school was pregnancy. This was one of the reasons why parents wanted the girls to start school early and leave before puberty.

Language
To promote unity among different ethnic groups and dissociate oneself from the racial and colonial past, Swahili was declared the language of instruction

Table 14: *Drop out reasons in 1991, total for all primary schools, Standard I–VII*

Reason	Boys	Percent	Girls	Percent	Total	Percent
Truancy	13 785	89	11 169	77	24 954	83
Pregnancy	0	0	1 710	12	1 710	6
Death	930	6	823	6	1 753	6
Others	773	5	732	5	1 505	5
Total	15 488		14 434		29 922	

Source: Ministry of Education and Culture BEST 1992; the same BEST 1992.

in all primary schools in 1967 (Brock-Utne 1993). The intention was to gradually introduce the use of Swahili in secondary schools and higher education from 1973 onwards. However, this was never realised, since the Minister of Education in 1983 announced that English should remain the medium of instruction at the secondary school level and above (Roy-Campbell 1991). The decision was not successful:

> One detrimental result of maintaining English as the medium of instruction for secondary school has been the blurring of the boundaries between language and knowledge. Language has proven to be a barrier in the acquisition of knowledge for many secondary school pupils, and indeed for some of their teachers (Roy-Campbell 1991, pp. 217).

Wort (1997) discussed the constraining effect of the use of English, in most cases a third language, in the distance training programme for primary school teachers. The problem, for both students and teachers, of using English as an instruction medium, still prevailed, in a society where there were more than 120 spoken languages and where Swahili was much more widely accessible than English.

Teachers' economy

The average annual salaries for teachers in 1983 (USD equivalent prices) was estimated to be 662 for Tanzania, 1,233 for Kenya, and a total of 2,255 USD for sub-Saharan Africa. As a multiple of corresponding per capita income these salaries were 2.8, 3.6 and 5.6 respectively. In 1987 the basic salaries for primary school teachers were raised to 4.4 times higher than the per capita income (UNESCO 1989). Since then Tanzania has devalued its currency considerably and together with the effect of inflation, the salaries have decreased. In late 1990, the exchange rate for USD 1 was about 190 Tanzanian shillings (TShs); in the beginning of 1994 it was TShs 500. In 1991 the average gross salary was 7,100 TShs per month for primary school teachers and 8,200 TShs for secondary teachers. The starting annual salary for a primary school teacher (without allowances) in 1994 was about 6,000 TShs. In other words, teachers' salaries are low.

The World Bank (1995) argued that the vast majority of Tanzanian primary school teachers were paid less than USD 20 per month (10,000 TShs), which was insufficient to feed the average household. Sideline activities are presented in Table 15.

In 1989, there were about 98,400 teachers in primary schools. It was widely believed in the society that the teachers were dissatisfied. But a survey of teachers' working conditions showed that 90 percent of the primary school teachers were satisfied with their jobs (World Bank 1991) and 92 percent of them intended to stay in their profession. Two thirds of them were Grade B or C teachers, which meant that they had received a short professional training. About 85 percent of them were between the ages of 25 and 44 years old. This indicates that many of them were trained during the 70s when Universal Primary Education was introduced in the span of a few hectic years. From 1973 to 1977 the number of pupils increased by 1,100,000. Between 1975 and 1980 the teaching force grew from 28,783 to 89,913. Wort's (1998) description of the training strategy used to supply the primary schools with teachers to meet the Universal Primary Education demand showed that this was done mostly through a distance education programme and, in the beginning, on a very basic level (Grade C). An in-service programme was developed during the 80s to upgrade the teachers to a B level as well as to A level. Much criticism of the low educational standard in the primary school was directed towards these teachers from the parents. However, Wort reported that studies neither supported nor verified the criticism (ibid. pp. 32, 79, 84–85).

Evidently teachers had notable difficulties surviving on their salaries. To be able to support a family and keep children in school, it was necessary to look for other sources of income. Lugalla (1993) conveyed the following reasons:

> The meagre salaries which teachers receive have forced them to either quit their jobs, or invest much of their time in sideline activities like selling vitumbua[1], chapati[2], ice-creams and cold drinks. Many participate in private teaching and tuition activities. In urban areas some teachers' houses have been turned into classrooms for evening tuition. The fees charged range from TSh 300 to TSh 500 per pupil per month. Worse, some of the teachers have fallen into corrupt practices and as a result examination paper leakage and tendencies toward favouritism are increasing (pp. 203).

The data in Table 15 indicates that the vast majority of the teachers (77 percent of the primary and 76 percent of the secondary school teachers) did have other income earning activities besides teaching. Many of them had more than one so-called 'project'. The dominating activity was growing food for their own (and their family's) consumption. Of the primary school teachers about 83

---
[1] A deep-fried rice dish.
[2] A kind of bread.

Table 15: *Other sources of income and earnings for teachers (percentage)*

Activity	Primary			Secondary		
	Total	Urban	Rural	Total	Urban	Rural
Outside activity	77.0	64.0	82.8	76.4	72.6	85.3
One activity	33.1	31.4	39.2	40.6	37.7	46.5
Grow food for own consumption	88.8	74.9	93.6	78.1	80.3	72.6
Grow commercial crops	23.9	14.1	27.2	20.8	19.3	23.7
Raise livestock	18.7	19.7	18.4	19.9	23.2	13.0
Petty business	17.8	25.2	15.2	18.6	19.2	17.0
Private tutoring[a]	8.8	17.9	5.7	35.3	28.9	47.4
Other	1.6	17.3	9.7	10.0	12.2	6.4
Earnings relative to salary						
Lower	50.5	49.7	50.7	–	–	–
Equal	4.4	5.0	4.1	–	–	–
Higher	45.1	45.3	45.1	–	–	–
Would quit if possible	38.2	36.9	38.5	53.2	53.6	52.5

[a] The figures are almost certainly an underestimate. Interviews with teachers carried out at three secondary schools in Dar es Salaam in October 1992 indicated that all teachers without exception participated in this activity, although they were reluctant to divulge this information through questionnaires (Lugalla, 1993).
Source: Lugalla 1993.

percent had an outside or sideline activity (activities outside their normal duties as teachers in a school), compared to 64 percent of the teachers in urban areas. The percentage was even higher for the secondary school teachers. In the rural areas farming was the main source of income, while in the urban areas activities were more diversified.

In 45 percent of the cases the outside activities were more economically beneficial than the salary as primary school teacher. About 50 percent of the outside activities, on the other hand, earned teachers lower income than their salaries. Table 15 indicates what has been said before—that a teacher was unable to survive on the teaching salary alone.

Further, Mrs Mema, in the introduction, gave us an example of the economical situation of the teachers which fits in with the findings of this survey.

Few primary school teachers with a higher education were satisfied with the salaries they received. The teaching profession was one of the last choices of able secondary graduates and this had a strong relation to wages (Ministry of Education and Culture 1992).

Teachers were posted—and at times rotated—throughout Tanzania, as all governmental employees, with the aim of blending all ethnic groups in order to promote unity and understanding.

But teachers in the primary school, especially women, wanted to stay in the urban areas rather than go to remote rural districts with few proper—if any—school facilities. One effect of this was that there were more female teachers in the towns and only about 20 percent male teachers. In the rural areas there was an equal distribution from the gender perspective. As a consequence the urban schools were overstaffed while the teachers in the rural areas had a heavier teaching load and received no extra remuneration.

In secondary schools teachers did not have the same job satisfaction as those in primary schools. In governmental schools only 46 percent of the teachers were satisfied with their jobs as compared to 51 percent in the private schools (World Bank 1991, Table 3.1, pp. 15). Most of those who were satisfied also planned to stay as teachers. However, they were dissatisfied with their salaries and did not look on their profession as something that could be recommended to the younger generation. In this context, the attitudes of the primary school teachers were strikingly different. The secondary schools were normally situated in much more physically attractive environments and the classes were smaller, but they had little if any contact with the surrounding community. As has been pointed out earlier, most of them were boarding schools.

The working environment in schools was not encouraging (Table 16). Primary school teachers worked under more severe conditions than their secondary school counterparts, even if they, too, were suffering. On the other hand, the absence of in-service training and promotion was felt much more by secondary than by primary school teachers. The latter were more satisfied with their salary than secondary school teachers. Class size was considered a problem by both groups. Surprisingly the dissatisfaction in relation to the surrounding community was felt to be more or less the same by both groups, at least statistically. Normally the secondary schools were alienated from the surrounding community due to the boarding system. Otherwise, the primary school teachers were more 'content' with their situation than their secondary counterparts—apart from the school facilities. One possible explanation is that the primary school teachers, especially in the rural areas, were better integrated in the surrounding community.

Attitudes towards the Education for Self-Reliance programme
If the educational philosophy behind Education for Self-Reliance was admired by international educationists, the policy aiming at a dominantly rural society and prioritising basic education for all, was not accepted by the Tanzanian society as a whole. Nyerere did not want to discuss the presence of social classes after independence. The concept of 'class' was not applicable in a rural society. However, Tanzania inherited an elitist Western educational system in which the more highly placed citizens and academics received their education abroad. This continued even after independence and ideas contrary to Education for Self-Reliance were brought back to Tanzania. This was an example of the contradictions in the educational and political development (Fägerlind and Saha 1983). The more educated should be those who were most motivated to take part in implementing the new educational policy. However, as has been indicated before, the highly placed officials sent their children to private sec-

Table 16: *Aspects of teachers' jobs found to be discouraging by teachers (percentage registering dissatisfaction)*

Aspect	Primary	Secondary
School facilities	81.9	68.8
Class size	55.7	52.7
Student achievement	32.7	58.3
Relations with community	30.3	29.6
Student discipline	29.8	50.1
Training and promotion opportunities	29.2	73.4
Salary	25.6	58.8
School administration	15.4	38.5

Source: Teacher Survey Data, 1990 cited in Lugalla 1993.

ondary schools and colleges to ensure their academic schooling. Both students and parents regarded schooling as a means of being able to leave the rural areas (Carnoy and Samoff 1990, pp. 252). The better-off children went to secondary school at a rate that was five times higher than that of worse-off children. Of those in governmental schools, 34 percent of the pupils came from the richest 20 percent, as compared to only 8 percent from the 20 percent poorest (World Bank 1995). The effect of this on the teachers' motivation to achieve the Education for Self-Reliance policy cannot be dismissed.

The changed social status of teachers was referred to by Mrs Mema in the introduction. In the 1970s teacher status was high but by the 1990s teachers are no longer met with the same respect from pupils and parents.

Summary

Teacher qualification was a constraining factor; diploma holders (two years teaching training after Form IV) were dominant in both secondary schools and teacher training colleges. The majority of primary school teachers were grade B teachers with four (although in some cases only two) years of training after Standard VII.

The pupil-centred and active-learning teaching methodology prescribed in the curriculum had become, in reality, mostly a lecture method.

It was necessary to look more into the teacher's situation to understand the conditions for teaching. The class composition, which is one frame factor according to Lundgren (1972), was complicated by a wide age variation, drop outs and repeaters. The teachers were not prepared for such a situation.

Economical conditions for teachers were difficult—salaries were low and a teacher had difficulties making do. As a consequence the vast majority of both primary and secondary school teachers had outside (or sideline) activities for generating income, which in 45 percent of the cases for primary school teachers gave them more than their salaries as teachers. This is an important factor in understanding the living conditions and life styles of teachers. Ivor F. Goodson has stressed the importance of teacher life styles for the accomplishment of the teacher profession (Goodson 1996).

Primary school teachers, especially those in rural areas (and they are in majority), were more satisfied with their jobs than secondary school teachers. Primary school teachers were dissatisfied with school facilities and class sizes while secondary school teachers complained about training and promoting opportunities, school facilities, salary, student achievement, class size and student discipline (in that order). The use of English as the teaching medium in secondary school had a constraining effect on both students and teachers.

The urban, especially higher-income, parents had not accepted the educational policy of Education for Self-Reliance which was directed at the rural population in an agricultural society (World Bank 1995, Ishumi & Malikyankono 1995). On the other hand, the children of the better-off parents were five times more likely to attend secondary schools than children of worse-off parents. This had an effect on attitudes and was not conducive to pupils' successful implementation nor assistance from the parents in helping teachers to realise Education for Self-Reliance projects in school. The teachers and the schools were not encouraged to develop projects according to aims stated by Nyerere, which would have changed the purpose of schooling. Education for Self-Reliance would have been preparation for a rural life and not for a continued 'traditional' academic career.

CHAPTER 7
Classroom accounts

Introduction

To enter the school and the classroom requires that the researcher have certain qualities. Considering that I was a foreign visitor from a different culture and not able to use my mother tongue, some aspects of behaviour were more important than others. In my own culture I can enter a school and ask for information whenever I wish. This is an effect of the principle of public access to official records. I can, as a parent or as a teacher trainer, enter classrooms without even asking the teacher for permission. In Tanzania I had to obey other rules and regulations of the school administration as well as cultural traditions. It was expected that everyone showed respect to social status and to elders (age). A woman had to follow a dress code in order to be respected. Greetings were exchanged in a certain way. Sara Delamont (1992, pp. 29) points out five common impediments to good fieldwork: not finishing the process, sexism, going native, being bored and reporting the familiar. Considering her views, I could ask myself to what extent I have tried to avoid these barriers. Delamont further discusses types of field notes, recording, how to gain access for example to schools and the behaviour of the researcher.

Visits to classrooms

As I have said in chapter 3, I intend to relate my interviews to a context. The interviews were carried out in the schools, in empty classrooms or staff rooms. The aim was not, however, to conduct ethnographic or anthropologic research but to be able to provide the reader with a background.

What kind of environmental education was implemented in the classrooms? In August 1995, I stayed one week each at Elimika[1], a primary school, Chuma, a secondary school, and Aminika Teacher Training College. The schools were not new to me. I had, during 1992–1997, stayed about 13 weeks at Aminika

---

[1] The names of places and persons have been changed.

(where I had conducted seminars for or together with them), followed the teaching in classes about eight weeks at Chuma (supervising student-teachers) but only passed Elimika a couple of times. Several of the teachers in the secondary school and the teacher training college knew me, and the teachers in the primary school had at least seen or heard about me.

I had asked the schools ahead of time for permission to come and do some classroom observations during one single school week. The school headmaster/mistress as well as the college principal were informed about my aim—to observe teaching and see if anything was going on that contained environmental education components—before they granted my request. I visited seven teachers during ten lessons during the week at Elimika and five teachers during fourteen lessons during the week at Chuma. During the week I had allocated to Aminika, there was no teaching at all because of cancellation due to financial constraints.

My objective was very humble since the time was very limited. How did the teachers perceive me? It is a difficult question to answer since I never asked them. I was treated as a guest in a very friendly way. That is a part of the Tanzanian culture but Swedes are normally well received and Swedish political and aid policy, at least up to the end of the 1980s, is well known. On the other hand, I represented a foreign country and an unknown authority. Some teachers were aware that I had connections with the University of Dar es Salaam.

I spent one entire week at each school, meaning that I went there in the morning and stayed as long as possible into the afternoon. I sat in the staff room during teas and sometimes during lunch. I walked around the school yard discussing with teachers during breaks. I was invited home by some teachers in the afternoons. I was, according to my interpretation of Tanzanian values, decently dressed without overdressing.

I entered classrooms only as agreed between the teacher and myself. Since the teachers were subject teachers even at the primary school level, I chose the subjects I was most interested in, namely agriculture, geography, biology, domestic science/home economics, and science. I went to mathematics or English only when nothing else was available. Sometimes other things occurred that cancelled a planned lesson or lessons (the schools, their context, resources and their daily routines are described in Appendices 7, 8 and 9).

During the lessons I took notes. After each lesson I had a discussion with the teacher about what had been taught. This was particularly important in the primary school, since the teaching medium was Swahili, a language I do not command. In the afternoons and evenings I organised and elaborated on my observations.

Primary school

In primary school, I observed seven different teachers during ten lessons in the span of one week.

In agriculture, the teacher Mr A. was in charge of the school farm. The only tool available was a spraying tool. There were no pesticides or insecticides. Pupils brought necessary tools from their homes when they were working on the school farm. The teachers most often did not have own copies of the syllabus. Normally, the head of the subject department had one copy at the secondary school. In primary school this was not always the case and nearby schools borrowed both syllabi and textbooks from each other.

Some topics in the syllabus were always taught theoretically[2] although practicals were suggested. Beekeeping was considered by Mr A. as too dangerous to practice. Digging a fish pond and keeping fish he felt was impossible. Agriculture was taught from Standard V to VII.

I observed practical application of theory on three occasions and two of them were related to environmental education. But I don't think this was very usual; at two of the occasions the other teachers as well as the head teacher came to see what was going on outside at the compound. The demonstrations and practicals were basically good according to my experience as a teacher trainer, although the 'design' was remindant of the drawings made at the blackboard or in the textbook.

During the 90s, the Ministry of Agriculture launched several campaigns such as 'Plant a tree. Cut a tree', 'Don't burn the forest' and 'Practice modern farming'. The head of the department at the primary school I visited told me that the campaign issues were observed in the school but they did not have accompanying materials such as posters and pamphlets.

In domestic science, there was one textbook per three pupils in Standard VII, but in Standard V there were only three books for 70 pupils. Sometimes other primary schools nearby had the books from the domestic science department, since they were borrowing them. The textbook in Standard VII was from 1991. The teacher taught only those chapters for which she had a scheme of work.

There was no copy of the domestic science syllabus. The staff tended to rely on the experience of one of the teachers, whose scheme of work was based on the 1969 syllabus. Needlework, which was part of the domestic science syllabus, was not taught. The reason was that the school could not afford to provide the pupils with material and not all pupils could afford to bring their own material to school. Before, too many were playing outside or being idle while those who could contribute to the material had needle work.

The practicals in cooking were still realised to some extent, but about one quarter of the class did not participate, since they could not bring contributions for the ingredients that were needed.

---

[2] Teaching theoretically or having theoretical lessons will appear not only in the text here but also in the next chapters. I am using the word 'theoretical' since that is what the teachers themselves use. It is a colloquial word in Tanzanian English. It means that the lesson is taught in the classroom using the lecturing method and by words only. A theoretical can be on an abstract level but it can also describe practices, habits or other very concrete things in daily life.

I found that the head of this department was very concerned and struggled to get funding to do at least a few of the essential practicals. I was able to contribute so that a farewell party for the Standard VII pupils could materialise. The cost involved was (comparatively) very low and the occasion was very important for the pupils.

In geography, the department had one textbook per two pupils in Standard VII. The teachers had the 1990 syllabus but the textbook was based on the syllabus from 1978. There was nothing in the 1978 syllabus on conservation, for example, or transportation and communication. By using books from the library of the teacher training college, teachers were able to prepare the necessary lesson content.

The geography teacher in Standard VII told me that lessons in primary school generally followed this pattern: 'discussion and presentation of the subtopic, reading the text in the textbook (if available), written questions on the blackboard, pupils write answers in their exercise books, the teacher walks around and correct all answers'. There was no note taking in primary school; pupils only took down answers to questions.

Discussion was defined as: 'the teacher presents a question, the pupils answer or give examples, the teacher gives the correct answer'. And so on. Using this technique, the content was presented to the pupils.

Summarising my observations, I would say that teachers based their work on syllabi from 1969–1990. The existence of textbooks varied. There were differences between the teachers in their preparation and teaching. Some read aloud from notes or books and others dramatised the content in a very good way. Questions and chorus answers were common. Teachers often wrote diagrams on the blackboard, which the pupils copied. The text on the blackboard for copying varied; some teachers gave a short text as well as questions to be answered (open or fill in blanks questions mostly), others only wrote the questions. Not all pupils had exercise books so some could not copy anything during the lessons. The class monitor collected the exercise books for correction. In Standard VII girls always gave their books for corrections while boys were less interested in doing so.

In agriculture and biology there were environmental education components but these were on a theoretical level with few possibilities for integration with earlier knowledge, real life or practice. In domestic science practice seemed to be much more common. Of course, the Education for Self-Reliance projects could be seen as part of the subject of agriculture, but the pupils seemed to be doing what they were told to do without explanation about the relationship between theory and practice.

Secondary school

In secondary school I observed five different teachers during 14 lessons in the span of one week.

One teacher in biology Mr B. explained the topics in the syllabus for me. He had been a teacher for 25 years. The topic of soil erosion and conservation was taught during four periods. The content was:

- The meaning of soil erosion (removal of the upper layer of soil which is suitable for plant growth).
- Types of soil erosion (sheet and gully erosion).
- Agents of soil erosion (wind in dry areas, water, animals).
- Conservation methods (crop rotation, terracing, contour farming, steep areas, afforestation, soil is conserved by planting trees; other methods: manuring the soil, mulching).
- Poor farming methods (ploughing down the slopes, burning of vegetation, overstocking, over-cropping).

The only teaching material used were some pictures from the geography books showing sheet and gully erosion.

The maize farm (one of the two school farms) had some areas with soil erosion (sheet and gully). Mr B. pointed them out to the students. Unfortunately, a tractor had been used in the preparation of the soil before planting, but the ploughing had at least been done along the ridges of the slopes. Sometimes there was too much water, he said. The topic was easily understood by the students from rural areas but was difficult for city students. Most of the pupils at Chuma Secondary School were from rural areas.

In biology, the topic of ecology was given 12 periods in total. It was normally taught in Form II but sometimes in Form IV depending on the teacher's convenience. It was possible to make some changes in the order of the topics in the syllabus.

'We don't go much into details', Mr B. said. Most time was spent on energy flow and nutrient circulation in the ecosystem and interdependence of organisms. He showed the students the food chain and the food web, which were new concepts for them. The only teaching aid was the drawing of diagrams on the blackboard.

In these topics he also talked about natural resources, which was everything that appeared natural: land, plants, animals, water, air, the use of these things and their economic value. 'We don't go much into details', Mr B. said once again.

In the sub-topic of pollution he taught the meaning, types, control (how to avoid pollution), alternatives to the use of fire wood, i.e. solar energy, and how far the technology had got. He also taught about water pollution in rural areas and that it was important to be careful in the use of water (animals in the same water as that used for washing and drinking was not a good thing).

There were some hand lenses and microscopes which could be used for very simple experiments. He said that teachers were not trained to use experiments as a teaching method. Since he had begun as a teacher in 1970, he had not attended one single seminar or in-service course.

The teacher in geography, Mr C., claimed that the syllabus was impossible to cover. He tried to cover East Africa in detail. When that was done, the rest of Africa was taught with a thematic approach (water management and energy).

The topic of 'soil erosion: factors and conservation' was taught during six periods. Mr C. started with the definition of soil erosion (which he defined as the removal of top soil) and continued with types of soil erosion, concentrating on sheet and gully erosion. He also mentioned land slides and agents of soil erosion such as water and wind. Factors causing soil erosion in East Africa, he said, were deforestation, methods of farming on hilly areas, overgrazing and burning of vegetation.

The conservation methods that Mr C. taught were terracing, farming in the highland areas, destocking, reforestation, planting grass on the ridges, blocking the water to run freely in gullies and contour farming.

He had no teaching aids for these lessons, so he drew diagrams on the blackboard. The school used its funds to buy food for the students and not for teaching aids. This contributed to making the teaching teacher-centred. The class made no field trips. There was a textbook available, produced by the Institute for Curriculum Development. There were not enough copies and Mr C. did not even distribute them to the students. He said he did not like the book because it had been written in a workshop where a number of geography teachers wrote one chapter each. He said it was very shallow and the diagrams in the book were taken from other books. The photos were poorly printed; it was hardly possible to see the pictures.

Mr C. told me that 'if you only teach what is in the syllabus, you will cover it'. However, he did not follow the syllabus; he added effects, problems and possible solutions ('how can you do to solve this problem?') to each topic and it took time. Within the topic of fishing, for example, he added coast problems (such as use of ammunition when fishing, which destroyed the coral reefs; destruction of mangroves; beach erosion). In agriculture he told of how far the farmers had to go to conserve the soil and how they managed the irrigation.

Mr C. also said that the National Council of Examination went beyond the content in the syllabus when they constructed the examination questions. Students in the country generally performed poorly in geography in the examinations. 'How can the teachers prepare?,' he wondered. The Council used to arrange seminars—he believed the last one was in 1984.

The teachers were working according to their schemes of work. It was evident to me, as seen above, that the syllabi overlapped each other concerning soil conservation and soil erosion, as well as in two major environmental education components. But even if the teachers were aware of this, the syllabus was the steering wheel.

I observed two common, only slightly different, types of lessons in the secondary school: 1) The teacher went orally through everything, asking questions more or less often, always writing on the blackboard. Then there was time set aside for taking notes from the blackboard. Before that, pupils generally did not copy anything into their exercise books. Finally there were written questions to be answered in the exercise books. 2) The teacher presented and wrote notes on the blackboard at the same time. Students copied continuously, were questioned by the teacher periodically and at the end were given written questions to answer. Of the fourteen lessons I observed, about half of them followed the first type and the other half, the second type.

Teacher Training College

I was unable to attend classroom teaching at the teacher training college, during the same time I visited the primary and secondary schools, due to the fact that the registration for the term had been postponed (see Appendix 9). Postponement was in fact not unusual, but a fairly common feature of the operational problems of the educational system. So, instead of attending lessons, I asked tutors about what they had been doing and they showed me their scheme of works[3].

The domestic science department had two tutors. They did not teach everything that was in the syllabus. An experienced tutor, Mrs G., said that she chose what was most important for the students to know. Most of it was taught by words only. It was only possible to do maybe two practicals during the entire certificate course.

The schemes of work in geography contained few topics related to environmental education. During the first year, I found nothing. During the second year, I noticed there were the topics of soil, forestry and economic development (wildlife and tourism). In the soil topics there was a sub-topic of soil erosion; 120 minutes were allocated to this issue.

The geography teacher, Mr C., had schemes of work from several years compiled in a file. His lesson plans from the previous year were neatly written in an exercise book.

Using the information gleaned from the lesson plans, the teaching methods taught to teacher students in Geography in the two-year diploma course were the following: Field study, Simulation (using maps, pictures, charts, diagrams etc.), Sample study method, Teaching materials (teaching aids), Chain survey field work and Survey.

There were not many teaching aids. Mr C. had a collection of maps made of locally available material. For the topic of soil erosion and soil conservation, he had a few photos and pictures in books. The department lacked the equipment they were teaching about (weather measuring instruments, compasses etc.). Normally the geography teacher teaches theory, Mr C. said. He cited examples and the students drew the equipment from the examples he himself drew at the blackboard. This was particularly true for the most recent years.

---

[3] I have stayed about 13 weeks at this particular college during a number of years, so I feel I am quite familiar with the context.

Sometimes, when there was time, Mr C. took the students to visit the surrounding area, looking at tree planting or farmers using a mulching technique in coffee growing. Terracing was widely practised in the region, he said, although the soil conservation officer would hardly agree.

Still, some practicals were done in the self-reliance projects which all students attended. Mulching, for instance, was done in the vegetable garden. Students had been planting trees to fence the college compound (still going on) and also at the college shamba, where they had planted species of trees suitable for dry land. The college compound was always green. Thus they had been exposed to two different planting techniques. The teacher was personally concerned about these projects and said that he told the students why they were doing these activities, for example, to prevent soil erosion.

The topic of soil erosion and conservation was taught in both the certificate and diploma courses, but with more details in the latter. The students had already been introduced to the topic in primary and secondary schools.

During recent years, terms had been shortened due to financial constraints. The teacher had to make priorities as to what to teach from the syllabus. He or she chose the topics that had been on the national examinations. They had first priority. If there was time, other topics were taught. By this method, the syllabus was not covered. The alternative, however, was to rush through everything.

Examination results from this teacher training college were usually good but there were a number of problems. Due to financial constraints, the terms ended earlier than planned or sometimes they started later. The teaching practice period was made shorter and after a time it disappeared entirely. In a few subjects, the alternative was micro-teaching (or peer-teaching) but this did not apply to all students and was often a repetition of what the tutor had already taught. The teaching had become theoretical with no practicals.

Through my own observations during several years, I was able to see and confirm the effect of environmental education work at the college compound. I also heard at the primary school that the geography teacher (Mr C.) was keen on this topic and helped them with seedlings and advice. The same teacher was the leader of the Malihai Club[4] with a relatively impressive number of environmental education activities.

Summary and personal reflection

The presence of environmental education components in the classrooms was not common. The topics in the syllabi were taught theoretically and without being put into practice. Overlapping in the syllabi was not corrected, so that the same content was taught in several subjects. The subjects of domestic science and home economics were, according to my observations, those that involved the most practical teaching and which made it more possible for the

---

[4] Malihai is the name of the club, which can be found all over Tanzania but with concentration in the northern part.

students to understand the meaning and relevance of what they were being taught. The subject of agriculture had the opportunity to relate its content to Education for Self-Reliance activities. This was done to some extent but only at the Teacher Training College level.

The teachers varied in teaching experience, training and interest. The teaching methods that were used were teacher oriented, e.g. the teacher planned and implemented the lesson, often through the lecture method. Focus was on recall of knowledge (to some extent with the exception of domestic science and home economics). Teaching aids and materials were rare. Students' learning at all levels was based on notetaking.

The difference which I observed between the teaching in primary and secondary schools was that the lessons in secondary school were more diversified. The teachers in secondary school had a more personal style and I got the impression that they did not follow a lesson 'model' in the same strict sense as the primary teachers often did. Note taking was, however, as important in secondary as in primary schools. Texts in secondary school were much longer and contained more information in whole sentences. The stereotyped model 'copy a small number of questions, write answers' did not exist in the lessons I observed.

What did the pupils learn? After my observations and interviews, it seemed to me that the knowledge pupils gained in primary school must have been fragmented and mysterious without relation to life outside school. One exception might be domestic science, which concentrated on everyday knowledge. In secondary school I found that the learning, in spite of all good intentions, tended to be based on memorisation of facts. Even if the teacher devoted time to explanation or asking questions, the fact that the majority of the students did not have textbooks meant that they had to rely on notetaking, i.e. copying the teacher's notes.

I was well-received at the schools. I was already known to the secondary school and the teacher training college but only slightly to the primary school. The Swahili language was not a complete barrier since I am used to observing what goes on in classrooms without fully understanding what is being said. My intention was to find out if environmental education was taking place and that was not primarily dependent on the language. I was not particularly surprised at the outcome of my observation, on the whole. I had been in and out of school classes many times earlier and thought I knew the conditions. I did, however, become more aware of the importance of the Education for Self-Reliance projects for primary schools. Regrettably the revenue of these projects was used more on administration costs at school than on pupils' welfare and educational needs. On the other hand, the idea of the projects was to contribute to the school budget. I also became more aware of the effect of financial constraints in primary school, both for the school itself and for the teachers. I was confronted with live examples.

Returning to the methodological aspect, although I have followed basic recommendations of data collection, I have not carried out analysing or theorising but rather a description of some of the things that I observed (Delamont 1992). This is in accordance with the aim of my classroom visits. I consider what I observed to be an illustration and a background description of the schools in which teachers work. The above account should be considered an introduction to the next section, which presents the interviews.

CHAPTER 8
Teachers and environmental education

Introduction

The teaching conditions are frame factors that constrain the implementation of the curriculum. From the frame factor theory approach aspect, these are external conditions or determinants that restrict teaching outcome. To get a picture of the teachers' conditions for implementation of environmental education, I used a short questionnaire asking about some of the physical frames. The results are presented in the first part of this chapter.

To understand teachers' thinking and reasoning another approach was used. Teachers' beliefs or ways of experiencing are internal determinants that are not captured in the frame factor theory approach (Lindblad, Linde & Näslund 1999). Thus, in the second part of this chapter, I describe the main outcome of the interviews; three categories of teachers' different ways of experiencing what environmental education is and two categories of different ways of experiencing why environmental education is important. As for the other main questions, namely learning/teaching strategies and the content of environmental education, no qualitative different ways of experience developed.

Teaching conditions for environmental education—answers from a questionnaire

The teachers who were interviewed were also asked to answer a questionnaire. The objective was to get an overview of a number of factors that had an impact on the teaching situation of the teachers. I got answers from 40 primary school teachers (of which 38 were interviewed) and from 35 secondary school teachers (although 37 were interviewed). The discrepancy is due to such factors as the fact that the teachers might have been called to perform other duties and were not available for interviews or did not hand in the questionnaire while I was still there. The answers reflect the teachers' own estimates and experiences, meaning that they might have remembered things correctly or incor-

Table 17: *Number of pupils in the classes where the interviewed teachers taught*
Primary school teachers, n=40; secondary school teachers, n=35

School	Mean number of pupils	Minimum number	Maximum number
Primary	78	35	150
Secondary	39	20	75

rectly. I did not verify the data with other sources of information. Still, it gives an illustration of the teaching conditions experienced by the group of teachers which I interviewed.

Class sizes

I was interested in knowing how many pupils/students they normally had in their classes. I found that there was a great difference between primary and secondary schools, the former with mean sizes which were double that of the latter (see Table 17).

Was there a difference between rural and urban schools regarding class sizes? The answers indicate that the urban primary classes were about 45 percent larger than those of the rural (see Table 18). There were several reasons for that: the number of people moving to urban areas exceeded the economical resources for construction of classrooms, the enrolment of pupils was higher compared to rural areas etc. The classrooms were normally built for about 40 pupils but desks, for example, were used by four pupils instead of two. For secondary schools there was no noticeable difference in class size.

Teachers' preparation and resources

I wanted to know if the teachers had any training in environmental education, pre-service or in-service; what teaching material was available; if they made study trips; if they engaged students in field work and if any other people from outside were involved in teaching environmentally related topics. After each question the teachers could answer 'yes' or 'no' and give comments. The result is shown in Table 19.

A large number of both primary and secondary school teachers said that they had no training in environmental education. Since there has never been any in-service training courses for teachers in the field, they had to obtain such knowledge through either their postservice training, courses arranged by non-governmental organisations like the Malihai Clubs or courses which trained them in the implementation of the Family Education Programme.

The teaching materials available in the primary schools consisted mostly of posters. There had been four nationwide campaigns during the previous years. During the campaigns posters were distributed all around the country to health

Table 18: *Distribution of interviewed rural and urban teachers, and their mean class sizes*

Primary school teachers, n=40; secondary school teachers, n=35

Variable	Rural primary	Urban primary	Rural secondary	Urban secondary
No of teachers	13	27	14	21
Mean class size	59,5	86,6	40	38,5

centres, local authorities, schools etc. In teaching about the environment teachers mentioned that they used tools like hoes, buckets etc. (for garden and shamba). In secondary schools a few teachers had access to an ecology book or a Family Education book. They also had some local material on soil formation, soil erosion or planting of trees. Posters on soil erosion were to be found in a few cases. The overall amount of teaching material however was less than in secondary school.

The use of study visits or field trips was said to be more common in secondary schools than in primary. In primary schools teachers went on picnics to the mountains (involving no cost) or made study visits to a nearby national park. Two teachers had made a visit to a place that was affected by soil erosion (no cost). The official main objective of the primary education was to prepare the pupils for their future life in the (rural) community. Hence, one would expect that visits or connections with the surrounding society would have been more frequent since it was an important part of the Education for Self-Reliance policy.

It is important to remember that the examples were given by individual teachers and that a single school did not actually have the whole spectrum of examples. Another thing to remember is that the schools, from which these teachers came, were also easy to reach in terms of transport, since this was one of my selection criteria. I can imagine that schools far away from the district centre did not have the same access to facilities for demonstrating environmental aspects.

In secondary schools it happened that students visited nearby national parks, at least if the school lay close to one. Other places visited were directly in the neighbourhood (some domestic science teachers took their students to a home to demonstrate how a house should be kept in good order and cleanliness), or farms or valleys. In most cases only visits to national parks required funding.

The use of field work was apparently more common in primary school than in secondary. In primary school pupils planted trees and fruit trees, grass and flowers. They also developed tree seedlings in a nursery. Primary school pupils practised at the school farm, which was one type of self-reliance project. Ex-

Table 19: *Interviewed teachers' answers to written questions on teaching conditions; in percent*

Primary school teachers, n=40; secondary school teachers, n=35

Questions Do you:	Primary school teachers answers		Secondary school teachers answers	
	No	Yes	No	Yes
Have any training in environmental education?	90	10	94	6
Have teaching material?	68	32	91	9
Use study trips?	65	35	57	43
Use field work?	35	65	65	35
Have outside involvement in environmental education?	18	82	26	74

amples of field work in secondary school were projects on public health and individual research in the students' home villages. Other examples given in the questionnaire were work on the school water source and the planting of trees around the school boundaries.

In primary school as well as in secondary, according to the teachers, there seemed to be quite a few people from outside school involved in teaching. The primary schools were visited, for example, by an agricultural officer, a forest specialist and the adult education officer (the answering teachers probably did not separate what was going on in the primary school and the adult education classes). They also made visits to the health centre in the nearby community. In secondary school visits were made by the agriculture, veterinary, forestry or community development officers, as well as by representatives of the Wildlife Conservation Society and the Red Cross. Some students visited farmers, although this was possible only in rural areas.

The results presented in Table 19 are not built on observations but based solely on the teachers' answers. They reflect how the teachers perceived the question and how I have interpreted their answers. The questionnaire was short and covered only a restricted part of possible alternatives.

Perceived problems

There were several explanations given by the teachers as to why they did not teach environmental topics in a desirable way. When asked about the greatest problem in teaching environmental education, an open-ended question, primary school teachers pointed to the lack of teaching material and their own lack of training as obstacles to teaching environmental education (see Table 20). The lack of teaching aids is common in all subjects but of course, an all-embracing topic such as environmental education which is not a subject in it self but infused in existent school subjects, will suffer all the more.

Table 20: *Answers to questions of what the interviewed teachers considered as the greatest problem in teaching environmental education. Note that it was possible to give several answers*

Primary school teachers, n=40; secondary school teachers, n=35

Problem	Percent	
	Primary	Secondary
Lack of teaching aids/facilities	90	46
Lack of knowledge (teacher's)	30	46
Lack of proper classroom	12,5	n.m
Too many pupils	10	n.m
Not in the syllabus	n.m	14
No funds for study trips	n.m	14
No practicals/field work	n.m	11
Lack of time	7,5	11
Lack of transport	7,5	8
Students' attitudes	5	5
Lack of areas for practicals	5	n.m

n.m.=not mentioned.

Some primary school teachers indicated that they did not have classrooms in which to teach and a few (4/40) complained over large classes. It was not surprising, as was shown in Table 17 above, to find classes with as many as 150 pupils. Reports from the school inspectorate confirm these observations.

The secondary school teachers primarily consider lack of teaching aids and training as problems with no mention of lack of classrooms. Generally, as has been stated above, the class size at secondary schools was not as high as in primary schools. A few teachers (5/35) pointed out that environmental education was not included in the syllabus, which indicates that their concept of environmental education is not clear. Overall, both primary and secondary school teachers experience the same type of problems. Lack of transport, for instance, is mentioned as a problem by both teacher categories. This is probably related to their conception that study visits (preferably to a national park) are part of the teaching methods of environmental education. Going on study visits is indeed mentioned as a suitable teaching method in both the school syllabi and in the teacher training syllabi.

Now, after this presentation of the teaching conditions, let us proceed to how the teachers are experiencing environmental education. The outcome of the interviews of primary and secondary teachers is accounted below.

Teachers' ways of experiencing environmental education—outcome of the interviews

What is environmental education? What perceptions or ideas of environmental education do teachers have today? The next part presents the result of the phenomenographic analysis of the content of the interviews.

Three different ways of experiencing environmental education

Environmental education, the phenomenon that I investigated, is to some extent included in the curriculum, but not identified as such. That is, it is fairly easy to find environmental education components (according to the definition used in Chapter 5) in most of the syllabi as has been showed in an earlier chapter, but they are not labelled 'environmental education'. Nor did I myself present a definition of environmental education since the whole idea of the investigation was to find out what *teachers* perceived as environmental education. The area was thus open for a discussion of steering factors such as how the curriculum is formed. Most curricula are subject oriented; in schools in general, 'life' is divided into different subjects and Tanzania is no exception. So, in school, the world is divided into geography, history, science etc. The teachers themselves experienced their education in such a way, i.e. they were trained in this paradigm and this was the way they continued to work. In Tanzania the primary school teachers too were trained as specialists in certain subjects. The effect of this condition *could* be seen in the interviews, but it cannot be generalised.

Three different categories of ways of experiencing what environmental education is emerged from the analysis of the interviews with primary and secondary teachers. The first category is related to a here-and-now perspective based on observations: this is what it is, what and who can be seen in the surroundings. The second category focused on how the environment can be exploited in order to get as much as possible from it. The third category was concerned about conservation and improvement of the environment, and meant that resources must be cared for since mankind depends on them for survival. What the second and the third category have in common is the consciousness that people are dependent on the environment for food and other basic needs.

Below I will present some examples within each category. I have chosen examples that illustrate the nuances in the ways of experiencing involved in each sub-category. I will try to explain these nuances. The ways of experiencing are on a collective level (Marton 1996).

1. Environmental education is about natural and social surroundings

People should learn about what surrounds them, both living or non-living things, physical and non-physical aspects and natural resources such as land, forests, lakes and water bodies. People should be aware, learn and understand what is going on in the area where they live and how they are interacting with their environment.

In this way of experiencing one is focusing on what exists, what can be seen and found in the surroundings. The surroundings could embrace the very close neighbourhood to the school or the local community. Different types of natural resources are included as well as different kinds of habitats for human beings, animals, fishes and other types of living organisms. This category was not difficult to detect, since the teachers' reflections touched on specific or concrete parts of the surroundings or the total surroundings as such.

Two main sub-categories crystallised, one where the reflections were centred around natural resources and another that embraced the surroundings of the school, the nearby area or the more unspecified 'anything around us.'.

Some examples[1]:

> — Environmental education is the condition, things, all those that surround a human being wherever he lives ... those things that surround human beings like oceans, rivers, lakes, weather which is that of heat, wind, sun ... also living things such as plants, animals etc. (Primary school teacher 3)[2].
> — Environmental education ... the way I understand it ... is the totality of things or all events which surrounds you at a place in which you live ... when I say things I mean things like ... natural vegetation ... things like rivers, mountains ... this is the meaning of things. When I say events I mean activities which one carries [out] everyday ... like farm activities or other activities. Also the behaviour of the events which occur in that environment or eating, clothing all these belong to the environment. Games, traditional dances ... all things done by a person, all these entail environment (Primary school teacher 32).
> — I understand ... that it refers to ... knowledge ... about what is going on around us ... where we live ... in our environment ... the surroundings ... usually think of the physical aspects ... the soil. ... the features ... and also ... maybe non-physical aspects ... like air ... I don't know if air is physical or chemical ... so ... that's what I understand ... (Secondary school teacher 34).

2. Environmental education is about how the environment supports human beings through its resources

People get their food and other necessary things through human activities in the environment. To be able to improve their standard of living, people should learn how to behave and properly use the natural resources in their environment.

This category emphasises the utility aspect of human beings' relation to nature. The environment is seen as a provider for satisfying basic needs as well as improvement of human beings' lives. Because of its importance, people should learn how to use natural resources in the best way to get as much output as possible. After several attempts, I could finally resolve what differed in the teachers' thinking. On one hand there was a group of reflections that concen-

---

[1] Note: the language is quoted as the teachers themselves wrote or spoke.
[2] The interviewees were given numbers as identification.

trated on how one should use the environment in such a way that it would not be destroyed. On the other hand there were reflections on how the environment did or could satisfy their needs. I have called the first sub-category 'proper use' and the second 'exploitation of the environment'.

This way of experiencing environment and the relation between human beings and nature, is called *anthropocentrism* (Sörlin 1992, Armstrong and Botzler 1993). Anthropocentrism is a philosophical perspective that puts human needs and interests in focus. It can be traced back at least to the time of Mesopotamia and is probably one of the oldest ethical positions in Western civilisation. Roots can be found in both religious and secular philosophies, for instance in the works of St. Thomas Aquinas (Armstrong and Botzler 1993, pp. 275).

Examples from the interviews:

> — I think this is the education when ... whereby we can educate people how to deal with the environment so that they can have ... their needs for their lives ... for example food and dressing ... it is the question where we teach people how to rule the environment so that they can have a good life ... how they can deal with the environment to conquer this problem ... poverty ... (Secondary school teacher 1).
> — Environmental education is the portion which surrounds a person, where he lives and he gets his everyday basic needs... (Primary school teacher 2).
> — ... we have the important things in life ... now environment ... gives us the needs ... so it includes all the surroundings ... where people are ... people need something from the environment ... and ... we try to do some activities in the environment ... so they have to know the things ... which are surrounding them ... and those things that can give them what they need ... for example food ... and water ... (Secondary school teacher 14).

3. Environmental education is about conservation and improvement of the environment

People are trying to live of the environment but it is being destroyed. People should be taught how to keep the environment fit for human needs, to use it correctly and solve problems, for example, soil erosion. The pupils should be aware of how their day-to-day activities—social and economic—are controlled by the environment and how their role is to conserve and make the environment better. Population pressure causes destruction. Training of mind and character is needed to take better care of the environment where man gets his needs and 'everything'.

Conservation of the environment is the main aspect or focus in experiencing environmental education. It is important that pupils and people learn how their (daily) interactions affect the environment. Thus an attitude change is necessary and the problem solving skill is vital. If human beings are not aware of how their actions affect the environment, then the result will be destruction and a lack of satisfaction with their (daily) life, since their needs will not be fulfilled.

This is the largest category of answers from a quantitative point of view. The comments all touch more or less explicitly on preservation and conservation of natural resources. Everyone's responsibility for future generations was mentioned by interviewees and particular concern was expressed about problems such as overpopulation. The interrelation between man and nature and the need for balance was pointed out. An ethical concern could be discerned, particularly in relation to our obligation to take care of what is found in the nature. This could be traced to what is said in the Bible, which is not surprising, since many churches are active in spreading the environmental message. In this category there was also strong reference to the food situation. From the perspective of the relation between human beings and nature, this category reflects *environmental ethics;* the attitudes towards ecological systems, the values and the nature of relationships. The ethical principles can be found in many religions and can truly be said to have a multicultural perspective (Armstrong and Botzler 1993). The nature of Islamic ethics are comprehensive and a number of references can be found in the Koran (ibid. pp. 527–533). In Buddhism it is difficult to find anything specific related to environmental care. However, the lifestyle as well as virtues that are advocated in Buddhism are non-exploitative, non-aggressive and gentle towards nature (ibid. pp. 534–538).

I experienced some difficulties in this category. The reflections were related to human activities in the environment, some very general and others more specific and concrete, such as agricultural practices. What differences are there between the concepts 'taking care of', 'preserve' and 'conserve'? What is the time perspective? Do they all include sustainability? This was the most difficult decision I had to take and I especially experienced the language and cultural differences here. Examples:

> — Environmental education is along with environmental conservation, the country should not be affected through many ways ... for example through agricultural practices such as cultivation along the hills instead of across hills or contour ploughing, also when it rains soil is eroded (Primary school teacher 14).
> — ... a person should know something about ... the environment where he lives ... and how he can help to make this environment good ... he should see that it helps him to have a better life ... and ... see that he profits from it and of course ... he has to take care of the environment itself also ... and what actually ... need to be done to improve ... his whole being there ... both for his own benefit ... and ... to help his children ... of course our lives depends on the areas where we are living ... we get our food from there and our necessities and all that ... therefore everybody is responsible to ... to take care of the ... of his surroundings ... not only for the present time even for ... to be in good condition for the future ... (Secondary school teacher 17).
> — ... the nature of mankind ... as mankind is a part of nature ... man's willingness to alter environment has also increased to the pace that does not cope with the supply from the bank mentioned ... (soil, water, air) ... problems has risen due to misunderstanding of the said environment ... man and the interaction with the nature ... man tries to take the nature in order to obtain his needs ... from soil man

WHAT IS ENVIRONMENTAL EDUCATION?

```
                    About natural and      How the environment      About conservation and
                    social surroundings    supports human beings    improvement

        Natural                        Proper use of   Exploitation
        resources     Total            environment     of environment        Care of       Conservation
                      surrounding                                            surroundings  for the future
                                                                       Preservation of the environment
        Around the
        school                  Anything around us
                    Nearby      including human
                    area        activities
```

Diagram 6. Ways of experiencing what environmental education is. Categories and sub-categories.

> has obtained ... food ... shelter... clothes ... machinery of all kinds ... during tapping ... he makes some mistakes ... problems associated with tapping of these resources ... from the soil ... for example ... upsetting the balance of the nature ... the environment is destroyed ... decrease in natural resources ... if the human being does not obtain his needs ... and he has quite a lot ... that is a problem ... (Secondary school teacher 20).

An overview of the three ways of experiencing environmental education can be seen in Diagram 6. The diagram shows the question as well as categories and sub-categories. The result indicates different ways of experiencing the environment. One could look upon it just as it is: it is here and it consists of different living and non-living things. A second perspective is awareness of our dependence on natural resources, what the environment can provide, how we get access to it and how we can utilise it. The third way of experiencing shows the caretaker's responsibilities in a short-time or long-time perspective. I find these three different categories reasonable in a society dominated by agriculture. In another context further perspectives might be found.

The difference between the three categories reflects to some extent what was shown in Table 1 in Chapter 1. The first category is mainly an information source, to observe and learn what could be found and done in the environment. The second category is oriented towards the technical interest and education for management and control while the third category approaches the emancipatory interest and education for sustainability. However, I do not claim that the categories correspond to the divisions in Table 1; what I am saying is that there is a tendency to correspondence.

Why is environmental education important?
Two ways of experiencing

Another way to further penetrate the concept of environmental education was through the question of why it is important. All primary school teachers, with the exception of one, commented on how environmental education makes students aware of conservation and sustainability. In 21 of 36 answers availability of rain, agriculture or food was indicated as important factors to having a sustainable environment. Food security was described as a great concern to the teachers.

There were two main categories: environmental conservation and survival. Each had a number of sub-categories. The primary and secondary school teachers' understandings of the importance of environmental education could thus be grouped into two categories: Environmental conservation and Survival.

1. Environmental education is important in order to conserve the natural resources—environmental conservation

Here the attitude was, for instance, that you should handle the environment so that you get a good life, free from diseases. To obtain sufficient food products or to get money were related to using the environment well. Such use would improve the living conditions. An economical aspect is indicated at a level above the family context. Teachers who thought of the negative consequences of misuse of the environment wanted environmental education as prevention.

Teachers in this group used words like *prevent, take care of, to keep in good condition, conserve* and *preserve* when talking about the surroundings, natural resources or environment. Some examples:

> — Environmental education is important because it helps us in upgrading our economy. For example if we don't care for our environment ... we can ... taking an example of oceans if they decide to kill fishes unreasonably our needs won't be satisfied ... or wild animals ... poaching ... can destroy our environment (Primary school teacher 19).
> — This environmental education is important so that the community can understand the importance of natural things we have around. So that they can take care of them and extending them. If they are not taught how to take care of these things they will destroy them and we shall end at a loss (Secondary school teacher 11).

2. Environmental education is important in order to attain people's daily needs—survival.

It is important to conserve the environment because it is not only important for our own lives but for those of coming generations.

Many comments from the secondary school teachers (in 17 of 36 interviews) belonged to this category while primary school teachers had very few comments related to survival. The interview answers included hints at dependence or interrelationship between human beings and nature, consequences for the future and the need for conservation. The secondary school teachers were very aware of the need to use the natural resources in such a way that they would not be depleted or destroyed. When asked to identify changes in the environment during the past five to ten years, in almost all of the cases, the changes were of a negative nature. They included rapidly decreasing forests in their home areas, soil erosion or (in Dar es Salaam and Morogoro) pollution of water sources by the industries. The relation between deforestation and drought was interpreted by the secondary school teachers in the same way as the primary school teachers and probably for the same reasons. Their views on wild life conservation reflected what was pointed out in the syllabus—that tourism brings foreign exchange to the country. Biodiversity was not a concept that was commonly mentioned. Here are some examples of answers in this category:

>   —... environmental education is vital because it makes the pupil understand on how to take care of the environment practically so as to keep it for the next generation and for their own uses. To keep fertile soil and at last overcome the possibility of our country to become a desert (Primary school teacher 8).
>   — Environmental education is important because it has been affecting a lot of things. For example famine that is accompanied by drought that is caused by trees cutting. Therefore it is important to avoid cutting trees because most African countries in the third world countries have been experiencing the problem of food shortage that is caused by drought (Primary school teacher 22).
>   — The pupils must be aware of what surrounds them, how to conserve what is valuable; what the use come from, what constitutes what they use, the forest as water resource, the minerals, the wildlife, the agricultural environment that gives them what they have ... To keep them intact, to use them with care, to protect them for their future use ... Also environmental education broadens ones mind in relation to other parts of the world. Environmental education is important, it makes every Tanzanian a guardian of the resources we have, somebody that protects (Secondary school teacher 6).

The difference between these two categories is similar to the difference between category two and three in the ways of experiencing what environmental education is. The category of survival has a longer time perspective than the category of environmental conservation, which concentrates on e.g. the preventive actions that should be taken. The notion of understanding the environment is not evident but the focus is more on how to handle the environment so that it can continue to support human beings now and in the future. The first category seems to reflect an anthropocentric perspective and the second category expresses ideas related to environmental ethics.

Learning and teaching strategies

How did the primary school teachers think that environmental education should be learnt? Five teachers did not say anything about learning strategies. The comments from the others are grouped as follows: learning can take place in schools, by making study visits, by practicals, by using specialists, through theory and practice or through theory alone, through mass media and through meetings in villages. It might be important to remember that many of the primary school teachers were still involved in adult education programmes in the afternoons. When the secondary school teachers discussed how environmental education should be learnt, they approached the topic in similar ways. Three teachers did not comment on learning approaches or did not know what was meant by it.

The suggestions were grouped into the three categories: learning sources and teaching strategies in school, learning through the society and learning through mass media.

1. What to do in school when teaching and learning about the environment
Study visits, such as going somewhere to study something in its natural context, were specified by a minority of primary school teachers as a good teaching method. Some of the teachers' suggestions were not economically feasible considering the school's financial situations. However, in teacher training and elsewhere, study visits were presented as a possible method of teaching.

The 1967 Education for Self-Reliance and the 1974 Musoma Resolutions stated that primary education was universal, compulsory and terminal and that it should prepare pupils for a life in a community which is predominantly rural. Each school should have a self-reliance project that should contribute to the finances of the school and make it possible for the pupils to be trained in skills that they would need in their future life. It was also expected that the primary schools would be close to the life of the community in which they were situated; and that theory would be related in this way, since this was vital to the education process. How was this reflected in the teachers' remarks?

A majority of the teachers believed that pupils learned best through 'seeing and doing' (22 of 38 primary and 21 of 37 secondary school teachers). They said that first you teach theory and then the pupils go out and practice it. Only three of the secondary school teachers advocated teaching theory alone although it was, de facto, the most practised teaching approach. Other comments showed the wish to implement what was recommended. As mentioned elsewhere, there were few resources for teaching and even less for making study visits. The following were some of the teachers' comments on the issue of theory and practice:

> — For the children to understand more about the environmental education, pupils are supposed to learn first theoretically and then practically so as to take care of the environment. Practically they can plant trees, grass and flowers. They can also try to practice terracing, tame animals and to have little plots for planting those few things for different exhibitions, they can also practice mixed agriculture whereby pupils can practice mixed crop mode of agriculture (Primary school teacher 2).
>
> — also while we are discussing about the afforestation ... we could have at least some ... places where we could plant trees and so on, but we don't have time

because the syllabus is too big and ... while the time is too little. So we are failing to ... make the implementation of what we are teaching there ... so we are dealing with more theory than practice ... and that is I think the disadvantage (Secondary school teacher 4).

It is clear that the teachers believe in other methods than what they are using in the classrooms. The teachers have ideas about what could be done, if they only knew how to realise it, or if it was possible considering the available resources.

2. Learning through the society

One frequent primary school teacher comment (21/38), when they commented on learning strategies, was associated directly with village life and adult people. It had to do partly with the fact that the primary school teachers were also conducting adult education classes and partly with the fact that Tanzania is an agricultural society where most people lived in villages. Up until 1992 during the one-party state, the party structure from top-down to grass root was well established. Meetings or seminars in villages were an important means of communication. Some of the primary school teachers probably did not feel comfortable with their own training. They suggested the use of specialists for environmental education.

Fifteen of 37 secondary school teachers pointed to the need to work at both school and community levels with environmental information. It was emphasised that the methods that were used in schools could not be applied to adults. Formal education was not enough. School was an important place but it takes time before the pupils grow up and become decision makers such as farmers or heads of households. There was also a belief that when the pupils finished school, they would return to their home villages and would teach their parents. This was expressed in many interviews and is a common conviction in educational situations.

> — Methods that we can use in schools ... especially in teaching in lower classes it is good to educate these children practically. In cleanliness we should teach them how to clean themselves and their surroundings, how a child can get balanced diet ... I mean nutrition. So they can go home and explain to their parents about what they do at schools. There is also a possibility of welcoming parents to school when they need any type of help about the environment and cleanliness in their houses and their environment (Primary school teacher 21).
> — Environment starts at home where we live ... you can find some places are overpopulated ... here should be a person who will educate them on how to live in such places ... also at school teachers should teach pupils ... these pupils will carry whatever they have been taught to their homes. Through this circulation we will spread the knowledge. (Primary school teacher 29).

However, there were exceptions. One important factor was cultural tradition. If the content that was taught in school differed from the traditional practices, there was a low probability that the pupils would have an impact on changing these practices. It was not easy to convince a pastoralist who is used to herding his animals over vast areas to change to the more environmentally friendly zero-grazing system (keeping cows in cow sheds and cultivating the fodder they need).

> — Last time I said you must practice it ... what you have learned in the class ... but they say it is very difficult ... because ... they told me that ... if you go to the Masai land from school ... and then you pretend you try to change things ... they do not like you ... they always ... keep their culture ... it is only very few people in Masai land ... who come to school. ... most of them do not ... they do not see the meaning to come to school ... some of them have gone to urban areas ... and have seen the different the differences which are there between this district with those other places ... but if they try to practice it in their land ... I know two of them that have tried to practice ... nobody appreciated it ... so they were all discouraged ... and they have decided to move ... from their home places ... (Secondary school teacher 12).

One suggestion made in the interviews was to educate people born in these areas and then employ them to teach their villagers.

> — perhaps the people who are born here ... of this district ... who are educated ... could be sent back ... to their.. home places to teach ... or try to change others ... that is the only solution ... because if I go there ... I come from Kilimanjaro ... and then ... now they feel that I am a foreigner (Secondary school teacher 13).

There were other ways to reach people in the community. It was suggested that during visits to health clinics, individuals should receive education about the environment along with treatment.

> — Also people who are not in school ... are told when they go to clinics they get education with any treatment. They get education how to get rid of these for example malnutrition problems, how to get rid of malaria (Secondary school teacher 1).

And in village meetings people would be told and taught about local problems. This was part of what the teachers called 'the governmental system'.

> — I do think according to my own view environmental education can be taught to every Tanzanian so that he understands well by meetings ... in villages ... among various age groups (Primary school teacher 17)

Through seminars from national to local levels, leaders would be taught, and they were expected to communicate the ideas at grass root level. The village leaders, party leaders and/or traditional leaders (elders) were expected to discuss environmental issues with the people in the village and also to instruct them on what to do.

> — Therefore the good way is to use the older people ... take maybe the chiefs ... they say the area of chiefs is not back ... because certain years back the so called chiefs ... their kingdoms maybe have been ... put into consideration by the government ... let's say they are ... for example around our school we have a certain man

> ... known as a mzee[3]... and he is a chief ... he is being respected by many people ... and therefore ... if you want to start a certain project ... you have to approach that man ... we want to do this and this and the benefit of this is this and this ... and when you inform the chief ... and he has accepted that idea ... then he can tell his people the importance of that project ... and the people follows that idea ... according to my view ... I think the best way is to use the older people (Secondary school teacher 18).

The reason for environmental education in the community was to improve living conditions. What this above all meant was that people would be able to secure enough food for their whole family.

> — because when we talk about the environment ... we think about the houses we live in ... and the food we eat ... we do have farms where we get our food ... we can't be able to live if there is no environment... (Secondary school teacher 37).

3. Learning through mass media

About 10 percent of the teachers believed in the use of mass media to teach people. Of these media, radio was considered to be the most effective. The newspapers had weekly articles about the environment but they were not always related to local conditions.

Teachers in the interviews suggested the use of radio programmes to spread the ideas of environmental education. The vast majority of the households in Tanzania have access to a radio even if each household does not owe one. Radio programmes during 1991–1993 frequently provided information about environmental problems and gave advice on how to handle them through dramatisation of actual situations (serial stories). People were used to listening to messages from different authorities through the radio. In the educational system, for example, calls for starting of terms or instructions for national examinations were sent by radio. The information in the broadcasts was spread around to other people. The use of posters was also frequent. Every campaign had its stock of posters which were sent out to the districts. In the campaign 'Plant a tree, cut a tree,' organised by the Ministry of Agriculture (with the main idea of reforestation), posters with crying trees were well remembered.

> — Mass media like radio should have a proper programme about environmental issues.This will easily reach a good number of people. (Primary school teacher 34).
> — ... we should have numerous radio programmes ... about proper fishing ... illegal fishing ... poaching. ... as a bad, bad attitude or a bad behaviour ... and other malpractice (Secondary school teacher 6).
> — ... but. ... as far as in the villages ... maybe you can try to use some posters ... like they use these trees ... the importance of a tree ... a tree crying ... people get the interest and they plant the trees ... when I went home I met some old people ... they said they (the trees) are crying ... they are going to die and (I should be) trying to plant a tree before I cut down this old one ... which my mother planted ... I think if they are educated in a way ... they have an idea ... (Secondary school teacher 33).

---

[3] Mzee is an elder man in Swahili language.

In Tanzania the radio has been an important channel of communication. Important messages were broadcasted, for example, announcements of when a new term started or was cancelled, celebration of Ramadan and other holidays, and rationing of electricity. It is natural to think of the radio in the educational situation as well.

Content of environmental education

All primary school teachers except one commented on the content of environmental education. A good half of the teachers suggested examples of topics that should be included in environmental education. The issue of cleanliness was talked about very often. Other frequent suggestions were related to agriculture and agricultural practices. How to conserve the environment was seen as important. Regarding this issue, teachers had taken into account the context in which the pupils were living. Three different categories could be seen: subject related topics, conservation and themes related to where the pupils were living.

All secondary school teachers, with no exceptions, commented on the content of environmental education. Their comments were, however, more elaborated when it came to scope and breadth. Categories to be distinguished are: reference to components of subjects in the present syllabi, different environmental issues that should be taught, the need for adaptation of the content to local conditions and an interdisciplinary approach. There was thus a correspondence between primary and secondary school teachers' understanding.

In eleven comments out of twelve, soil erosion and/or soil conservation measures were mentioned as important topics. Avoiding environmental destruction or damage and pollution was also frequently mentioned. From this I draw the conclusion that the topics, which were not directly related to the teachers' own subjects, indicated a general view about what content was needed.

The teachers suggested that teaching about the methods of conservation should include describing how the soil should be utilised, how to plant trees, how to protect the forest, how to control disturbances etc. The emphasis was on teaching methods and ways to prevent or handle problems.

In Education for Self-Reliance ideology it was said that the content in school should be related to the community in which the pupils lived. Likewise, the teachers said that it was important to relate the content of the lesson to the area where the students were living. This is not difficult in primary school education since the school was closely related to the community in many aspects. The governmental secondary schools, however, as mentioned earlier, were boarding schools with students who were recruited nation-wide. Although the interviewed teachers were working in these governmental schools, they seldom mentioned the fact that the secondary school students were strangers to the local school environment. It might indicate that the school was isolated from the surrounding community, despite the education policy intentions expressed in the curriculum.

The following examples show some of the teachers' answers to the question what the content of environmental education should be.

1. Subject related content

From the subject of biology interdependence, transpiration, photosynthesis, natural resources, soil conservation, pollution, evolution and health are referred to. From physics only energy is mentioned. The domestic science/home economics subject inspired answers on cleanliness, health, keeping of a good environment in order to have a good life, good manners, nutritious food and the use of needle work. Soil erosion, afforestation, overgrazing, and faulty farming were answers that came from the subject of agriculture. From the syllabus of geography we find soil erosion, climate, natural resources and population pressure. The teachers' answers reflect what is already mentioned in the syllabi. The examples below were taken from the subjects of domestic science and agriculture and/or geography (depending on level).

> — Cleanliness of the body; cleanliness of the environment in which he lives around the house, school and village. Various types of diseases spread by insects or by germs. How to overcome environmental destroyers for example bad agricultural practices, soil erosion and so on. (Primary school teacher 11).
>
> —... have the grazing of animals ... the methods that are used in grazing destroy ... the soil fertility ... for example encouraging soil erosion...again we come back to soil erosion. Some of the methods discourage the growth of vegetation ... because you are overgrazing and not planning the way to graze ... so the animals will destroy all ... the vegetation ... and they remain with nothing ... for the animals. (Secondary school teacher 14).

Cleanliness was an important part of domestic science and the aim was to improve the health of the population. Education and health were the sectors that were prioritised by the socialist state of Tanzania. Agriculture was the dominant production form. It is thus logical that these areas were emphasised in the curriculum.

2. Content focused on environmental issues

The second category consists of three groups of issues: conservation, environmental problems and what I have chosen to call 'single issues' (not related to a context). The conservation issues concern maintenance of the environment, soil conservation (especially related to food security and farming practices), natural resources such as water and conservation in general. The environmental problems mentioned were cutting down forests, life style, pollution, agricultural practices, marine life, wild life protection and the scarcity of water. Single issues were, for instance, cleanliness, planting of trees, use of chemicals in agriculture and family life education, e.g. spacing the birth of children. Here are some quotes:

— .. it is now going to be a problem ... because most of the people are being instructed...to use chemicals as fertilisers ... herbicides maybe ... or they are being instructed to use ... any kind of chemical which ... at least activate or increase the ... production of agricultural commodities ... o the ... chemicals which are being left, which are being used they are somehow ... poisonous (Secondary school teacher 4).

— Maybe disposing waste ... to be able to conserve our environment we should know how best we can dispose some of the waste products ... either from industries ... from factories ... or domestic waste ... it would be more useful ... and sometimes how to use the by-products from the industries ... (Secondary school teacher 27).

— Things should be taught to the pupils so that they can be good instructors in their future society. They will know the importance of trees and the environment. They should avoid practices that can cause drought which will persist generation after generation (Primary school teacher 22).

—... the reasons ... why is this happening...why people are poaching ... why people are cutting trees ... maybe they are cutting trees so that they get land ... but will that land suffice their needs ... will they get what they expect by cutting trees or will it create a certain problem ... when we educate people on environmental education ... we should think of ... their problem also ... because we cannot tell someone to stop cutting trees ... when he is looking for a piece of land or he is looking for firewood ... if we tell a person to stop cutting trees ... we should give him or her ... another alternative ... stop cutting trees ... use this ... that is what I believe the environmental education should lead the people ... of what is to be done ... (Secondary school teacher 12).

The teachers have mentioned environmental issues and problems that were a concern of the Tanzanian society. They seemed to be well informed and seldom hesitated in expressing their ideas.

3. Content related to the local community

The third group of suggestions mirrors the ideology of the Ujamaa philosophy—the future of Tanzania should be built on agriculture and improvement of living conditions in the rural areas as well as development of the industries in the urban sector. The impact of domestic science (in primary school) or home economics (in secondary school) is strong concerning health education. The content should consider the needs of the people, analyse the environment or be related to problems in Tanzania.

— As a Science teacher I think things that are to be taught are first we should teach about the immediate child environment when at home. For example here in town one house is surrounded by many other houses and maybe very few trees so he has to be aware of his environment. After knowing his environment when he comes to school also he has to know his school environment. He can compare home and school he must be able to apply what he is taught at school to her or his home. For example the topic of Ecology in Science. Animals depend on plants for food and these plants have to grow well. Manure comes from animals which are kept well. So if at home his mother keeps chicken he will be able to help to keep well these chickens and use their faeces as manure in his farm. Here he will be applying what he has learnt at school. (Primary school teacher 28).

> — the content should ... depend ... on the environment in which ... the people who need the education are ... let's take an example of our case in Tanzania ... we should look at rural people and the urban people ... how we use these resources ... how we can conserve them so that we can go on using them for a longer time what is disturbing the environment and these resources and ... it is more related to the ecosystem ... man and his environment ... (Secondary school teacher 33).

4. An interdisciplinary approach

The last category is small. Only one teacher suggested an interdisciplinary approach to environmental education:

> — Another thing is what should be the content of environmental education. I think the content should be connected with the physical environment, the biological environment and ... I think that the economical environment also because ... these sectors interplay ... so when we study about them we know how one affects the other and in that way we will be able to manage the environment very well ... (Secondary school teacher 7).

The ideas teachers had about the content of environmental education, while not constituting qualitatively different ways of experiencing it, ranged from regarding the content as it already exists to focusing on environmental issues, relating the content to the local community and using a thematic approach involving several subjects.

Experienced changes in the environment

To further explore the concept teachers have of environmental education, I asked 19 of the primary school teachers what changes they had seen in the environment during the last five or ten years. More than half of the answers indicated that they tended to see negative changes, such as the cutting of trees, lack of rain and related difficulties. The positive changes were few and mostly related to health issues, many of which needed improvement.

When asked to describe their observations of changes during the last five years or so, the teachers' answers show a broader concept of environment and environmental problems than when asked about what environmental education is. In other words, they had 'practical' knowledge but they were not used to formulating it in an abstract way. Their knowledge was based on observations but they had not always been given an explanation of the cause behind the changes nor had they formulated one themselves.

One of the changes was an increase in deforestation and drought spells. This situation was very common in communities of Tanzania. The issue was brought to people's attention through the various campaigns against the custom of using fire when collecting wild honey or clearing land and the indiscriminate cutting of trees for a variety of reasons. Slogans or simple messages were used, but a deeper understanding of the problem was not promoted.

Still, the observations were very valid and pointed to current environmental problems in Tanzania. As the teachers indicated, the problems were how to survive on a daily basis, how to get rain so that food could be produced, how to have better health, how to improve living conditions and how to cope with the available resources.

Summary and conclusions

External determinants—frame factors

There is little doubt that the teachers in my case study experienced the *external* determinants as problems in implementing environmental education. The class sizes must constitute an obstacle to using teaching methods which demand active participation, for example problem solving. It is surprising that only 10 percent of the primary school teachers answered that too many pupils was a problem considering that, according to Table 20, the mean number of pupils was 78. On the other hand, if the teachers were not familiar with other teaching methods than one-way communication by the use of words and dictating or writing down notes for the pupils to copy, then the number of pupils does not matter.

The classrooms were built for half that group size and the problem of lack of desks and chairs was persistent (see Table 10 in Chapter 4). The lack of teaching resources and personal knowledge of the issues were perceived as the dominating problem. This cannot be solely related to environmental education but applies to other areas as well, since in-service training programmes are very scarce.

Table 19 shows that 65 percent of the primary and 35 percent of the secondary school teachers who were included in my interviews declared that they were using field work. Of the secondary school teachers, 11 percent feel that the absence of practicals is a problem in teaching environmental education. According to my observations, I doubt these optimistic estimations. The questionnaire did not ask about the frequency of field work or practicals. It could have been done once a year or once a month—or not at all. In the syllabi field work is indicated but in real teaching situations, there are many factors that obstruct implementation. Are field work and practicals considered to be the same thing? The answer is yes, more or less. Both could be done on the school farm or school compound but also in the surrounding community.

The overall conclusion is that the teachers point to several problems that are considered obstacles to implementation of environmental education, although some of the problems are common for all subjects. It is important to remember that the agriculturally productive and industrial regions, where these teachers worked, also enjoyed better educational services in comparison to the dry regions such as those of Lindi, Mtwara and Dodoma. This fact suggests that the situation for teachers in other regions might be similar or even worse.

Internal determinants: What environmental education is

When focusing on the *internal* determinants and the teachers' thinking and reasoning and by analysing the interviews with the teachers, three qualitatively different ways of experiencing *what environmental education is*, were found:

— environmental education is about natural and social surroundings.
— environmental education is about how the environment supports human beings through its resources.
— environmental education is about conservation and improvement of the environment.

The first category concerned physical and some ecological aspects as well as certain human activities in the environment. The second category could be interpreted as an orientation towards a technical interest (in relation to the divisions in Table 1). Its focus was mainly on education for management and control. Education for sustainability was clearly expressed in the third category, which was also critical of existing practices; a first step towards an emancipatory interest. The relation between human beings and the nature in the second category appeared to fall into the category of anthropocentrism and in the third category to be more related to environmental ethics.

The categories varied from physical/ecological to social, political and economic aspects of the world. The environment is what surrounds us, materially and socially. The interaction between our physical surroundings and the social, political and economic forces that organise the context for our lives can thus be said to be the base for viewing the environment as a social construct. Practices and structures in the society will then be the cause of environmental problems.

This means that environmental education should focus on reflection, preventive measures, conservation and improvement of the environment according to the emancipatory interest.

Why environmental education is important

As for the question, *Why is environmental education important?* I found two qualitatively different ways of experiencing, albeit closely related:

— environmental education is important in order to conserve the natural resources—environmental conservation.
— environmental education is important in order to get people's daily needs—survival.

The difference between these two ways of experiencing is that one is concerned with a longer time perspective than the other. Environmental conservation is about care of the environment, learning how to live in the environment and avoiding destruction and pollution, while the survival category also encompasses a need to take care of the environment because people today and the future generation cannot survive without it. The two categories reinforce the opinion that environmental problems are socially constructed. In the perspective of the relation between human beings and nature, anthropocentrism is reflected in the first category while the second might be more oriented towards environmental ethics.

In comparison with the ways of experiencing what environmental education is, where three qualitatively different categories were found, the categories of the importance are only related to the third category; environmental education is about conservation and improvement. It gives a more profound description of ways of experiencing that particular category. But teachers who 'belong' to the two first categories in the first sense also belong to the categories in the second sense. Does this mean that there is a contradiction? As mentioned earlier, Ference Marton has explained that we are talking about the qualitatively different ways of experiencing the phenomena, regardless of whether the differences are within or between individuals (see Chapter 2). Thus, following his interpretation, there is no contradiction.

Learning and teaching strategies

Concerning *learning and teaching strategies*, teachers' perceptions were categorised in the following groups: what to do *in school* when teaching and learning about the environment; learning through the *society*; and learning through *mass media*. These categories are not qualitatively different.

There was a strong belief in connecting theory (teaching by using words) with practice, at least at a rhetorical level. This is what is said in Education for Self-Reliance and the syllabi written during the 1970s. The examples that were given were practical activities related to a school farm or self-reliance projects and not to, for example, a constructivist learning approach. Studies (Nyerere 1967b, Linde 1987, Mbilinyi & Mbughuni 1991, Temu 1995) and my own observations have indicated that the relation between theory and practice has not materialised. The most common teaching method is lecturing in the classroom. What was going on in the classroom was very seldom connected with what was going on outside the classroom (mainly related to the self-reliance projects).

The ideas about learning through the society reflect the existence of adult education and informal education in Tanzania, at health centres and village meetings, for example. It is interesting to note the importance and status of elders. However, my perception is that this is not utilised in the schools to any notable extent. The use of mass media in environmental education is also related mainly to adult and informal education. Schools were infrequently sent posters. If the schools were supplied with radios or even one radio, or (rarely) a television, it was locked up in a cupboard or in the house of the head teacher/master. The teachers, however, believed very much in the use of radio programmes for spreading environmental messages.

The teachers' suggestions of suitable teaching methods reflect their own training or directives in the syllabi more than their own practice. They were talking about what they were supposed to do without always knowing how to implement or use the suggested methods in their classrooms.

The content of environmental education

Regarding the *content,* the teachers' ideas were grouped into four categories: *subject related* content, content focused on *environmental issues*, content related to the *local commun*ity and an *interdisciplinary* approach. These categories were not qualitatively different.

The suggestions on subject related content were related to what could be found in the syllabi. Content focusing on environmental issues was about conservation, environmental problems and single environmental issues. It was notable that the conservation issues were much related to *food security*. There was a strong impact from the subjects of domestic science and home economics on health education. Teachers felt the content should consider the needs of the people. Here, too, Education for Self-Reliance had clearly left its mark when the teachers reflected upon how the content should be related to the surrounding community. The interdisciplinary approach, showing the interplay between physical, ecological and economic sectors, was suggested by one teacher only.

Comments

Teachers have an understanding of what environmental education is and of its importance. The relation between humans and nature is anthropocentric or reflects environmental ethics. They have ideas about teaching strategies even if they do not always know how to carry them out. Primary school teachers' comments were related to village life and adult learners while secondary school teachers tended to point to the need for school and community to act together. But they did not know how to integrate these two parts of the society. One teacher disclosed in an interview:

> — ... we don't give practicals because of some reason ... one of the reasons that makes us not doing practicals is that ... we are not used to ... we are just teaching for the sake of teaching ... (Secondary teacher 22).

Teachers have a variety of opinions about what should be taught. The suggestions are related to what is already in the curriculum or to issues that seem to be more closely related to ongoing discussions about environment and society.

To improve teachers' environmental education strategies it seems important to consider the same wisdom as for successful learning: find out what the learner already knows, ascertain this and build on it.

CHAPTER 9
What do pupils understand about the environment?

Introduction

Environmental education components can be found in the syllabi of primary and secondary schools in Tanzania. But is the curriculum implemented? How well informed are pupils on environmental matters? The answers to such questions could contribute to my understanding of the realisation of the curriculum.The tool of a questionnaire with open-ended questions was used to get a random sample of answers. The questions were given to pupils and students in the same schools as where I interviewed teachers.

In this section, the choice of questions and the results are described and discussed. The reason why I analysed each single question is that I wanted to know pupils' knowledge and awareness of particular topics. Questions were chosen according to existence in syllabi, intentions on national and international policy level as well as current discussion in the Tanzanian society at that time.

I have separated the results from primary and secondary schools. Primary school is intended for all children but less than ten percent are selected for secondary school, which might have an impact on the result. I have analysed the results in urban and rural schools to investigate if there is any difference. Primary schools are mixed while secondary schools normally are gender separated (boarding schools), although mixed schools exist (only in day-schools). I have tried to explore if there are any differences in the results in the boys' and girls' secondary schools.

A questionnaire study

The objective of using a questionnaire was to get a description of the distribution of pupils' understanding of certain issues. In this particular case, one advantage was that I could collect information effectively during a short period of time and with a high response rate. The use of the questionnaire has its limitations, though. It must be brief and the questions cannot be deeply probed or followed up (Chadwick, Bahr & Albrecht 1984).

The same questionnaire was given to 672 Standard VII pupils (questions in Swahili) and 738 Form IV students (questions in English) in the Arusha, Dar es Salaam, Kilimanjaro and Morogoro regions. Whole classes participated and the only pupils who did not participate were those that did not, for one reason or other, come to school that particular day. I experienced the classrooms as 'crowded' so the missing pupils in all likelihood were not a significant number in relation to the total number of pupils. I estimate that the non-attendance on average was less than ten percent. Pilot testing was done in the Morogoro region. The students were given no time in advance to prepare for the questions since I wanted their immediate recall of knowledge. The questions followed a pattern of what, how and why, as well as a request to give examples. The time given for answering the questions varied between 45 and 60 minutes, depending on the students. Answers were collected between February 1992 and February 1993, always during the same period from the primary and secondary schools in a specific region.

Why were these particular questions chosen?

To set the context for the pupils the first question, *What is meant by 'environment'?*, was of a general nature. It is sometimes claimed that pupils in the primary school could have difficulties in perceiving the difference between 'environment' and 'surrounding,' since the same word for both (mazingira) is used in Swahili. On the other hand, 'mazingira' is used on posters and in the radio programmes in environmental campaigns. The concept is part of the syllabi of primary and secondary schools.

The second question, *Where did you learn things about the environment?* was used because I knew that there was a very popular programme series on the radio during the year I collected the data. The radio is much more accessible to the broad population than the newspapers with articles on environmental matters. Newspapers can only be purchased in the larger cities. I also knew that some church leaders had participated in environmental campaigns. In analysing the answers to this question, it is important to remember that there is a tacit knowledge among the farmers, for example about traditional soil conservation methods. The answers to this question are presented in a separate table below.

The third question, *Why is knowledge about the environment important?*, was an attempt to stimulate the pupils to think for themselves. It was also a check to see if they could reflect upon the question or if their knowledge mainly came through rote learning.

The fourth question, *How can you reduce soil erosion?*, was an attempt in the same direction. In my pilot version I asked about the factors that cause soil erosion and received long lists of answers which I guessed were learned by heart. The question is important, since the soil erosion problem is expanding and the population growing, hence the need for more food. Soil erosion is part of the syllabi of agriculture, geography and home economics/domestic science in both primary and secondary schools.

Question five, *Give some examples of endangered animals (animals threatened by extinction) in Tanzania!* is a question that is much cherished in Western societies. I was interested to see if this was also an issue in Tanzania. Did the teachers mention endangered species when they taught about the natural resources of the country?

The same cherished attitude in Western society applies to question six, *Give three examples of pollution of the environment!.* Although there are comparatively few industries in Tanzania, I knew that there had been local resistance towards a plan to establish a certain industry in Moshi because of the consequential outlet of chemicals into the river system and that this had been addressed in the mass media. The outlet of wastes from the central national hospital of Dar es Salaam and the textile factories into the nearby rivers were also familiar to some extent. In Morogoro, too, there was an industry that polluted the lake which the local community used for many purposes. Pollution was mentioned in the syllabi.

The seventh question, *What is the 'green-house effect'?,* is the third typical Western concern in environmental education. I wanted to know how well this concept was known.

The concept included in question eight, *What is an ecosystem? Please give an example,* should be familiar to the pupils since it is part of the syllabi for both primary and secondary school.

Question nine, *Where should a garbage dumping site be situated? Explain why.,* was a subject taken up in home economics at both school levels. Shortly before I collected data, it had been a big issue in Dar es Salaam, since the town authorities wanted to open a new dump site close to a densely populated area but it was stopped due to the resistance of residents. This had been widely debated in the mass media, both in radio and newspapers.

Fishing along the coast of the Indian Ocean and along the shores of Lake Victoria and other lakes was an important contribution to the food supply. The fishermen were increasingly using dynamite to get as large a catch as possible and the coral reefs were being affected. The law was constantly violated. This is why I chose question ten: *Why is it forbidden for fishermen to use dynamite to catch fish?.*

The last and eleventh question, *What are the causes of deforestation?* took up another of the large environmental problems in Tanzania. During the years before and during my data collection, there had been a large tree planting campaign and the issue was also part of the syllabi in primary and secondary schools. The radio programme referred to above dramatised what happened when the trees were cut.

Administration of the test

I administrated the questionnaires myself (in primary schools with the assistance of an interpreter). The pupils and students were asked to participate during the school day which meant that they had to leave their lessons. They were informed by the head of the school or by a teacher about the event. Then I told them about the purpose of the questionnaire and about the research. I emphasised that it would have no effect on their grades in school and that they were free to guess as much as possible if they did not know the answers. I also emphasised that they might have knowledge that they had got outside school. I tried to explain the concept of research and also asked them to try to answer all questions. If anything was unclear, they were allowed to ask me for clarification and in such cases I re-phrased the question. The pupils and students were always co-operative and tried to answer as many questions as possible.

Results

The data processing was very simple, consisting of frequency distribution, median value and percent. The students' responses to the questions have not been processed in a qualitative way but according to a traditional scoring system with right-or-wrong aspects. This is in correspondence with the examination system of the schools. There is one difference though; in examinations multiple-choice questions are common and open-ended question more rare. I have used the following criteria, based on what was possible to learn as compared to what was included in the syllabi, when marking the responses:

— No idea at all or wrong idea = 0 points.
— Presenting a few words with some connection with the topic = 1 point.
— An answer with some basic main points but not complete = 2 points.
— An answer with the basic main points = 3 points.

Table 1 and 2 in Appendix 10 show the frequency of the marking scores for each question (except for question 2 which will be presented separately in Table 21 below). Examples of typical answers to question 1, what is meant by 'environment', in primary school were:

> 0 p
> — It means a place which is completely built, with houses, water, toilets and it should be near a hospital.
> — Environment is a certain type of cleanliness of a place or land environment.
>
> 1 p
> — It is a place where man lives.
>
> 2 p
> — Environment is a place in which people live and carry out various activities and hence get their food.
> — A place where people are living and living things and non-living things in the world also in the country.

3 p
— Environment is a collection of all those things concerned with living things. Environment is a general word that explains the totality of natural resources, atmosphere, air, heat etc.
— The earth and all things in it. For example: ocean, lakes, rivers, plants, animals etc.

And in secondary school:

1 p
— Environment is areas or places around us on the earth surface around the people.

2 p
— Environment means living and non-living within the surface of the earth.
— Environment means man's surroundings where he lives and plants corps and where animals live.

3 p
— Environment means all the features over the earth's surface including natural and manmade features which surround us.
— Environment are all things which surround man and contain components such as air, water, soil and rock and atmospheric gases. All of these can affect both habitat and living organisms.

The answers to questions 4, 5, 6 and 11 involved examples and consequently the marking has been different, i.e. one point for each example (maximum 3 p).

The first question, What is meant by 'environment', is, as said before, a general question. Both primary and secondary school students attained similar median values, 1.95 and 1.98 points. The question can be considered as belonging to the category of *correct explanation*—the answer lies in the ideas behind the curriculum. The environmental literacy level is *nominal*.

On question 2, 'Where did you learn things about the environment?' the answers (in percent) are as follows in Table 21. The students were free to give as many answers as possible.

As an overall summary, it is evident that primary and secondary school students experience that they have learnt more about environmental education topics from other sources than those available in school. The ratio between in-school and outside-school learning sources is 1/1.9 for primary and 1/1.6 for secondary school students. For primary school leavers, their families were the wells of information about environmental issues. The mass media, too, played an important role. It is surprising that the newspapers were named to be such large contributors, considering the low circulation in the country. In primary school pupils do not have access to newspapers but somehow they are still apparently familiar with their content. Of the school subjects, the pupils pointed out the domestic science and the science subjects as the largest contributors to their environmental knowledge.

Table 21: *Answers in percent to question 2, Where did you learn things about the environment? Note that it was possible to give several answers*

Source of knowledge	Primary school, n=672	Secondary school, n=738
School	8	6
Science	51	Non-existent subject
Biology	Non-existent subject	58
Chemistry	Non-existent subject	5
Physics	Non-existent subject	1
Geography	43	89
History	6	21
Agriculture	41	13
Domestic science	70	Non-existent subject
Kiswahili	2	Non-existent subject
Political Education	2	1
Total in school	32 [a]	39 [b]
Family	98	60
Newspaper	77	83
Radio	84	89
Youth organisation	37	18
Church	41	30
Other, incl. mosque	33	20
Total outside school	68 [c]	61 [d]

[a] Based on absolute numbers
[b] See previous footnote
[c] See previous footnote
[d] See previous footnote

In secondary school, the mass media was said to be the largest informants but the subject of geography was assessed to be as important as the radio. In secondary schools pupils normally have access to newspapers in the school library although the papers might be weeks old. The family, along with the biology subject, were identified as vital contributors.

Among the school subjects there is a difference between primary and secondary schools. In primary school domestic science was said to be the most important and in secondary school geography was pointed out as a major source of information. These opinions correspond to the occurrence of environmental components in the syllabi.

Analysing the responses from the pupils, one can draw the conclusion that formal education is not regarded as a major contributor to their knowledge—at least, as they themselves assess the situation. Another conclusion is the important role of radio programmes in spreading knowledge and information, even though the pupils themselves said that newspapers also had had an impact, a fact that was unexpected, since about 80–90 percent of the population in Tanzania have access to radio while the circulation of newspapers is very low.

It is important to stress that the answers on question 2 are based on the experiences and immediate remembrances of the students and not on an in-depth analysis of their learning sources.

Turning to the answers to question 3, we note that the pupils showed that to some extent the knowledge about the environment is important for their lives. The secondary school pupils scored higher than the primary school. This question is more complicated than the first one.

The question on how to reduce soil erosion is the one that has been easiest to answer by all. The median values are about two points for primary and close to three points for secondary school. This indicates that the answers to the question are well known. The answers have a practical content and are action oriented. Of course, it remains to be seen if the pupils are able to apply the knowledge they have about reduction of soil erosion. In the syllabi of agriculture, science and geography in primary school we find factors that cause soil erosion and how to prevent it. These subjects are taken by all pupils. In secondary school syllabi this topic can be found in agriculture (for those that have chosen this bias[1]), geography and biology (the latter are studied by all students).

When the pupils were asked to give some examples of endangered animals (animals threatened by extinction) in Tanzania, they may have confused the word 'endangered' with 'dangerous'. The primary and the secondary school students answered on the same level of understanding, even though the only extra-curricular club[2] oriented towards wild life (Malihai[3]) is for secondary schools only. Furthermore, there is nothing in the primary school syllabi on endangered animals. In secondary school syllabi, it could be taught in geography (wild life and its conservation).

When asked to give three examples of pollution of the environment, we see that there is little difference between the answers from primary and secondary schools. Generally they tended to have only a slight notion of what pollution is. There was nothing in primary school syllabi about it. In secondary schools it was mentioned in home economics and biology.

The issue of the 'green-house effect' is not found in any of the syllabi for primary and secondary school. It is also the question that was most difficult to answer, although the pupils tried to do so in very creative ways. It is quite clear that almost none of them knows what it is all about.

The concept of an ecosystem is basic in understanding the environment. It can be found in the science syllabus in primary school and in biology and agriculture in secondary school. The question is almost exactly the same as the formulation in the syllabi. There was almost no difference between the two school levels and the result showed little understanding.

---

[1] In secondary school four different biases can be chosen in Form III and IV: agriculture, commercial, home economics and technical.
[2] Clubs in the afternoon with voluntary participation.
[3] Malihai is the name of the club. It can be found all over Tanzania but is especially concentrated in the northern part.

Where a garbage dumping site should be situated and the reasons why, is an area where the primary school pupils scored higher than the secondary, who had a median value of zero. The issue can be found in the science syllabus in primary school and in the home economics (which not all students took) syllabus in secondary. The topic is important for improving the living conditions of the people of Tanzania and to help them to avoid diseases, all of which are important in the policy of Ujamaa. From this point of view of basic knowledge, it is natural that the primary school pupils should have higher results—but all students in secondary school have passed through primary school and should have known this issue.

Nothing can be found in the syllabi about why it is forbidden for fishermen to use dynamite to catch fish. Primary school pupils scored higher than secondary (who had zero) but many showed a confusion about the concept of dynamite. The issue is however, as mentioned above, an acute problem for the conservation of beaches and coral reefs in Tanzania.

Deforestation and its causes were covered in agriculture, science and geography classes in primary schools and in agriculture (in agriculture bias schools) and geography in secondary schools. It is a burning problem in Tanzania and has been a focus for several nation-wide campaigns. It was the main message in the very popular radio programme series during the time this questionnaire was handed out. Deforestation is linked to question four. Tree plantation is one of the measures to reduce soil erosion. Primary school pupils scored higher (about median value 2) than secondary school students (close to median value 1). The difference between the secondary students' answers to question 4 and 11 was surprisingly large.

In Table 22 the questions are categorised in correspondence with the two curricula emphases that were used for the analysis of the syllabi—Roberts' curriculum emphasis and Roth's environmental literacy (see chapter 5). As can be seen, the questions have basically the same emphasis as in the syllabi. The question with the best result, both in primary and secondary school, was question 4, which required a correct answer or explanation. The second best result for primary schools, question 11 and for secondary schools, question 1, are of the same character concerning the curriculum emphasis. Looking from another aspect, that of environmental literacy, questions 4 and 1 are on *nominal* levels while question 11 is on a *functional* level.

Is there a difference between rural and urban schools?
When comparing results between rural and urban schools a few differences could be noticed. The primary school pupils were from areas near the school. Rural pupils in Standard VII had higher results on questions 1, 4, 8, and 11. Urban pupils scored higher on questions 3, 5 and 6 when comparing the median values. In total, the urban pupils had higher results.

In secondary schools, the school itself was located in a rural or urban area but the pupils did not come from the surrounding area except in Dar es Salaam

Table 22: *Comparison of median values in primary and secondary school (max. score: 3). Relation to curriculum emphasis and environmental literacy*
Primary school, Std VII, n=672. Secondary school, Form IV, n=738

Question	Median primary	Median secondary	Roberts' curriculum emphasis	Roth's environmental literacy
1. What is meant by 'environment'?	1.95	1.98	Correct explanations	Nominal
3. Why is knowledge about the environment important?	1.05	1.99	Science, Technology and Decisions	Functional
4. How can you reduce soil erosion?	2.07	2.89	Correct explanations	Nominal
5. Give some examples of endangered animals (animals threatened by extinction) in Tanzania!	1.03	1	Everyday coping	Nominal
6. Give three examples of pollution of the environment!	1.05	0.95	Everyday coping	Nominal
7. What is the 'green house effect'?	0	0	Everyday coping	Nominal
8. What is an ecosystem? Please give an example.	0.95	0.91	Everyday coping	Functional
9. Where should a garbage dumping site be situated? Explain why.	1.04	0	Correct explanations	Functional
10. Why is it forbidden for fishermen to use dynamite to catch fish?	0.93	0	Correct explanations	Functional
11. What are the causes of deforestation?	2.01	0.96	Correct explanations	Functional

urban secondary schools, where there were day schools. The rest were boarding schools with a national intake of pupils (although during the last few years the intake had been more from the nearby region due to the economical constraints). Rural secondary schools did not necessarily have pupils from rural homes and they did not have the same contact with the local community as the primary schools had. But schools with an agricultural bias were naturally located in a rural setting. Furthermore, pupils in secondary schools generally came from better-off families (see Chapter 4).

With this in mind we have to be cautious in our analysis of the results. Urban schools (with a dominance of Dar es Salaam schools) did score higher on questions 1, 3, 6, and 10 when comparing the median values. Questions 6 and 10 reflect discussions in newspapers which are more easily accessed in towns. The higher result on questions 1 and 3 might be due to the existence of afternoon clubs with environmental focus, especially in Dar es Salaam.

'Rural' schools had a higher median value on questions 5 and 11. The rural schools included those with agriculture as a bias and would thus be expected to have a higher result on these questions compared with the urban schools, which were more generally biased. My conclusion is that the agriculture subject doesn't seem to have had a higher impact than other subjects regarding environmental education components.

Is there a difference between gender?
For the secondary schools, I have looked at the gender difference. Schools can be gender differentiated or mixed. I have only analysed the results of 346 students (69 percent of the total number) in boys' and 152 students (31 percent of the total) in girls' secondary schools. Boys tended to score better on questions 1 (What is meant by 'environment'?), 3 (Why is knowledge about the environment important?), and 10 (Why is it forbidden for fishermen to use dynamite to catch fish?), while girls had a higher score on questions 5 (Give some examples of endangered animals in Tanzania!) and 9 (Where should a garbage dumping site be situated? Explain why.). In the total result, however, there was no gender difference. In 1992, the number of girls in public secondary schools was 5,950 (40 percent of the total) while the number of boys was 8,911 (60 percent of the total) (Ministry of Education and Culture, BEST 1993). I consider the number of girls too small and the discrepancy in the gender relation in my sample too large to pay much attention to the result.

Summary and discussion of results

A questionnaire with eleven open-ended questions was administrated to 1,410 pupils in Standard VII in primary school and Form IV in secondary school. My main aim was to explore the teaching conditions of the teachers. The aim of the questionnaire was to get some notion of the state of environmental awareness among the pupils in the school where I interviewed their teachers. In total I got about 14,000 answers to ten questions. How did I handle this cumbersome situation? I chose not to categorise the answers in a similar way as was done with the teachers but evaluated the answers according to the traditional approach of school tests, namely deciding upon a 'criteria' for grading, in this case, from 0 to 3 points.

Summary of the results
In primary and secondary schools in Tanzania environmental education components are infused into the subject syllabi. By using a questionnaire some of the components were tested. The result is confusing; primary school leavers scored on average higher on three questions compared to secondary school leavers. On five questions there was no difference. In other words, secondary school students, with four more years of schooling, scored higher on only two of the questions, when considering median values. Generally the scores on the questionnaire were low, with a few exceptions. This will be the subject of a discussion below.

If we consider two points out of three as a fairly good result on the questionnaire (because it included some basic main points) and with that as a starting point, I have shown that primary school pupils in Standard VII perform well considering the question about the meaning of the environment, soil erosion and deforestation. Secondary school students in Form IV answered well about the meaning and importance of environment and very well about soil erosion.

Low results were obtained from primary schools on why knowledge about the environment is important. Both primary and secondary school students had about one point as a median value on the questions regarding endangered animals, pollution and ecosystem. Secondary school students got about one point on the causes of deforestation.

Median values around zero were obtained by both primary and secondary school students concerning the meaning of the green house effect. There were very few students who had any idea at all of this issue. The secondary school students also had a median value of zero regarding placement of a garbage dump and the use of dynamite in fishing but there were some who could give more elaborated answers.

On three issues, primary school pupils had higher results than secondary school students, namely: placement of garbage dump, the use of dynamite in fishing and causes behind deforestation.

Greenhouse effect, a question reflecting present discussions in Western countries, got very low response and there was a low result on other current Western focuses, namely pollution and endangered animals (which, however, are not in the syllabi). Best results were found on the issues that were prominently debated environmental problems in mass media and elsewhere in Tanzania: soil erosion and deforestation.

There is no clear connection between the results of the questionnaire regarding a certain issue and the presence of that issue in the syllabi, with the exception of question 4, about soil conservation, and question 11, on deforestation. Because it is included in the syllabi, the students ought to have had a higher result on question 8 on ecosystems, but that topic came last in both the syllabus for Standard VII and the one in Form IV, and the classes did not always reach that point before the final examinations. The conclusion is two-fold: the pupils have knowledge that probably is acquired from elsewhere and they have not learnt everything that is in the syllabi.

In the national examinations at the primary level, in 1992, there was a question related to the ecosystem but apparently the pupils were not yet prepared for that (my questionnaire was administrated 1–7 months before that examination). In the national examinations at secondary level in 1992 there were at least (depending on the school bias) two questions related to soil conservation that same year. I imagine that the students should have been able to answer correctly.

One would expect pupils in rural primary schools to have better results than those in urban schools because of their close connection to the local communities, but that is however not clearly the case. Rural schools have Education for Self-Reliance projects while urban schools do not always have that possibility. There was no difference in the overall results of the rural and urban secondary schools although one would expect that rural secondary schools would score higher since they include schools with an agricultural bias.

Environmental literacy was, in half of the questions, on a *nominal* level, i.e. recognition of basic terms and in the other half, on a *functional* level, i.e. showing a broader knowledge and understanding, according to Roth's categories. On average there was no difference between the results on questions on the *nominal* or *functional* level for the primary school but secondary school students gave higher answers to questions on the *nominal* level compared to those on the *functional* level.

Discussion of the results
Why was the scoring generally so low? One can always discuss the validity of the questionnaire, starting with the choice of questions. I have explained the background to my choice in the beginning of this chapter. Six of the questions were related to the syllabi, two were directed to the experience of the pupil and two reflected environmental issues in Western countries. On the other hand, all questions were in accordance with environmental problems observed by the National Environment Management Council in Tanzania. From 1991 the council was supposed to see to it that environmental education was carried out. The content of the question was thus not out of the Tanzanian context.

The language, too, is of importance for the validity. For most pupils, Swahili is a second language, taught and used as a teaching medium in primary schools. English is a third language, taught a few hours in the upper classes in primary schools. When entering secondary school, where English is the teaching medium, this language is still new and the skills in using it are not developed.

The results in school, and in this questionnaire, are dependent on the pupil's language proficiency even though in this case the questionnaire was administrated to the final classes. Could the comparatively higher results in the primary schools be related to language proficiency? Do primary school pupils master Swahili better than secondary school students master English? I find this very likely and believe it to have had a negative effect on the validity of the questionnaire. Does the language barrier also affect the generalisability of the result? The language situation will affect the results on the national exams which are in Swahili for primary and English for secondary schools and from that point of view, the results of the questionnaire are fairly representative considering the selection of schools and their performances.

Is the result a reflection of what the students really know about the environment and environmental concepts? I find this doubtful. The result only shows what the students answered on the questions in the particular situation when the questionnaire was administrated, as well as showing that primary school pupils and secondary school students gave different answers on certain questions.

Only one of the questions requires integration of what has been learnt and what is going on in the society, namely the question on why it is important to have knowledge about the environment. The rest requires that one has learnt the 'correct explanation' or else they are related to daily activities, according to Roberts' curriculum emphasis. On average, the pupils got higher results on questions with a correct explanation emphasis than on the questions concerning everyday coping. Could this be an effect of the teaching they have experienced? Is that teaching concentrated on giving the 'right' or 'correct' answers? Or is it an effect of the researcher's way of asking or grading the answers? When I formulated the questions, I was not familiar with Roberts or his curriculum emphases. I constructed the questions in such a way that they would not be very different from the type of questions that are usually used in schools, based on my earlier experiences in Eastern Africa. I had studied the syllabi, but not analysed them. I got access to the examination questions at a later stage, when I had already started to collect data.

This issue is related to teaching methods. Were the students taught in such a way that they were able to relate the topics to the environment? Were the teachers equipped to teach about environmental issues? Was the surrounding society or community, including parents, knowledgeable about environmental issues? Do primary schools through their Education for Self-Reliance projects and other activities give a more concrete and practical interpretation of the content? Were the pupils used to answering these types of questions or not? I think that these are points that had a great effect on the outcome.

Another important question is whether the pupils were motivated to answer the questionnaire in the face of the fact that it was not something related to their assessment in school. However, I was present and administrated the test on all occasions but one and I do not feel that the pupils regarded the questionnaire as insignificant.

I think that the most interesting answer is the indication of where the students had learnt and understood something about the environment. The answers show that, according to the students, the school was not the sole or even the most important source. The family and the mass media were perceived as powerful transmitters. Single subjects taught in schools such as domestic science (primary school) and geography (secondary school) seemed to have benefited students, according to their own testimony, and this shows that the schools were also to some extent, slowly but surely, doing their jobs. Another reflection is: are the schools and mass media pulling together towards the same aim?

CHAPTER 10
Summary, conclusions and reflections

Introduction

This study is a single case-study involving several variables. The aim has been to explore the conditions for teachers' realisation of the environmental education components in the curriculum and the impact of the frame factors.

Is it possible to generalise anything from such a single case-study? Yes, as Robert K. Yin (1994) says, it *is* possible—case studies are generalisable to theoretical propositions but not to populations. It is thus possible to expand and generalise theory by studying aspects that have been overlooked or not previously investigated. In this final chapter I will summarise some of the findings and present possible conclusions and reflections.

First I will give a short summary of the educational policy background. Next I contrast the external determinants in frame factor theory with internal determinants in teachers' thinking, that is teachers' understanding of environmental education. My findings suggest that there are other factors that are important for the learning outcome than those stipulated in the frame factor theory approach. These additional frame factors are, among others, teachers' access to syllabi and teaching material (textbooks and teaching aids), pupils' language proficiency and access to textbooks and the teachers' socio-economic status.

My answers to the research questions are:

- there are a large number of environmental education components in the syllabi in primary schools but considerably less in secondary schools.
- these components are strongly related to the Education for Self-Reliance policy developed during the period 1967—early 1980s.
- the teachers' ways of experiencing environmental education indicate that they have an understanding of what environmental education is and its importance.
- the frame factors in Tanzania for the realisation of the curriculum do not function in the same ways as in Sweden; the state-defined frames do not play the same role and other factors are more dominant.
- the impact of environmental education seems to be very limited.

– the findings should been seen in the light of the fact that the research tools were developed in one cultural context and used in another and therefore might not be fully valid.

In the final part I submit my reflections on the prospects of education for sustainability in the least developed countries.

Critical view of the researcher

Knowledge is something that people construct together. The researcher participates in the construction of information and data from interviews and questionnaires. To what extent does the researcher's pre-conceptions and interpretations influence the result?

I find the question difficult to answer. To some extent I have been aware of my biases. I had my own opinion about what the environmental problems were in Tanzania and what environmental issues I thought should be taught in school. This opinion was strongly influenced by my experiences from the agriculture and forest sector. I also had an opinion about how the subject should be taught effectively: through active pupil participation in the learning process. From the beginning I was not aware of the magnitude of the financial constraints on the school sector and did not understand its effect on the teachers' conditions both in school and at home. As time went by, I developed a better understanding.

I felt frustration at times when my 'plan' was not possible to carry out due to events that I felt should not 'disturb' the daily school routine. The cultural differences were felt at such times. However, how much it influenced my observations or interpretations is hard to say.

There are two crucial points when my pre-conceptions might have influenced the outcome. One is the analysis of the curriculum and the other the analysis of the interviews. My idea of what environmental education components are is accounted for in the appendices. Of greater interest is my analysis of the curriculum emphases. Did I see it the way Roberts and Roth intended? Did I understand their concepts or did I transform them into an interpretation 'suitable' to me?

As for the second crucial point, I realize I was not knowledgeable enough on Education for Self-Reliance when I implemented the interviews. It was only afterwards that I studied the original source, that is the texts and speeches of Nyerere. When analysing the interviews, however, I was conscious of this educational philosophy—and positive towards it. Did I manage to control this bias or not? The situation is even more complex because of the cultural and language differences between the parties. I am quite certain that it has been impossible for me to truly reflect the opinions of the teachers in the analysis of the interviews. They were in their transcribed forms already a distortion of what was said. Then, in my interpretation, my biases played their roles.

Social transition through education

The driving force in the development of the Tanzanian society after independence was the sole political party, Chama Cha Mapinduzi (CCM). The overall aim of education, according to the directives of the party, was to develop a society which was independent of external economic and political powers, and to create a self-reliant society based on domestic agriculture. The state funded schools achieved certain admirable results concerning equity but not the main objective of an education system where peasants and workers would profit from the fruits of education and be able to change and improve their living conditions. Changes in society through education was what the Tanzanian government had hoped for, but it did not materialise.

It is clear that there were conflicting interests in Tanzania when Education for Self-Reliance was the dominating educational policy. The elite groups in Tanzania found other ways in which to ensure that the education of their children would enable them to fit into a capitalist and elitist Western-oriented political and economic system. This system was introduced by the colonial powers. Education was modelled on a British prototype (Nyerere 1967a), but the elite groups never accepted the Nyerere educational philosophy for a socialistic society. What remained unclear, however, was the role of the administrative apparatus. Did they fight or not for the implementation of the curriculum? Or were the constraining factors too overwhelming? According to the World Bank (1990, 1995) the managers were not trained or qualified for their jobs, management of resources was inadequate and the controlling system weak. Chama Cha Mapinduzi had a strong position at both the central and local levels, but not everyone agreed with the educational policy. The party was (and still is) strong in the rural areas where the lower socio-economic groups lived. The question of what kind of education might be suitable for peasants and what kind suitable for the elite was not discussed thoroughly by Nyerere and the party leadership. Both Education for Self-Reliance and the Universal Primary Education programmes were aimed at providing mass education for an agricultural society through formal education. An example of considerations that could have been made was the opinion which was much later expressed by Negash (1996), who argued for focusing on in-formal education for the needs of the peasants. His views were related to the Ethiopian context and, according to him, what the peasants there needed the most, were inputs such as better technology, demonstration centres, infrastructure, tenure laws and better prices for agricultural products. Negash was of the view that scarce resources should not be used on attempts to combine formal education with vocational or practical subjects.

In 1985, there was a shift in the educational policy, based on the report of the Presidential Commission and supported by the Cost Recovery Programme (see Appendix 2). The aim of education was now to provide Tanzanians with a proper education, that is, knowledge and understanding as well as important skills and attitudes, whereas the Education for Self-Reliance (1967) and the Musoma Resolution (1974) had stated that the aim of education was to liberate man (Samoff 1990, pp. 268). This new political goal for education implied a shift from the Ujamaa policy[1], which concentrated on the development of the agricultural sector, to a mixed economy policy and structural adjustment through development of a market economy. For schools, cost sharing and partnerships at local levels were introduced. Instead of the primary school focusing on preparation for rural life, the function of preparing pupils for secondary school education was emphasised (Ministry of Education 1984). Individualism and elitism were encouraged as well as the establishment of private schools. Parts of the self-reliance policy were retained, for example improving daily life by using local resources, preserving cultural traditions, human dignity and national unity.

Environmental components in the curriculum

The expectations of environmental education as stated in the Presidential Commission on Education of 1982 and based on the Arusha Declaration were formulated in the Education for Self-Reliance policy. The content of the curriculum in schools was supposed to be integrated into the daily life activities of a mainly rural community. New syllabi in all subjects were developed during the 1970s. Most of them were still in use in the early 1990s.

In this dissertation, the syllabi for primary school in agriculture, domestic science, geography and science where chosen for analysis because they were most likely to contain environmental components. Besides identification of these components, I have also analysed the syllabi according to two curriculum emphases, namely Roberts' curriculum emphasis and Roth's environmental literacy level. The curriculum emphasis analysis was carried on the whole of the syllabi while the environmental literacy level was done only on the identified environmental education components.

The environmental education components in primary school (see Appendix 4) were concentrated on soil science, soil conservation, soil conservation methods, hygiene and health. Very few questions related to environmental issues appeared in the national exam. The curriculum emphasis reflected the Education for Self-Reliance policy. The level of environmental literacy, according to Roth's definitions, was mainly basic.

The same analysis was made for the secondary school syllabi in agriculture, home economics, geography and biology. The environmental education components are listed in Appendix 5. The agriculture subject reflected the Education for Self-Reliance and contained a number of environmental issues on both soil conservation and agricultural practices but this subject is taken only in the schools with an agricultural bias. The home economics subject was mainly a

---

[1] Co-operation in the community.

repetition of the primary school syllabus. In geography the environmental education components were few as they were in biology as well, although ecology was included in the fourth year. In the national examination environmental questions appeared only in the agriculture subject, which was taken, as mentioned, by a minor part of the students. Thus the knowledge in this matter, which these students were intended to develop, was very restricted. The curriculum emphasis was similar to that of primary school with the difference that instead of some scientific skills development, there was an emphasis on 'correct explanation,' especially in geography but also to some extent in biology. The environmental literacy level was basic, with some broader aspects in agriculture and biology.

For teacher training, analysis of the syllabi in education and geography was done. Education for Self-Reliance was taught through the education subject. The geography syllabus was richer in environmental components (see Appendix 6) than in both primary and secondary school syllabi. The curriculum emphasis was likewise more diversified with four different foci, while at the lower levels only two were represented. The environmental literacy reflected all levels: nominal (basic), functional (broader) and operational. In short, the teacher training syllabus was more environmental and implied different kinds of learning methods and a broader and more action-oriented knowledge than the primary and secondary school syllabi.

What factors had an impact on implementation of the educational aims? Below I will present my reflections on this, starting with some comments on the methodological approaches of my study.

Frame factors and teachers' thinking

In frame factor theory approach the frames are seen as determinants of the implementation of the curriculum, i.e. teaching and learning, as stated by Dahllöf and Lundgren (see Chapter 2). The frames are related to the political, educational and economic policies of a government. In a one-party state as post-independent Tanzania mainly has been, the frames were defined by the central government and the ruling party, at least during the first decade. Later the country's aid dependency brought other actors onto the scene. For the individual teacher the conditions of teaching included not only the context of school but also the context of one's personal economic situation or standard of living.

The frame factor theory approach does not consider internal determinants, such as teachers' thinking, understanding, reflections, intentions, practical reasoning and alike. Does their thinking play a role for the outcome of the educational process? Are the teachers' understandings of a phenomenon related to or a guarantee of the result of field implementation of the curriculum? These are some of the questions I will consider.

The difference between the formulated and the realised curriculum

It was expected that the education system would foster young Tanzanians for a life in a rural context and develop knowledge, skills and attitudes relevant for a community life.

It was also expected that the primary school would combine education and production through self-reliance projects. The objective was not to reproduce the past but prepare the students for the future.

In 1974, Chama Cha Mapinduzi decided on a Universal Primary Education programme for all Tanzanians, which was implemented in 1977. This was an enormous challenge for a poor country. Education (and health) was a priority for the government and a quarter of the budget was allocated to education and the educational reform, not only for Universal Primary Education but also for adult education.

The main actors involved in the context of formulating the curriculum were Chama Cha Mapinduzi and its leader, Julius K. Nyerere. The administrative apparatus, such as the Ministry of Education and the Institute for Curriculum Development, were not involved in the decisions. In 1972, a decentralised policy was adopted and the local authorities became involved in educational planning and implementation but the financial resources came mainly from central levels.

Lindensjö and Lundgren (1986) have stressed the discrepancy between the central and local levels as an obstacle for implementation. Conflicting interests and differences in political ways of thinking could counteract the educational intentions. In the case of Tanzania responsibility for the primary school was delegated to the local administration (regional and district). Up to 1992 the ruling party, CCM, was an important political power at all levels but the local branch did not always share the ideas of the central leadership and this was of course reflected in how engaged they were in the realisation of the curriculum. The ruling system during the period from 1967 (the year of the Arusha declaration) to 1992 (when the decision on a multi-party system was passed) was based on a centralised one-party model and the educational reforms came from the top, sometimes without preparation or discussions in the parliament.

Here, an important factor was the degree to which the aims of the curriculum were understood and accepted. Ishumi and Maliyamkono (1995) stated that the main reason why the education system did not achieve its aims was the failure by the schools to translate the curriculum objectives into reality (ibid. p. 52). Systematic strategies for implementation were lacking and leaders were not actively working on implementation. One advantage, though, was a decline of inequalities between regions through the quota system to secondary schools (Mosha 1990).

The gap between the context of formulation and the context of realisation complicates not only the outcome of a curriculum but also the professionalisation of teachers, i.e. their position and status in the society. The field-implementation is carried out by teachers. How do they interpret the curriculum? What are their intentions? What possibilities do they have to realise the curriculum? In Table 23 I have summarised the context of formulation and realisation and the actors involved.

Revisiting the frame factor theory approach, we see that the constraining factors in Tanzania, such as finance and physical frames, have had a great impact on the implementation of the educational reform of the Education for Self-Reliance philosophy. The financial situation had not only affected the salaries of teachers but also their living conditions. Teachers were not able to survive on their salaries but had to find side line economical activities, thus affecting their motivation and possibility to engage fully in their school work. The resources of schools were meagre and in-service training, textbooks and teaching aids were not available.

The attitude of the society toward the country's educational reform varied. The large majority, the rural population, was positive but the urban population and the elite were negative. Some parents and communities never accepted the aims of primary schooling for they saw such schooling as terminal and not aimed at preparation for secondary school, which they wanted for their children. Even among the political leadership there was resistance (World Bank 1995, Ishumi & Malikyankono 1995). Education was seen as an opportunity to make a career and a way to reproduce the society as it was and those who embraced these values were not eager to accept the Education for Self-Reliance philosophy of equality. Further, the local authorities, too, varied in their aspirations to fulfil the aims of the reform.

Nonetheless, there was a success story during the first decades after independence, for example concerning the ideological part of Education for Self-Reliance and literacy. In 1967, 69 percent of the population was illiterate according to the National Literacy test. In 1986, the rate of illiteracy was reported to be 9.6 percent. However, in 1996 the illiteracy rate had increased again, to 21 percent among men and 45 percent among women.

Returning to the question of frame factors and transmission of knowledge in the formal educational system, the influencing factors and agents can be summarised as in Table 24.

It was not easy for teachers to shift their educational paradigm. This was pointed out by Dan C. Lortie in his classical study on schoolteachers in the beginning of the 1970s (Lortie 1975). Most teaching that takes place in Tanzanian schools today seems to be theoretical, fragmented and reproduce what teachers have learnt themselves at the teaching training institutions. It was assumed that teachers learnt different teaching methodologies during their training and that the Education for Self-Reliance philosophy was thoroughly taught. The possibility of actually seeing and experiencing different teaching and learning methods must have been very limited. It appears that teachers received almost no help in how to develop pupil activities such as discovery

Table 23: *The context of formulation and realisation and comments related to the one-party state of Tanzania up to 1992*

	Level	Comments
The context of formulation		
Implementation of political intentions	Political level	Actors: The political party and its key organs.
Formulation of curriculum/ syllabi, aims, objectives and content	Central administrative level	Main actor: The political party. Assistant actors: Ministry of Education and Culture, Tanzania Institute of Education (Curriculum Development), curriculum panels.
–	Local administrative level	Actors: The political party. Assistant actor: The local government.
Preparation for implementation by teachers		Actors: Curriculum developers, teacher training colleges.
The context of realisation		
Guideline writing (interpretation of political decisions)	Administrative level	Actors: Local authorities.
–	Local administrative level	Actors: Local government. District educational officers and school inspectors.
Field implementation		Actors: Teachers.

learning, problem-oriented or problem-solving methods. Their own teaching practice was short—two or maybe four weeks if the financial situation was good. Few of the teachers I interviewed had any training in environmental education, which most likely reflects the situation in the whole country.

In the frame factor theory approach, as formulated by Lundgren, teacher thinking is not included. So how did the teachers reason in the classroom? On what did they found their intentions and actions? What role did the curriculum play? Did they base their actions on their own experiences as students and/or expectations from the surrounding community? What did they see as important in the execution of their profession? Such questions have been studied and discussed in Sweden by, among others, Lindblad (Lindblad 1994, pp. 121–130, Lindblad, Linde & Näslund 1999). There has been no similar research on teachers' thinking in Tanzania. In my study I have interviewed teachers on how they perceive the concept of environmental education. A discussion of the findings of teachers' ways of understanding environmental education will now follow.

Table 24: *Content, agents, steering and limiting factors in the Tanzanian schools*

The content	Agent	Steering and limiting factors
How it is chosen	The Govern-ment	The political party CCM (up to 1992). After 1992: IMF/World Bank. Donor agencies. Political parties. Pressure groups.
How it is constructed	Tanzania Institute of Education	Subject Panels. Ministry of Education and Culture. Professional advising groups.
How it is taught	Syllabus	Availability of latest syllabus or not—different editions could be found in schools.
	Scheme of work	Developed by teachers, controlled by school inspectors. Not always found.
	Teacher	'Time loss' due to: – practical work (Education for Self-Reliance). – teachers' absence due to collection of salary, staff meetings, other duties or errands, private 'projects', social events such as funerals and weddings, unforeseen activities such as campaigns, etc. – lack of competencies in certain subjects. Inadequate or lack of professional training. Lack of teaching material. Communication problems due to language differences. Teacher vocational motivation depended on—salary—working conditions—in-service training options—posting station.
	Learner	Teaching methodology. Pupil's motivation. Parents' attitudes (gender, political, vocational prospects). Socio-economical circumstances. Absence/presence of textbooks.

How teachers understood environmental education

The environmental problems in Tanzania, and East Africa in general, were mainly related to land degradation. Referring to the earlier discussion, we can observe that the ideas of the teachers seemed to reflect an adequate perception of the problem. Land degradation affected agricultural production and food security. What happened was that the water cycle was disturbed and the loss of rain (water supplies) meant loss of food. Soil erosion was, to a large extent, accelerated by humans themselves, and could only be reduced by applying proper agricultural practices. Population pressure, both animal and human, was not under control, making it difficult to promote sustainable use of natural resources.

The difference between the primary and secondary school teachers was marginal when comparing them at a general level. Their different ways of experiencing environmental education were similar. Their perceptions were closely related to rural living conditions in an agricultural society. I have argued a) that the teachers had different ways of experiencing what environmental education was; b) that their experiences were qualitatively different and c) that their experiences were to a large extent connected to rural living conditions in an agricultural society. This latter point was not surprising, since more than 85 percent of the population lived in rural areas and agriculture was the main source of income. The teachers in town schools referred to rural contexts when answering the questions. Tanzanians looked upon their birth place as 'home' and often returned there for celebrations. When they retire most of them 'go home.' Thus, their ways of thinking about environmental education were to a large extent related to agriculture. Food security was a common concern in a country where food provision was dependent on the yearly rainfall. If the rains did not come, the result was immediate food shortage in communities with little to no storage of food.

One way to present an overview of the ways of experiencing environmental education is to relate the different categories (concept definition, importance, content and methods of environmental education) to each other, as follows below. The objective of my analysis, however, was not to focus on the relation between different categories but on receiving qualitatively different categories for the phenomena.

Qualitatively different categories
Concept definition:
What is meant by environmental education? The basic category is the way of experiencing or understanding environmental education itself. I found three qualitatively different categories:

– Environmental education is about natural and social surroundings.
– Environmental education is about how the environment supported humans through its resources.
– Environmental education is about conservation and improvement of the environment.

Importance:
Why should we have environmental education? What is its importance? The ways of experiencing this appeared to be similiar, although qualitatively different. The first category implied actions in a short-time perspective, for us people living now, while the second category emphasised a longer-time perspective.

Table 25: *Tentative categorisation of ways of experiencing environmental education in relation to Jürgen Habermas cognitive interests*

Horizontal Cognitive interest based on Jürgen Habermas *Vertical* 1–3: Categories of understanding the concept of environmental education. A–B: Categories of rationale for environmental education	Technical interest; controlling and managing the environment	Practical interest; understanding the environment	Emancipatory interest; empowerment to engage in actions—self-reflection
1. Environmental education is about natural and social surroundings	Possible position	Doubtful position	–
2. Environmental education is about how the environment supports humans through its resources	Possible position	–	–
3. Environmental education is about conservation and improvement of the environment	–	–	Possible position
A. Environmental education is important in order to conserve the natural resources—environmental conservation	Possible position	–	–
B. Environmental education is important in order to attain people's daily needs—survival	–	Possible position	Doubtful position

– Environmental education is important in order to conserve the natural resources—environmental conservation.
– Environmental education is important in order to attain people's daily needs—survival.

To what extent have the ways of experiencing and understanding environmental education been influenced by the Education for Self-Reliance philosophy? It seems that they are close to each other but it is difficult to argue for a straight correlation due to the limitations of my research. The concept of knowledge in the Education for Self-Reliance philosophy was based on skills, knowledge and attitudes in the daily life practice of individuals. The thoughts in these categories reflect the same perspective (see Appendix 3).

What kind of pedagogical practices could be expected if they were based on the teachers' ways of experiencing environmental education? Returning to the Jürgen Habermas three basic cognitive interests (see Chapter 1), a tentative categorisation could look like what is seen in Table 25.

If we try another perspective, the relation between human beings and nature, what do the categories express? The second 'concept' as well as the first 'importance' category, appear to reflect an *anthropocentric* perspective, i.e. nature is there to satisfy the needs of the human being. This is a very old perspective, expressed by St. Thomas Aquinas and others. The third 'concept' and the second 'importance' category seem to express *environmental ethics*. In a multicultural perspective, the ethics in these categories might be more clearly pronounced in Islamic than in Christian beliefs. It might be relevant to remember that the Tanzanian society consists of three large religious groups: Christians, Muslims and followers of indigenous religions.

Not qualitatively different categories
Since environmental education is an important issue, what content should be taught in school? There were four, not qualitatively different, categories. The first one mirrored what was already taught in school. The second focused on environmental problems and measures, especially conservation. Content related to the local community contained suggestions about analysing the needs of the people and the existing environmental problems. That latter is an approach that was part of the Education for Self-Reliance policy.

Content:
– Subject-related content.
– Content focused on environmental issues.
– Content related to the local community.
– An interdisciplinary approach.

Finally, how should this content be taught in school, what ideas and suggestions do the teachers have? I found three, not qualitatively different, categories. The first one is to a large extent related to teaching methods in the school where the necessity to relate theory and practice was underlined (although not executed). The second most probably shows the influence from Education for Self-Reliance. The belief in the power of mass media, especially radio programmes, was strong.

Teaching methods:
– What to do in school when teaching and learning about the environment.
– Learning through the society.
– Learning through mass media.

The ideas about content and methods seem to be influenced by what was suggested in the Education for Self-Reliance programme. What other opportunities did the teachers have? Through their training at teachers' training colleges, they were indoctrinated with the educational philosophy slant on pedagogy. The course goal of pedagogy was dominated by the Ujamaa philosophy and more than 1,000 hours were allocated to this course. Moreover, the syllabi, which they had as a base for their studies of subjects, reinforced the same philosophy. Considering the declining number of teaching practice hours when the financial situation deteriorated, the student teachers learnt the words but not the practise. The only other source of information they had was their own school experiences as pupils. No wonder they thought that they needed text books and/or more knowledge in environmental education. They did not know what else to ask for.

Relation to other research of interest
I have compared the findings on the meaning of environmental education with two other studies mentioned in chapter 1. Alistair S. Robertson (1995) focused on teacher students' conceptualisation of 'environment' (environment was equated with surroundings) in South Africa. The result was categorised in five different ways of thinking, see Table 26. Leif Östman (1995) analysed Swedish textbooks in chemistry and biology. One of the approaches to teaching science was with the objective of explaining the relation between humans and nature. He found that he could identify four different ways to teach students (four different subject foci): exploitation of nature (teaching how human beings have used or can use nature to further their material prosperity); nature as a precondition (teaching how people are dependent on nature, how nature is a prior condition for human life); the human being as a threat (teaching that the human race is threatening itself and nature and how it is doing so); and the survival of Homo sapiens (teaching a responsible attitude to nature on the basis of an anthropocentric line of reasoning).

Environmental education is a social construction and variations between different social contexts are to be expected. However, similarities could exist. Robertson's study was carried out on South African teacher students in close connection to environmental education sessions during their first twelve weeks of the 1992 (ten students) and 1993 (twelve students) teacher education programme. The interviews were implemented at several occasions during the course while their knowledge of environmental issues gradually increased. This meant that the students, unlike my interviewees, were very aware of environmental problems and issues. English was not their first language and it was interesting to me to learn that they translated 'environment' to mean 'surroundings'. I met the same language problem in Tanzania ('environment' is translated as 'surroundings' in Swahili). Robertson used a phenomenographic approach in analysing his interviews. I found many similarities but also differences between our two contexts. Östman, on the other hand, studied textbooks used in a totally different cultural, political, economic and educational context. His research approach, text analysis, concentrated on written discourse in natural science. The content of the textbooks was of course adapted to a Western industrialised society with its specific environmental problems and issues.

Table 26: *Comparison between three different research on environmental education (Lindhe 1999, Robertson 1995, Östman 1995)*

Lindhe Interview with teachers in Tanzania	Robertson Interview with teacher students in South Africa	Östman Text analysis of textbooks in Sweden
Environmental education; about natural and social surroundings.	The natural world, human effects on bio-physical features.	No immediate applicability.
Environmental education; about how the environment supported humans through its resources.	Environment in social terms, where interpersonal behaviour in social settings was the main focus of interest in one's surrounding.	'Exploitation of nature' and 'nature as a precondition'.
Environmental education; about conservation and improvement of the environment.	Environment as integrated systems.	'Human beings as a threat' and 'the survival of Homo sapiens'.
No immediate applicability.	Environment as part of one self.	No immediate applicability.
No immediate applicability.	Political factors in the South African social environment and relationships between economic impoverishment and lack of access to natural resources.	No immediate applicability.

In Table 26 the different categories are compared. It appears that there are similarities even though the focus and the context of the research are different. There are also differences, since not all categories overlap each other. For example, I found no reference to philosophical aspects or the political conditions as Robertson did.

I have found that the motive for teaching environmental education is basically understood by teachers. Ference Marton related the qualitative differences of ways of understanding to the nature of knowledge, i.e. qualitatively different processes of learning, in his early studies (see for example Marton, Dahlgren, Svensson & Säljö 1981). If the motive here is basically understood, it is probably at a level where the teacher can memorise certain aspects and talk about them (atomistic approach) and not at a level which reflects deeper understanding of concepts (holistic approach).

The way they experienced environmental education was relevant and closely connected with a Tanzanian context. The teacher had an opinion about what environmental education was, why it was important and what the content should be despite the fact that this has not been explicitly included in their training. This is one of my most gratifying findings. It appears that a good deal of the teachers' interpretations are related to or influenced by the Education for Self-Reliance philosophy.

Were the teachers' ways of experiencing or understanding environmental education a sufficient factor for a successful implementation of the environmental education components in the curriculum? I will come back to this but first let us look at the impact of environmental education.

The impact of environmental education

To attain an apprehension of the level of pupils' understanding of some environmental issues, I conducted a simple survey by using a questionnaire. The results of the questionnaire, given to 672 pupils in Standard VII and 738 students in Form IV, show that the question on how to reduce soil erosion got the highest median values at both levels. The second highest was an explanation of the concept of environment. The third highest was, in primary school, a recall of causes of deforestation and, in secondary school, an explanation why environmental knowledge is important. However, on the whole, scores on the questionnaire were low. The secondary school students scored higher on only two questions while the primary school pupils scored higher on three of the questions, in spite of a difference of four years of schooling and a tough selection to secondary education. Both primary and secondary school students declared that their sources of information on environmental issues were mainly outside school (a ratio of 1/1.9 for primary and 1/1.6 for secondary). Families and mass media played important roles. In primary school domestic science was said to be the most important and in secondary school geography was pointed out as a major source of information.

These factors motivate us deeply to ask why the impact of formal education is so small.

Factors of importance for the learning outcome of environmental education

One strong factor of importance for the learning outcome of environmental education is the national examination, which expressed the kind of knowledge, skills and attitudes that were valued. Teachers taught and students learnt what was expected to be asked in the exam. Time in school during the last month before examination was allocated to repetition. I witnessed that even the vacation before the last term was used for the same purpose. Teachers admitted to me that they gave priorities to what they thought would appear in the examination. It was important to cover those aspects in the syllabi. As late as November 1998, when I visited Tanzania, the Form IV national examinations were cancelled after the first week since it had been discovered that the content of the questions had 'leaked out' to certain parents (and pupils).

Even the construction of the questions had an impact. In the primary school examination multiple-choice questions were the overall dominating type. The pupils did not have to formulate sentences themselves, only make a marking. Almost no questions at all were related to the environment. Only 15 percent of the primary school leavers were able to go on to the secondary school level. So the conclusion is obvious: in order to succeed, teachers and pupils concentrated on what they thought would appear in the examination papers. In the secondary school examination there were also open-ended questions and a few more environmental education questions, but only in the subject of agriculture which a minority of the secondary school students took.

Another important factor was whether the teacher had access to the most recent syllabus in the subject she or he was going to teach. This was not usually the case. I found teaching being planned according to syllabi from 1969 although much more recent ones existed. On the other hand, from an environmental education point of view, the old syllabi might have been more 'environmental' than the new ones. But as a principle, it reflected the gap between educational planning and implementation.

A third factor is the lack of training, both concerning content of and teaching methods for implementation of environmental education. The teacher training colleges were suffering from the same constraining factors as the schools. Environmental education, although not called as such, was to be taught and related to the surrounding community but the teachers (and the teacher trainers) lacked experience in doing so. In the Education for Self-Reliance policy, close connection with the community was emphasised but implementation was left to the teachers without necessary preparation. This has been verified by several sources. Underlying the lack of environmental knowledge and skills in schools seems to be the teaching methodology that was learnt at the teacher education colleges and practised in schools. In the Education for Self-Reliance policy, there were ideas about pupil participation and active learning. The curriculum was, however, more teacher- and subject-oriented than pupil-oriented, particularly in the secondary school syllabi. The syllabi developed after the Arusha declaration were more oriented towards active learning than the most recent ones. In the classroom, the dominating method tended to be 'lecturing,' defined generally as verbal delivery of a piece of information that should be taken down in note books as questions with written answers or, in secondary schools, as a short text which served as a substitute for a textbook. 'Discussion' was in effect a question from the teacher and if the answer from the pupils was not correct, the answer also came from the teacher. The practice in the classroom was thus contradictory to the intention of the Education for Self-Reliance policy. What the pupils learnt was to adapt to the authority in the form of the teacher and the head of the school, to be a passive receiver of information which was later to be reproduced in the way the teacher considered to be the correct way and not to discuss or question what was going on. Due to the language barrier, the content and the concepts might not even be understood but just memorised. This practice was once again an example of the so-called 'hidden curriculum'

(Broady 1985) and a view of knowledge as fragmented and de-contextualised.

Only on a few occasions did a demonstration or a study visit take place. Practice, which was an important part of the Education for Self-Reliance policy, was seldom implemented for several reasons, among them, the time constraint. Laboratory work, practicals in domestic science etc. could only be implemented on very few occasions because of a lack of necessary material. In secondary schools, a new concept, 'theoretical practical,' was introduced even in the national exam due to shortage of laboratory material. A fourth factor, of course, was the lack of text books and teaching aids. But environmental education shared this problem with most of the topics or subjects in the Tanzanian schools.

An effective school needs some basic resources such as trained teachers, classrooms, textbooks and other teaching material. In the industrialised countries, these fundamental basics exist and an increase of textbooks, for example, is not related to better performance. But for the least developed countries, the situation is different; a basic 'kit' consisting of these resources is necessary (Lockheed & Levin, 1993).

So what was the impact of the environmental education of the formal education system? Through overlapping in the syllabi, it appears that some basic knowledge about soil erosion and soil conservation was learnt, but not practised, apart from what was in the agriculture subject at secondary school. In primary schools this was only learnt if students had access to a trained teacher. In domestic science and home economics, basic information about health and diseases were learnt theoretically and also, to some extent, practically. Tree nurseries in primary schools were quite frequent, according to statistics. However, the practical work that actually was implemented—for example, work on the Education for Self-Reliance projects—was seldom explained or referred to in theoretical lessons. Thus the impact of learning in school was restricted and the informal and non-formal educational systems appear to have had a greater impact.

One could ask, why should there be any impact at all? What is the meaning of school in the rural areas? Nyerere wanted it to prepare for a life in the village. Others, such as Carnoy and Samoff, 1990, claim that the meaning of schooling is to escape rural life. Holger Daun (1992a) has shown that the meaning of school differs in different systems (indigenous, Islamic and Western) or social groups. Mikael Palme (1993) has found differences in social groups, while Tekeste Negash questions the need of formal education for all (Negash 1996). According to Negash non-formal education would be much more relevant for an overwhelmingly rural majority. The conclusion is thus that the question is very complex and an overall answer is difficult to formulate.

Now let us focus on the methodological approach. I will consider the tools I have used and how they might have affected the result.

Theoretical and methodological approaches versus findings

In this study I have used Western theories and research tools. Have they been useful to me when trying to understand the Tanzanian situation? In what ways were they not useful?

Starting with the *frame factor theory approach*, I have experienced it as a useful tool but also seen limitations. Since the frame factor theory was developed in Sweden, I will make comparisons between Tanzania and Sweden.

The regulating factors were of similar kinds in Tanzania and in Sweden. In the 1970s there were many similarities between the two societies. Both had a centralised educational system with socialistic goals. During the 1980s both started to decentralise the school system while retaining the governmental system. A difference was that Tanzania in the 70s had a more revolutionary aim to change the society.

The constraining factors were likewise similar, since Tanzania inherited the Western system from its former colonial power concerning organisation and physical frames. But in Tanzania the factors had stronger effects. As late as 1991, on average 45 percent of the primary schools had no furniture in their classrooms. The shortage of instructional material was serious. The time allocated to teaching and learning for the pupils was shortened due to several factors, among them financial constraint and lack of teachers. The classes were large and variation in age was common. A study of successful primary and secondary schools in Tanzania (Temu 1995) has verified that the physical environment of the school is as important as the economic status and the sociocultural values of the surrounding communities. Schools with locations in more resourceful areas were likely to be better equipped and students there performed better. My study was mainly carried out in areas where agricultural and industrial productions were above average in Tanzania, but in spite of that, the performance of the schools varied. The role of the community, such as support to the school infrastructure, parental support and parental participation in decision making, was also one of the factors which Temu pointed to as important for school success. Temu's findings confirm the role of constraining factors.

The governing factors were more problematic. The curriculum is meant to steer the educational process. It is supposed to represent the production system in the society and should function as a reproduction tool. If the syllabi are not always available to the teachers (which I have found), what will then govern their teaching? And if the actors in the context of realisation do not accept the educational goals, what forces are governing? It is clear that in the Tanzanian context the syllabus was not a self-evident governing factor as stated in the frame factor theory approach.

Ideally, things should have worked as in Diagram 7. The state-defined frames should steer the curriculum and provide conducive physical and administrative conditions. The local authorities should supplement and implement

```
┌─────────────────────────────────────────────────┐
│              STATE DEFINED FRAMES               │
│  Educational policy   Economic policy   Political policy │
└─────────────────────────────────────────────────┘
                         ▼

                              ╱  Textbooks and teaching aids
           Curriculum  ─────<
                              ╲  National exams

                                          ╱  Time
    Physical and administrative frames  <
                                          ╲  Class size
                         ▲
          ┌──────────────────────────┐
          │  Local government policy │
          │      LOCAL FRAMES        │
          └──────────────────────────┘
```

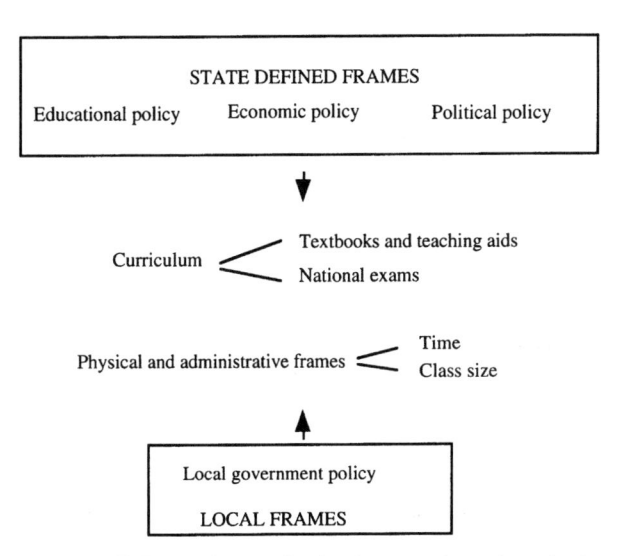

Diagram 7. Frame factors for implementation of curriculum.

the national goals. This concords with the intentions of the post-independence educational policy designed by Julius Nyerere. He appeared to believe in a causal connection, i.e. a political policy could be implemented through education with suitable curricula, a large financial allocation in the governmental budget and a sufficient number of teachers and schools.

Now, the situation is more complicated than the one described in the diagram. There is a difference between what is decided at the central level and what is happening at the local level. The centre, i.e. the elite and the decision-makers, decides on the frames of education (Dahllöf 1971, Lundgren 1972, Daun 1992, Lindblad 1994). The periphery consists of the teachers (Lindblad 1994) and the parents or common people, often in the rural areas (Daun 1992).

The teachers are in the periphery but they are the actors and implementers. To ensure that what they are doing is in accordance with the aims formulated at the central level, Lindblad points out possible strategies: attempts to force changes, re-educate the teachers or use experts or other actors working at the local level. These strategies have changed over time but no successful model has hitherto been developed.

The relation between the centre and the periphery is complex in Africa, according to Daun, and he points to some important factors that must be considered: ecology (existence of monocultures), production (dependence of world market prices), the state (decisions and actions of international non-governmental actors) and culture (for example Christian and Islamic activities). The school is different from the culture in which the pupils live and are to be successful, which means that pupils must change their understanding of reality, especially since the content of teaching and learning is not adapted to the local conditions.

```
                                                    ┌─────────────────────────┐
                                                    │ Non-governmental actors │
                                                    └─────────────────────────┘
   Educational policy  ◄──►  Economic policy  ◄──►  Political policy    ◄──┘
                                    │
                    Physical and adminstrative frames
                         ╱          ▼          ╲
   ┌──────────────────┐    ┌──────────────────┐    ┌──────────────────────┐
   │ Access to syllabi│    │ Parents' attitudes│    │Socio-economic status │
   │ Access to teaching│ ─ │ Language profiency│ ─  │Cultural values       │
   │ material         │    │ Access to textbooks│   │Teacher training      │
   │ National exams   │    └──────────────────┘    └──────────────────────┘
   └──────────────────┘
        CURRICULUM              PUPIL                    TEACHER
```

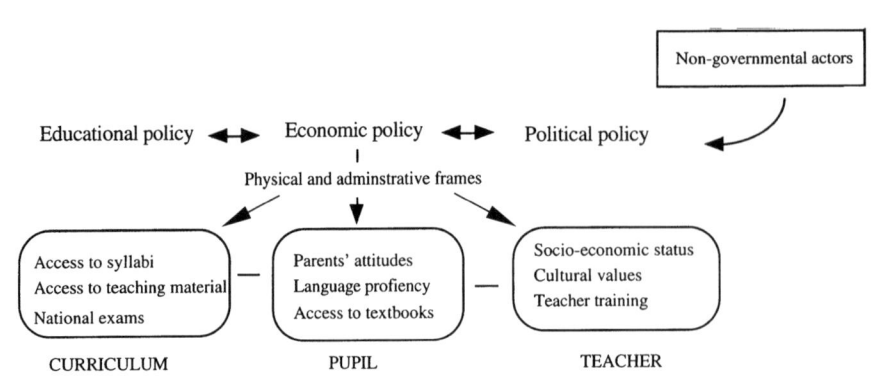

Diagram 8. Factors influencing the field implementation of curriculum in Tanzania.

My findings appear to show that the frame factor concept does not function in the same way in Tanzania as in Sweden. Instead, several other factors have an influence on teaching and contribute to the final relation. The teachers' preparation for the teaching profession, their access to syllabi and teaching material, their social status and economic situation, cultural values (the family and relatives have maximum priority, the role of elders and of males/females in the community, etc.) and the national exams are frame factors for realisation of environmental education in the Tanzanian educational system. Other factors are the parents' attitudes, the pupils' language proficiency (or, from the other way round, the language used as the medium of teaching) and their access to textbooks. Finances at the macro level are an important factor since aid dependency involves other actors[2], who all have strong influences. All these factors limit the teachers' actions in the classroom. Diagram 8 shows an adaptation of the frame factor theory for the Tanzanian context.

The *phenomenographic research approach* for understanding how teachers understand and think about environmental education has been, as a whole, useful to me. I have complemented this approach with field-visits over a span of several years, visits to schools for observation and participation in different activities as well as analyses of relevant documents. The main limitation was the language barrier, i.e. neither the interviewer nor the interviewees spoke their mother tongue. Also, the way of formulating the questions followed a Western tradition. What effect did it have? What impact did it have on the mutual understanding? As for the phenomenographic analyses, which are a decontextualised description of various ways of experiencing environmental education, the variation in my study was on a collective level and had little or no relevance for individual actions. Differences between cultures and subcultures within the same society have not been part of this analysis. The descriptions present a possible picture of possible ways of thinking about a phenomenon,

---

[2] DANIDA (Denmark), DGIS (the Netherlands), GTZ (Germany), IMF, NORAD (Norway), ODA (UK), EU, Irish Aid, Sida (Sweden), UNESCO, UNICEF, and the World Bank.

limited by the fragmentation of thoughts during the analysis, by the language barrier and by the transcription from oral to written language. On an individual level these ways of experiencing environmental education are likely to change over time. Still, the outcome is important. It indicates that the limited result of environmental education in schools did not mainly depend on teachers not understanding the concept or disregarding its importance, even if they experienced lack of knowledge.

My conclusion is that theories that have originated in the developed countries might not fully be applicable to an understanding and explanation of questions in the least developed countries, particularly when confronting other cultural ways of life and education. The limitations to such theories are actually quite clear but for the moment they are all that we have. There is a need to take the discussion further and develop new theories. In the field of environmental education research, there is a need to find ways to study how people involved in education understand the environment, what patterns of thought exist and the practice and the role of cultural values.

I will conclude this chapter with some reflections on issues of interest for further action or/and research.

The prospects of education for sustainability[3] in the least developed countries

The most widely used definitions of sustainability focus on the relationship between population, poverty, environmental degradation, democracy, human rights, peace and improving the quality of life for all, especially the poor and deprived, within the carrying capacity of ecosystems (UNESCO 1997). It thus embraces relationships between social, economic and natural systems and processes. Agenda 21, in the Rio Declaration at United Nations' Conference on Environment and Development in 1992, states that education is critical for promoting sustainable development and that environment and development education should deal with the dynamics of both physical/biological and socio-economic environment (Agenda 21, Chapter 36).

What possibilities do the least developed countries have to follow these guidelines? And what credibility do they have? The least developed countries represent 10 percent of the world population and their GDP per capita, which was 1 USD in the early 1990s, is in decline in recent years (Sida 1996b). Poverty, environmental problems and economic development are interlinked. 'Knowledge' is becoming a new production factor. Does every country possess sufficient requirements for development? And what can be done to improve the conditions?

---

[3] Environmental education as a concept has broadened in the discussions during the 1990s and education for sustainability (EfS) is more and more used internationally.

Environmental problems are aggravated by poverty. Frederick Kijage and Anna Tibaijuka (1996) have studied poverty and social exclusion in Tanzania. They argue that during the socialist period (after the Arusha declaration) the state emphasised equity and seriously tried to address poverty and redistribute resources in the society. Education was seen as an important role-player in this transformation. So far strategies to improve conditions in the social sector have not been successful, due to heavy reliance on donor support, among other things. Low-income groups today are hit harshly by cost-sharing in the education sector, which has contributed to social exclusion.

Education as a tool for transformation was discussed earlier in this dissertation. I concluded that the expectations of development have rarely been realised and I pointed to the restricting effect of different factors in the formal educational system. It is not sufficient that the teachers appear to have understood the concept and importance of environmental education.

What role does the political ideology play for sustainability? This has not been discussed in depth here, being outside the scope of the research, but naturally there is a difference between socialist, liberal and conservative ideas on the exploitation of natural resources in relation to the economy and use of technology. There is no agreement on the meaning of sustainability; meaning differs according to political orientation.

How then should the curriculum be developed? What kind of education should be focused on and for whom? How is curriculum related to life and what kind of life should that be? When should the aim of education for sustainability be considered? Should it be an education for management and control based on causal explanations? Or should it be an education for environmental awareness and interpretation based on understanding? Or should it be an education for sustainability with self-reflection and empowerment?

Application of the ideas of the critical theory of Jürgen Habermas has been explored in the Deakin-Griffith Environmental Education Project, which resulted in some basic characteristics of defining education for sustainability. The project is a collaboration between the Deakin and Griffith Universities in Australia. According to John Huckle and Stephen Sterling (1997), a socially critical pedagogy should include active and experiential learning and a classroom dialogue which introduce elements of critical theory. Pupils should be encouraged to think critically. They should become aware of themselves and their life history and they should develop the power to shape their lives. This will make it possible for them to reflect on the forces that influence and restrict their lives and on democratic alternatives, as well as develop knowledge and skills to act democratically with others to build a new social order.

What society today is prepared for this? If education for sustainability is to be used in a transition process, it assumes that the society will accept these aims and that teachers will be trained in learning approaches that enable the students to develop such knowledge, skills and attitudes.

An effective education for sustainability needs a co-operative approach from the formal, informal and non-formal educational systems. Non-governmental organisations play an important role in many countries (Vinke 1992). They provide in-service training for teachers and supply supporting materials. However, such efforts have remained confined to a limited number of teachers and schools. A co-ordination between the efforts of different non-governmental organisations would be more effective. Partnerships between non-governmental organisations in the developed and the developing worlds have been known to be successful (Hale 1992).

Is Education for Self-Reliance of importance today?
During the Education for Self-Reliance policy, the project was important as preparation for the future life as adult and member of the community. Education with production has also been a key concept for national reform work after independence in Zimbabwe in 1980 (Gustafsson 1987). It was also considered a relevant concept in 'new' South Africa for solving one of its most pressing problems among out-of-school children and the unemployed (Lawrence and Parker 1995). As for education for sustainability, particularly in a country dominated by the agriculture industry, education for production is still a feasible approach, particularly in terms of formal education. While the content could be extended to encompass more environmental issues, the methodological approach is still quite acceptable.

Other suggestions for further research
Another area for further research is the role of girls and women in the society and how they contribute to caring for the environment at a personal, local and global level. In Tanzania, and other developing countries as well, women are involved in the environment in a number of ways, for example as farmers, consumers of energy, responsible for health and hygiene in the families, educators and decision-makers. How can their experiences contribute to our understanding of sustainability? What kind of education do they need to be able to participate in the development of a sustainable society? The gender perspective has not, thus far, been in focus in environmental education. The feminist perspective on both content (gender stereotyping in curricula) and ethics (ecofeminism) would be a fruitful contribution to our knowledge.

The value of traditional or indigenous knowledge in environmental matters should be appreciated to a greater extent. The communities around the schools have this knowledge and it has traditionally been transmitted through the informal education system, i.e. families and clans. Since it has been indicated that the surrounding communities are aware of the current environmental problems, the formal school system should develop their capacity to relate to the communities. This could mean co-operation with or adaptation to indigenous education systems. These traditional values were once honoured by Nyerere in the Education for Self-Reliance but only on a general level and the aims did not fully materialise. Since the learning systems vary among local cultures, as shown by, for example Holger Daun (1992), formal primary schools should be given the possibility to develop a local version of the curriculum in consistency with the existing learning systems. Further research should study the possibilities of formal, informal and non-formal approaches to develop a more effective education for sustainability together.

Research on how teachers understand the curriculum, how they talk about it, their intentions and how they act in the teaching situation would contribute to an understanding of the complex situation of realising the curriculum. The relation of these factors to the social, cultural, economic and historical context appears obvious. One issue that has not been researched, as far as I know, is environmental ethics in religious beliefs in sub-Sahara. What role do they play? To explore this domain further would be useful and particularly relevant to developing countries. Also, the teacher as a reflective practitioner in education for environmental development would be a field of great interest.

Finally, a word on what I should have answered the people who told me that 'nothing much' was being done concerning environmental education in schools and that 'teachers are ignorant.' Today I would say, 'It's no use blaming the teacher'! It is now obvious that there are many other actors and factors on the arena.

References

Adedayo, A. & Olawepo, J.A. (1997). Integration of Environmental Education in Social Science Curricula at the Secondary School Level in Nigeria: problems and prospects. *Environmental Education Research*, Vol. 3, No. 1.

Adu Boahen, A. (ed.) (1990). *General History of Africa, VII. Africa under Colonial Domination 1880–1935.* Abridged edition. Unesco International Scientific Committee for drafting of a General History of Africa. Unesco. London: James Currey Ltd and University of California Press.

Agenda 21, Chapter 36: Education, Training and Public Awareness. http://iisd.ca/rio+5/agenda/chp36.htm (April 1999)

Alerby, E. (1998). *Att fånga en tanke. En fenomenologisk studie av barns och ungdomars tänkande kring miljö.* Institutionen för pedagogik och ämnesdidaktik. Centrum för forskning om lärande. Luleå: Luleå tekniska universitet.

Alexandersson, M. (1994). Den fenomenografiska forskningsansatsens fokus. I Starrin, B. & Svensson, P.-G. (red.): *Kvalitativ metod och vetenskapsteori.* Lund: Studentlitteratur.

Anderson, G. (1997). *Fundamentals of Educational Research.* London: The Falmer Press.

Arcury, T.A. & Christianson, E.H. (1993) Rural-urban differences in environmental knowledge and actions. *The Journal of Environmental Education* 1993, Vol. 25, No. 1, pp. 19–25.

Armstrong, S. J. & Botzler, R.G. (1993). *Environmental Ethics. Divergence and convergence.* New York: McGraw-Hill, Inc.

Atieno Odhiambo, E.S., Ouso, T.I. & Williams, J.F.M. (1988). *A History of East Africa.* Essex: Longman Group UK Limited.

Axelsson, H. (1997). *Våga lära. Om lärare som förändrar sin miljöundervisning.* Göteborg Studies in Educational Sciences 112. Acta Universitatis Gothenburgensis.

Bak, N. (1995). Green Doesn't Always Mean 'Go': possible tensions in the desirability and implementation of environmental education *Environmental Education Research,* Vol. 1, No. 3, pp. 345–352.

Bakobi, L.M.M. (1994). Environmental Education in Tanzania. Consultancy report for SADC. Environment and Land Management Programme.

Bloom, B.S. et al. (eds.). (1956). *Taxonomy of Educational Objectives, Handbook I: Cognitive Domain.* New York: David McKay Co. Inc.

Boerschig, S. and de Young, R. (1993). Evaluation of Selected Recycling Curricula: Education the Green Citizen. *The Journal of Environmental Education* 1993, Vol. 24, No.3, pp. 17–22.

Bowden, J. A. (1996). Phenomenographic research—Some methodological issues. In Dall'Alba, G. & Hasselgren, B. *Reflections on Phenomenography. Toward a Meth-*

odology? Göteborg Studies in Educational Sciences 109. Acta Universitatis Gothenburgensis.
Boyes, E., Chambers, W., & Stanisstreet, M. (1995). Trainee Primary Teachers' Ideas about the Ozone Layer. *Environmental Education Research*, Vol. 1, No. 2, 1995, pp. 133–145.
Broady, D. (1985). *Den dolda läroplanen.* Stockholm: Symposion.
Brock-Utne, B. (1993). *Education in Africa.* Vol. I. Education for self-reliance or recolonization? Oslo: Universitetet i Oslo. Pedagogisk forskningsinstitutt.
Brock-Utne, B. (1994). *Indigenous forms of Learning in Africa.* Rapport Nr. 7. Oslo: Universitetet i Oslo. Pedagogisk forskningsinstitutt.
Brody, M., Chipman, E. & Marion, S. (1988–89). Student Knowledge of Scientific and Natural Resources Concepts Concerning Acidic Deposition. *The Journal of Environmental Education*, 1988–89, Vol. 20, No. 2, pp.32–42.
Brody, M.J. (1990–91). Understanding of Pollution among 4th, 8th, and 11th Grade Students. *The Journal of Environmental Education*, 1990–91, Vol. 22, No. 2, pp. 24–33.
Bruhn, A. & Lindberg, O. (1996). Kvalitativ metod och datateknologi. I Svensson, P-G. & Starrin, B. (red.). *Kvalitativa studier i teori och praktik.* Lund: Studentlitteratur.
Buchert, L. (1994). *Education in the Development of Tanzania 1919–1990.* Eastern African Studies. London: James Currey Ltd.
Buchert, L. (1997). *Education policy formulation in Tanzania. Coordination between the Government and International Aid Agencies.* Paris: UNESCO. International Institute for Educational Planning.
Calderhead, J. (1993). The Contribution of Research on Teachers' Thinking to the Professional Development of Teachers. In Day, C., Calderhead, J. and Denicolo, P. (eds.) (1993). *Research on Teacher Thinking: Understanding Professional Development.* London: The Falmer Press.
Cantrell, D.C. (1993). Alternative Paradigms in Environmental Education Research: The Interpretive Perspective. In Mrazek, R. (1993): *Alternative Paradigms in Environmental Education Research.* Monographs in Environmental Education and Environmental Studies. Volume VIII. The North American Association for Environmental Education, Troy, Ohio.
Carlgren, I. (1990). Relations in Thinking and Acting in Teachers' Innovative Work. In Day, C., Pope, M. & Denicolo, P. (eds.) (1990): *Insight into Teachers' Thinking and Practice.* London: The Falmer Press.
Carlgren, I. (1996). Professionalism and Teachers as Designers. In Kompf, M., Bond, R.W., Dworet, D. and Boak, R.T. (eds.) (1996). *Changing Research and Practice: Teachers' Professionalism, Identities and Knowledge.* London: The Falmer Press.
Carlgren, I. and Lindblad, S. (1991). On Teachers' Practical Reasoning and Professional Knowledge: Considering Conceptions of Context in Teachers' Thinking. A contribution to the 1991 AERA meeting in Chicago.
Carlgren, I., Handal, G. and Vaage, S. (1994). Introduction. In Carlgren, I., Handal, G. and Vaage, S. (eds.) (1993). *Teachers' Minds and Actions: Research on Teacher Thinking and Practice,* London: The Falmer Press.
Carnoy, M. & Samoff, J. (1990). *Education and Social Transition in the Third World.* Princeton, New Jersey: Princeton University Press.
Carr-Hill, R. (1984). *Primary education in Tanzania. A review of the research.* Education Division documents. No 16. Stockholm: SIDA.
Chadwick, B.A., Bahr, H.A. & Albrecht, S.L. (1984). *Social Science Research Methods.* New Jersey: Prentice Hall Inc.
Chonjo, P.N. (1992). Summary of the main findings of perceptions of afforestation by primary school pupils and their teachers and how the schools can be used to protect the environment. Paper presented at a Workshop at University of Dar es Salaam, December 15-16 1992.

Connel, S. (1997). Empirical-Analytical Methodological Research in Environmental Education: response to a negative trend in methodological and ideological discussion. *Environmental Education Research,* Vol. 3, No. 2, pp. 117–132.

Cottrell, S.P. & Graefe, A.R. (1997). Testing a Conceptual Framework of Responsible Environmental Behavior. *The Journal of Environmental Education,* 1997, Vol. 29, No. 1, pp. 17–27.

da Silva, C. (1996). Building Bridges: Traditional Environmental Knowledge and Environmental Education in Tanzanian Secondary Schools. In Leal Filho, W., Murphy, Z. and O'Loan, K. (eds.) (1996). *A Sourcebook for Environmental Education. A Practical Review Based on the Belgrade Charter.* London: The Parthenon Publishing Group.

Dahllöf, U. (1967). *Skoldifferentiering och undervisningsförlopp.* Stockholm: Almqvist & Wiksell.

Dahllöf, U. (1971). *Ability Grouping, Content Validity and Curriculum Process Analysis.* New York: Teacher College Press, Columbia University. New York.

Dahllöf, U. et al. (1991). *Dimensions of evaluation in higher education.* London: Jessica Kingsley Publishers.

Daun, H. (1992a). *Childhood Learning and Adult Life. The Functions of Indigenous, Islamic and Western Education in an African Context.* Studies in Comparative and International Education 24. Stockholm: Institute of International Education. Stockholm University.

Daun, H. (1992b). Education and parental strategies for survival. In Buchert, L. (ed.). *Education and training in the third world. The local dimension.* CESO paperback no. 18. The Hague: Centre for the Study of Education in Developing Countries (CESO).

Daun, H. (1996). *National Forces, Globalization and Educational Restructuring.* Stockholm: Institute of International Education 104. Stockholm University.

Day, C. (1993). The Importance of Learning Biography in Supporting Teacher Development: An Empirical Study. In Day, C., Calderhead, J. and Denicolo, P. (eds.) (1993). *Research on Teacher Thinking: Understanding Professional Development.* London: The Falmer Press.

Disinger, J.F. & Roth, C.E. (1992). Environmental Education Research News. *The Environmentalist,* Vol. 12, Number 3, pp. 165–168.

Earl Todt, D. (1995). *An investigation of the environmental literacy of teachers in south-central Ohio using the Wisconsin Environment Literacy Survey, concept mapping and interviews.* Ph.D. thesis. The Ohio State University.

Edgren, G. (1996). A Challenge to the Aid Relationship. In *Aid Dependency. Causes, symptoms and remedies.* Stockholm: Swedish International Development Cooperation Agency.

Faulconer, T. (1993). *Situating Beliefs and Trends in Environmental Education within the Ecological Debate.* Paper presented at the Annual Meeting of the American Educational Research Association, Atlanta, GA, April 1993. ED 361 231.

Fien, J. & Rawling, R. (1996). Reflective Practice: A Case Study of Professional Development for Environmental Education. *The Journal of Environmental Education,* 1996, Vol. 27, No. 3, pp. 11–20.

Fien, J.F. (1992). *Education for the environment: a critical ethnography.* Ph.D. thesis. University of Queensland.

Francis, H. (1996). Advancing phenomenography—Questions of method. In Dall'Alba, G. & Hasselgren, B. *Reflections on Phenomenography. Toward a Methodology?* Göteborg Studies in Educational Sciences 109. Acta Universitatis Gothenburgensis.

Franke-Wikberg, S. & Lundgren, U.P. (1980). *Att värdera utbildning. Del 1.* Stockholm: Wahlström & Widstrand.

Furley, O.W., Watson, T. (1978). *A History of Education in East Africa*. New York: NOK Publishers.
Fägerlind, I. & Saha, J.S. (1983). *Education and National Development: A Comparative Perspective*. Oxford: Pergamon Press.
Galabawa, C.J. (1990). *Implementing Educational Policies in Tanzania*. Washington D.C.: World Bank Discussion Papers; 86. Africa Technical Development Series.
Goodson, I.F. (1996). *Att stärka lärarnas röster. Sex essäer om lärarforskning och lärar-forskarsamarbete*. Didactica 5. Stockholm: HLS Förlag.
Gough, A. (1997a). *Education and the Environment: Policy, Trends and the Problems of Marginalisation*. Australian Education Review No. 39. Melbourne. Australian Council for Educational Research Ltd.
Gough, A. (1997b). Evaluation of Australian Government Literature on the Environment. *The Journal of Environmental Education*, 1997, Vol. 28, No. 4, pp. 18–25.
Gough, N. (1993). Narrative Inquiry and Critical Pragmatism: Liberating Research in Environmental Education. In Mrazek, R. (1993): *Alternative Paradigms in Environmental Education Research*. Monographs in Environmental Education and Environmental Studies. Volume VIII. The North American Association for Environmental Education, Troy, Ohio.
Greenall Gough, A. and Robottom, I. (1993). Towards a socially critical environmental education: water quality studies in a coastal school. *Journal of Curriculum Studies*, 1993, Vol. 25, No. 4, pp. 301–316.
Grundy, S. (1987). *Curriculum: Product or Praxis*. Deakin Studies in Education Series: 1. London: The Falmer Press.
Gustafsson, C. (1994). Antalet utvärderingsmodeller är oändligt ... I Gustafsson C. & Selander, S. (red.) *Ramfaktorteoretiskt tänkande. Pedagogiska perspektiv. En vänbok till Urban Dahllöf*. Uppsala: Pedagogiska institutionen, Uppsala universitet.
Gustafsson, I. (1987). *Schools and the Transformation of Work. A Comparative Study of Four Productive Work Programmes in Southern Africa*. Stockholm: Institute of International Education, University of Stockholm.
Habermas, J. (1972). *Knowledge and Human Interests*. London: Heinemann.
Hale, M. (1992). Towards more effective support for environmental education in developing countries. Paper prepared for the OECD Development Centre. April 1992.
Hamilton, M.L. (1993). Think You Can: The Influence of Culture on Beliefs. In Day, C., Calderhead, J. and Denicolo, P. (eds.) (1993). *Research on Teacher Thinking: Understanding Professional Development*. London: The Falmer Press.
Hanselman, D. & Yuec, C. (1978). Recent Master's Thesis Work in Environmental Education and Communication. *National Association for Environmental Education*, Troy, Ohio. ED 226 973.
Hansen Nelson, M. (1993). Teachers' Stories: An Analysis of the Themes. In Day, C., Calderhead, J. and Denicolo, P. (eds.) (1993). *Research on Teacher Thinking: Understanding Professional Development*. London: The Falmer Press.
Hart, P. (1993). Alternative Perspectives in Environmental Education Research: Paradigm of Critically Reflective Inquiry. In Mrazek, R. (1993): *Alternative Paradigms in Environmental Education Research*. Monographs in Environmental Education and Environmental Studies. Volume VIII. The North American Association for Environmental Education, Troy, Ohio.
Hasselgren, B. (1996). Tyrri Soila and the phenomenographic approach. In Dall'Alba, G. & Hasselgren, B. *Reflections on Phenomenography. Toward a Methodology?* Göteborg Studies in Educational Sciences 109. Acta Universitatis Gothenburgensis.
Hawes, H. et.al. (1979). *Curriculum and Reality in African Primary Schools*. Harlow: Longman Group.
Helldén, G. (1995). Environmental Education and Pupils' Conceptions of Matter. *Environmental Education Research*, Vol. 1, No. 3, pp. 267–277.

Hillcoat, J., Forge, K., Fien, J. & Baker, E. (1995). 'I Think It's Really Great that Someone Is Listening to Us ...': young people and the environment. *Environmental Education Research,* Vol. 1, No. 2. pp. 159–171.

Huckle, J. & Sterling. S. (1997). *Education for Sustainability.* London: Earthscan Publications Ltd.

Huckle, J. (1993). Environmental education and sustainability: A view from critical theory. In Fien, J. (ed.): *Environmental Education. A Pathway to Sustainability.* Geelong Deakin University Press.

Hurry, L. B. (1980). *Environmental Education in Transvaal Secondary School and its Relation to the Teaching of Biology and Geography.* Master Thesis, University of South Africa. ED 234 992.

Hurry, L. B. (1992). *Directions in Environmental Education and Their Implication for the Training of Primary School Teachers in the Transvaal: Towards a Synthesis.* Ph.D. thesis, University of South Africa. ED 234 991.

Iliffe, J. (1979). *A Modern History of Tanganyika.* African Studies Series 25, Cambridge: Cambridge University Press.

Iliffe, J. (1997). *Afrika. Historien om en kontinent.* Lund. Historiska Media. AB. (Africans—the History of a Continent. Cambridge University Press)

Instituto del Tercer Mundo (1992). *Third World Guide 93/94.* Uruguay.

Iozzi, L.A. (1989a). What Research Says to the Educator, Part One: Environmental Education and the Affective Domain. *The Journal of Environmental Education,* 1989, Vol. 20, No. 3, pp. 3–9.

Iozzi, L.A. (1989b). What Research Says to the Educator, Part Two: Environmental Education and the Affective Domain. *The Journal of Environmental Education.* Vol. 20, No. 4, pp. 6–13.

Ishumi, A.G. & Maliyamkono, T.L.(1995). Education for Self-Reliance. In Legum, C. & Mnari, G. (eds.): *Mwalimu. The Influence of Nyerere.* London: Britain-Tanzania Society in association with James Currey, London, Mkuki na Nyota, Dar es Salaam and Africa World Press, Trenton.

IUCN, UNEP, WWF (1980). *World Conservation Strategy: Living Resource Conservation for Sustainable Development.* Gland, Switzerland.

IUCN, UNEP, WWF (1990). *Caring for the Earth: A Strategy for Sustainable Living.* Gland, Switzerland.

Johansson, B. (1989). *Hem till Tanzania:* boken om Barbro Johansson berättad för Anna Wieslander. Stockholm: Raben & Sjögren.

Jones, T. Jesse (1925). *Education in East Africa.* A study of the East, Central and South Africa by the second African Education Commission under the auspices of the Phelps-Stokes Fund, in cooperation with the International Education Board. New York and London. London: Edinburgh House Press.

Kaijage, F. & Tibaijuka, A. (1996). *Poverty and social exclusion in Tanzania.* Geneva International Institute for Labour Studies, United Nations Development Programme. Research Series 109.

Kaiser, P.J. (1996). Structural Adjustment and the Fragile Nation: The Demise of Social Unity in Tanzania. *The Journal of Modern African Studies.* Vol. 34, No. 2, pp. 227–237.

Keltchermans, G. (1993). Teachers and their Career Story: A Biographical Perspective on Professional Development. In Day, C., Calderhead, J. and Denicolo, P. (eds.) (1993). *Research on Teacher Thinking: Understanding Professional Development.* London: The Falmer Press.

Keltchermans, G.(1994). Biographical Methods in the Study of Teachers' Professional Development. In Carlgren, I., Handal, G. and Vaage, S. (eds.) (1993). *Teachers' Minds and Actions: Research on Teacher Thinking and Practice.* London: The Falmer Press.

Knowles, J. G. (1993). Life-History Accounts as Mirrors: A Practical Avenue for the Conceptualization of Reflection in Teacher Education. In Calderhead, J. and Gates, P. (1993). *Conceptualizing Reflection in Teacher Development*. London: The Falmer Press.

Kogut, B.H. (Ed.) (1982). Recent Master's Thesis Work in Environmental Education and Communication. Vol. V. *National Association for Environmental Education*, Troy, Ohio. ED 227 431.

Komba, D. & Temu, E. (1995). Tanzania: education for self-reliance dimension of Education with Production. In Hoppers, W. & Komba, D. (eds.) *Productive work in education and training. A state-of-the-art in Eastern Africa*. CESO Paperback no. 21. Centre for the Study of Education in Developing Countries (CESO), The Hague.

Kompf, M., Bond, R.W., Dworet, D. and Boak, R.T. (eds.) (1996). *Changing Research and Practice: Teachers' Professionalism, Identities and Knowledge*. London: The Falmer Press.

Krathwohl, D.R., Bloom, B.S. & Masia, B.B. (1964). *The Taxonomy of Educational Objectives, Handbook II: Affective Domain*. New York: New York: David McKay Co. Inc.

Kvale, S. (1997). *Den kvalitativa forskningsintervjun*. Lund: Studentlitteartur.

Lane, J., Wilkie, R., Champeau, R. & Sivek, D. (1994). Environmental Education in Wisconsin: A Teacher Survey. *The Journal of Environmental Education*. Vol. 25, No. 4, pp. 9–17.

Larsson, S. (1982). *Studier i lärares omvärldsuppfattning: Ett försök till integration*. Rapport nr 1982:15. Pedagogiska institutionen, Göteborgs universitet.

Larsson, S. (1986). Learning from experience: Teachers' conception of changes in their professional practice. *Journal of Curriculum Studies*, 19, 1, pp. 35–43.

Lawrence, M., Parker, B. (1995). Education with Production—Taking Root in South Africa. A Report from a Seminar in September 1995. In *Development Dialogue* 1995:2. Published by the Dag Hammarsköld Foundation, Uppsala, Sweden.

Leeming, F.C., Dwyer, W.O., Porter, B.E. & Cobern, M.K. (1993). Outcome of research in Environmental Education: A critical review. *The Journal of Environmental Education*, 1993, Vol. 24, No. 4, pp. 8–21.

Lindblad, S. (1983). Hur studerar man lärares omvärldsuppfattning? Eller: En diskussion av fenomenografin som normalvetenskap. *Tidskrift för Nordisk Förening för Pedagogisk Forskning* nr 2, pp. 27–38.

Lindblad, S. (1994). *Lärarna—Samhällets och Skolans Utveckling. Utforskningar och analyser av lärarledd verksamhet*. Stockholm: HLS förlag.

Lindblad, S., Linde, G. & Naeslund, L. (1999). Ramfaktorteori och praktiskt förnuft. *Pedagogisk Forskning i Sverige*, under utgivn. 1999.

Linde, G. (1987). *Yrkesutbildning i Tanzania. En fallstudie av Dar es Salaam National Vocational Training Centre*. Forskningsgruppen för läroplansteori och kulturreproduktion. Stockholm: Högskolan för lärarutbildning. Institutionen för pedagogik.

Lindensjö, B., Lundgren U.P. (1986). *Politisk styrning och utbildningsreformer*. Forskningsgruppen för läroplansteori och kulturreproduktion. Pedagogiska institutionen. Högskolan för lärarutbildning i Stockholm. Gymnasieskola i utveckling B 86:3. Skolöverstyrelsen. Stockholm: Liber

Lisowski, M. & Disinger, J. F. (1991). The Effect of Field-Based Instruction on Student Understandings of Ecological Concepts. *The Journal of Environmental Education*, 1991, Vol. 23, No. 1, pp. 19–23.

Lockheed, M. E. & Levin, H. M. (1993). Creating Effective Schools. In Levin, H. M. & Lockheed, M. E. (eds.) *Effective Schools in Developing Countries*. The Standford series on education and public policy. London: The Falmer Press.

Lortie, D.C. (1975). *Schoolteacher. A Sociological Study*. Chicago: The University of Chicago Press.

Loubser, C.P. & Ferreira, J.G. (1992). Environmental Education in South Africa in the Light of the Tbilisi and Moscow Conferences. *The Journal of Environmental Education*, Vol. 23, No. 4, pp. 31–34.

Lugalla, J.L.P. (1993). Structural Adjustment Policies and Education in Tanzania. In Gibbon, P. (ed.) *Social Change and Economic Reform in Africa*. Uppsala: The Scandinavian Institute of African Studies.

Lundgren, U.P. & Pettersson, S. (eds.) 1979. *Code, context and curriculum processes*. Stockholm: Stockholm Institute of Education. Department of Educational Research.

Lundgren, U.P. (1984a). Ramfaktorteorins historia. I Broady, D. & Lundgren, U. P. (red.) Skeptron 1. Tema: Rätten att tala. Stockholm: Symposion förlag, pp. 69–81.

Lundgren, U.P. (1984b). *Between Hope and Happening: Text and Context in Curriculum*. ECS802 Curriculum theory. Victoria: Deakin University Press.

Lundgren, U.P. (1972). *Frame Factors and the Teaching Process*. A contribution to curriculum theory on teaching. Stockholm: Almqvist & Wiksell.

Lundgren, U.P. (1981). *Model Analysis of Pedagogical Processes*. 2nd edition. Studies in Curriculum Theory and Cultural reproduction/5. Stockholm Institute of Education. Lund: CWK Gleerup.

Lybeck, L., Strömdahl, H. & Tullberg, A. (1985). *Students' conceptions of amount of substance and its SI unit 1 MOL. A subject didactic study*. Report no. 1985:04. Department of Education and Educational Research, Gothenburg University.

Marcinkowski, T. (1993). A Contextual Review of the 'Quantitative Paradigm' in EE Research. In Mrazek, R. *Alternative Paradigms in Environmental Education Research*. Monographs in Environmental Education and Environmental Studies. Volume VIII. The North American Association for Environmental education, Troy, Ohio.

Marton, F. (1981). Phenomenography—describing conceptions of the world around us. *Instructional Science*, 10, pp. 177–200.

Marton, F. (1990). Phenomenography: A Research Approach to Investigating Different Understandings of Reality. In Sherman, R.R. & Webb, R.B. (eds.) *Qualitative Research in Education: Focus and Methods*. London: The Falmer Press.

Marton, F. (1992). På spaning efter medvetandets pedagogik. *Forskning om utbildning*. Nr 4, 1992. pp. 28–40.

Marton, F. (1996). Cognosco ergo sum—Reflections on reflections. In Dall'Alba, G. & Hasselgren, B. *Reflections on Phenomenography. Toward a Methodology?* Göteborg: Studies in Educational Sciences 109. Acta Universitatis Gothenburgensis.

Marton, F., Dahlgren, L-O., Svensson, L. & Säljö, R. (1977). *Inlärning och omvärldsuppfattning*. Stockholm: Almqvist & Wiksell.

Mbilinyi, M. & Mbughuni, P. (eds.) (1991). *Education in Tanzania with a Gender Perspective. Summary Report*. Education Division Documents No 53. Stockholm: SIDA.

Ministry of Education (1982). *Basic Facts about Education in Tanzania*. Dar es Salaam.

Ministry of Education (1984a). *Educational System in Tanzania towards the year 2000*. Recommendations of the 1982 Presidential Commission on Education as Approved by the Party and the Government. Dar es Salaam.

Ministry of Education (1984b). *Some Basic Facts about Education in Tanzania*. Dar es Salaam.

Ministry of Education (1989). *Biology Syllabus for Secondary Schools*. Institute of Curriculum Development. Dar es Salaam.

Ministry of Education (1990a). *Geography Syllabus for Secondary Schools*. Institute of Curriculum Development. Dar es Salaam.

Ministry of Education (1990b). *Basic Education Statistics in Tanzania (BEST) 1985–1989*. Dar es Salaam.

Ministry of Education (1990c). *The Development of Education: 1988–1990.* National Report of the United Republic of Tanzania. International Conference on Education. 42nd Session, Geneva 1990. Dar es Salaam.

Ministry of Education and Culture (1992a). *The Development of Education: 1990–1992.* National Report of the United Republic of Tanzania. International Conference on Education. 43rd Session, Geneva 1992. Dar es Salaam.

Ministry of Education and Culture (1992b). *Basic Education Statistics in Tanzania (BEST) 1987–1991.* Dar es Salaam.

Ministry of Education and Culture (1992c). *Basic Education Statistics in Tanzania (BEST) 1991 Regional Data.* Dar es Salaam.

Ministry of Education and Culture (1993). *Basic Education Statistics in Tanzania (BEST) 1992.* Dar es Salaam.

Ministry of Education and Culture (1994). *Basic Education Statistics in Tanzania (BEST) 1989–1991.* Dar es Salaam.

Ministry of National Education (1976a). *Applied Sciences. Agriculture, Home Economics biased schools, Home Economics non-biased schools, Technical Subjects, Fine Art & Light Crafts. Volume V: Secondary School Syllabuses.* Dar es Salaam.

Ministry of National Education (1976b). *Social Sciences. Geography, History, Economics. Secondary School Syllabuses.* Dar es Salaam.

Ministry of National Education (1980). *A Geography Syllabus for Diploma in Education Course.* Institute of Education. Dar es Salaam.

Mokhtar, G. (ed.) (1990). *General History of Africa. II. Ancient Civilisations of Africa.* Abridged edition. Unesco International Scientific Committee for drafting of a General History of Africa. Unesco. London: James Currey Ltd and University of California Press.

Mosha, H.J. (1990). Twenty Years after Education for Self-Reliance: A Critical review. *International Journal of Educational Development,* Vol. 10, No. 1, pp. 59–67.

Mrazek, R. (1993). *Alternative Paradigms in Environmental Education Research.* Monographs in Environmental Education and Environmental Studies. Volume VIII. The North American Association for Environmental education, Troy, Ohio.

Mucunguzi, P. (1995). Environmental Education in the Formal Sector of Education in Uganda. *Environmental Education Research,* Vol. 1, No. 2, pp. 233–240.

National Environment Management Council (1994). Tanzania National Conservation Strategy for Sustainable Development (National Environmental Management Council). Proposal January 1994.

Ndunguru, S. (1989). Environmental Education. Unpublished paper by the Chairman of National Environment Management Council, Dar es Salaam.

Negash, T. (1996). *Rethinking Education in Ethiopia.* Nordiska Afrikainstitutet Uppsala. Stockholm: Almqvist & Wiksell International.

Neuman, D. (1987). *The origin of arithmetic skills: A phenomenographic approach.* Göteborg: Acta Universitatis Gothenburgensis.

Nkonoki, S.R. (1978). Achievements, Problems and Tasks a Ahead in Implementing Education for Self-Reliance. *The Tanzania Educational Journal,* No. 16.

Nshubernuki, L. (1986). Conservation Attitudes of Schoolchildren in the Kondoa District of Tanzania. *Environmental Conservation,* Vol. 13, No. 2, pp. 161–164.

Nyerere, J.K. (1965). Agriculture is the Basis for Development. In Nyerere, J.K. (1968). *Freedom and Socialism. Uhuru na Ujamaa.* A selection from writings and speeches 1965–1967. Dar es Salaam: Oxford University Press.

Nyerere, J.K. (1966). The Role of Universities. In Nyerere, J.K. (1968). *Freedom and Socialism. Uhuru na Ujamaa.* A selection from writings and speeches 1965–1967. Dar es Salaam: Oxford University Press.

Nyerere, J.K. (1967a). Education for Self-Reliance. In Nyerere, J.K. (1968). *Freedom and Socialism. Uhuru na Ujamaa.* A selection from writings and speeches 1965–1967. Dar es Salaam: Oxford University Press.

Nyerere, J.K. (1967b). Progress in Schools. In Nyerere, J.K. (1968). *Freedom and Socialism. Uhuru na Ujamaa.* A selection from writings and speeches 1965–1967. Dar es Salaam: Oxford University Press.

Nyerere, J.K. (1967c). The Arusha Declaration. In Nyerere, J.K. (1968). *Freedom and Socialism. Uhuru na Ujamaa.* A selection from writings and speeches 1965–1967. Dar es Salaam: Oxford University Press.

O'Donoghue, R. & Taylor, J. (1988). Towards participant-centered resource development in Environmental Education. *Southern African Journal of Environmental Education,* No. 7, pp. 3–5.

O'Donoghue, R.B. & McNaught, C. (1991). Environmental Education: the development of a curriculum through 'grass-roots' reconstructive action. *International Journal of Science Education,* Vol. 13, No. 4, pp. 391–404.

Odora Hoppers, C.A. (1998). *Structural Violence as a Constraint to African Policy Formation in the 1990s. Repositioning Education in International Relations.* Studies in Comparative and International Education 43. Stockholm: Institute of International Education. Stockholm University.

Odora, C.A. (1992). *Educating African Girls in a Context of Patriarchy and Transformation.* A Theoretical and Conceptual Analysis. Master's Degree Studies from the Institute of International Education No 7. Stockholm: Institute of International Education. Stockholm University.

Orr, D.W. (1992). *Ecological Literacy.* Education and the Transition to a Postmodern World. State University of New York Press. Albany, U.S.

Othman, H. (1995). The Union with Zanzibar. In Legum, C. & Mmari, G. (eds.) *Mwalimu. The Influence of Nyerere.* London Britain-Tanzania Society in association with James Currey, London, Mkuki na Nyota, Dar es Salaam and Africa World Press, Trenton.

Palme, M. (1993). *The Meaning of School Repetition and Drop Out in the Mozambican Primary School.* Education Division Documents No 60. Stockholm: Sida.

Palmer, J.A. (1993). Development of Concern for the Environment and Formative Experiences of Educators, *The Journal of Environmental Education.* Vol. 24, No. 3, pp. 26–30.

Payne, P. (1997). Embodiment and Environmental Education. *Environmental Education Research,* Vol. 3, No. 2, pp. 133–153.

Pomerantz, G.A. (1990–91). Evaluation of Natural Resource Education Materials: Implication for resource Management. *The Journal of Environmental Education.* Vol. 22, No. 2, pp. 16–23.

Pope, M. (1993). Anticipating Teacher Thinking. In Day, C., Calderhead, J. and Denicolo, P. (eds.) (1993). *Research on Teacher Thinking: Understanding Professional Development.* London: The Falmer Press.

Ramsey, J.M. (1993). The Effects of Issue Investigation and Action Training on Eight-Grade Students' Environmental Behavior. *The Journal of Environmental Education.* Vol. 24, No. 3, pp. 31–36.

Riddel, R.C. (1996). Aid Dependency. In *Aid Dependency. Causes, symptoms and remedies.* Stockholm: Swedish International Development Cooperation Agency.

Roberts, D. A. (1982). Developing the Concept of 'Curriculum Emphases' in Science Education. *Science Education* 66 (2): 243–260.

Roberts, D.A. (1988). What Counts as Science Education? In Fensham, P. *Development of Dilemmas in Science Education.* London: Falmer Press.

Robertson, A. (1994) : Toward a Constructivist Research in Environmental Education. *The Journal of Environmental Education,* 1994, Vol. 25, No. 2, pp. 21–31.

Robertson, A.S. (1995). *Student-teachers' Conceptualisations of Environment and Human-nature Relationships.* Unpublished PhD thesis. Department of Mathematics and Science Education, Ottawa.

Robottom, I. & Hart, PP. (1993). Towards a meta-research agenda in science and environmental education. *International Journal of Science Education*, 1993, Vol. 15, No. 5, pp. 591–605.

Robottom, I. & Hart, PP. (1995). Behaviorist EE Research: Environmentalism as Individualism. *The Journal of Environmental Education* 1995, Vol. 26, No. 2. pp. 5–9.

Robottom, I. (1987). Two paradigms of professional development in environmental education. *Environmentalist.* 7 (4), pp. 291–298.

Robottom, I. (1992). Matching the Purposes of Environmental Education with Consistent Approaches to research and Professional Development. *Australian Journal of Environmental Education,* Aug. 1992, Vol. 8, pp. 133–146.

Roth, C. E. (1992). *Environmental Literacy. Its Roots, Evolution and Directions in the 1990s.* ERIC ED 348 235. ERIC/Datafil Educational Resources Information Center Boston Silver Platt 1975–

Roy-Campbell, Z.M. (1991). The Politics of Education in Tanzania: From Colonialism to Liberalisation. In Campbell, H., Stein, H. (ed.). *The IMF and Tanzania. The Dynamics of Liberalisation.* Harare: Southern Africa Political Economy Series (SAPES) Trust.

Samoff, J. (1990). 'Modernizing' a Socialist Vision: Education in Tanzania. In Carnoy, M. & Samoff, J. (1990). *Education and Social Transition in the Third World.* Princeton, New Jersey: Princeton University Press.

Samoff, J. (1991). The Façade of Precision in Education Data and Statistics: A Troubling Example from Tanzania. *The Journal of Modern African Studies*, Vol. 29, No. 4, pp. 669–689.

SIDA (1993). *Tanzania. Landinformation.* Stockholm: Swedish International Development Authority.

Sida (1996a). *Aid Dependency. Causes, symptoms and remedies.* Stockholm: Swedish International Development Cooperation Agency.

Sida (1996b). *Country Analysis Tanzania.* Department for East and West Africa. Stockholm: Swedish International Development Cooperation Agency.

Simmons, D. (1993). Facilitating Teachers' Use of Natural Areas: Perceptions of Environmental Education Opportunities. *The Journal of Environmental Education.* Vol. 24, No. 3, pp. 8–16.

Simpson, E.J. (1966). *The classification of educational objectives, psychomotor domain.* Urbana Ill.: University of Illinois.

Smith-Sebast, N.J. and Fortner, R.W. (1994). The Environmental Action Internal Control Index. *The Journal of Environmental Education.* Vol. 25, No. 4, pp. 23–29.

Sobhan, R. (1996). Aid Dependency and Donor Policy. The case of Tanzania with lessons from Bangladesh's experience. In *Aid Dependency. Causes, symptoms and remedies.* Stockholm. Swedish International Development Cooperation Agency.

Spork, H. (1992). Environmental Education: A Mismatch Between Theory and Practice. *Australian Journal of Environmental Education.* Vol. 8, pp. 147–166.

Stake, R. E. (1998). Case Studies. In Denzin, N.K. & Lincoln, Y.S. (Eds.) (1998). *Strategies of Qualitative Inquiry.* Thousand Oaks: Sage Publications.

Sterling, S. (1992). *Coming of Age—A Short History of Environmental Education (to 1989).* National Association for Environmental Education (UK). University of Wolverhamton.

Sutherland, D.S. and Ham, S.H. (1992). Child-to-Parent Transfer of Environmental Ideology in Costa Rican Families: An Ethnographic Case Study. *The Journal of Environmental Education.* Vol. 23, No. 3, pp. 9–16.

Svendsen, K.E. (1995). Development Strategy & Crisis Management. In Legum, C. &

Mmari, G. (eds.) *Mwalimu. The Influence of Nyerere.* London: Britain-Tanzania Society in association with James Currey, London, Mkuki na Nyota, Dar es Salaam and Africa World Press, Trenton.

Säljö, R. (1996). Minding action—Conceiving of the world versus participating in cultural practices. In Dall'Alba, G. & Hasselgren, B. *Reflections on Phenomenography. Toward a Methodology?* Göteborg Studies in Educational Sciences 109. Acta Universitatis Gothenburgensis.

Sörlin, S. (red.) (1992). *Humanekologi.* Stockholm: Carlssons bokförlag.

Tanganyika African National Union (1976). Proceedings of the National Executive Committee Meeting held at Musoma, November 1974. Directive on the Implementation of 'Education For Self-Reliance'. In *The Africa Review*, vol. 6, no. 1, 1976.

Taylor, R.J. (1997). *SHARE-NET. A Case Study of Environmental Education Resource Material Development in a Risk Society.* Unpublished Ph. D. thesis, Rodhes University, Republic of South Africa.

Temu, E.B. (1995). *Successful Schools in Tanzania. A Case Study of Academic and Production Programs in Primary and Secondary Schools.* Studies in Comparative and International Education 34. Stockholm: Institute of International Education. Stockholm University.

Thompson, A.R. (1981). *Education and Development in Africa.* London: The Macmillan Press Ltd.

Treaty on Environmental Education for Sustainable Societies and Global Responsibility (1992). Paper presented to the plenary session of the International NGO Forum, Rio de Janeiro, Brazil, June 9.

Tyler, R. (1949). *Basic Principles of Curriculum and Instruction.* Chicago: University of Chicago Press.

Uljens, M. (1989). *Fenomenografi—forskning om uppfattningar.* Lund: Studentlitteratur.

UNESCO (1978). *Intergovernmental Conference on Environmental Education: Tbilisi (USSR),* 14–26 October 1977. Final Report. UNESCO Paris.

UNESCO (1989). *Education in Tanzania.* Volume I and II. Report No 135 and 136. Paris.

UNESCO (1991). *Education for All: Purpose and Context.* Monograph 1. Roundtable Themes I. World Conference on Education for All, Jomtien, Thailand. France.

UNESCO (1993). *World Education Report.*

UNESCO (1997). *Educating for a Sustainable Future: A Transdisciplinary Vision for Concerted Action.* November 1997. EPD.97/CONF.401/CLD.1. http://unesdoc.unesco.org/ulis/ged.html (March 1999)

United Republic of Tanzania (1991). *National Report for the 1992 United Nations Conference on Environment and Development (UNCED).* Dar es Salaam.

United Republic of Tanzania (1993). *The Tanzania Education System for the 21st Century.* Report of the Task Force. Ministry of Education and Culture & Ministry of Science Technology and Higher Education.

United Republic of Tanzania (1995). *Tanzania Education and Training Policy.* Dar es Salaam. Ministry of Education and Culture.

van Rensburg, E.J. (1995). *Environmental Education and Research in Southern Africa.* Unpublished Ph.D. thesis. Rhodes University, Republic of South Africa.

van Rensburg, P. (1974). *Report from Swaneng Hill. Education and Employment in an African Country.* Uppsala: The Dag Hammarsköld Foundation.

Vinke, J. (1992). Analytical overview of actors and approaches in environmental education in developing countries. Paper. OECD Development Centre, Paris. March 1992.

Walker, D.F., Soltis, J.F. (1986). *Curriculum and Aims.* New York: Teachers College Press.

Walker, K. (1997). Challenging Critical Theory in Environmental Education. *Environmental Education Research*, Vol. 3, No. 2, pp. 155–162.

Wals, A.E. & Alblas, A.H. (1997). School-based Research and Development of Environmental Education: a case study. *Environmental Education Research*, Vol. 3, No. 3, pp. 253–267.

Wals, A.E.J. (1993): Critical Phenomenology and Environmental Education Research. In Mrazek, R. (1993): *Alternative Paradigms in Environmental Education Research.* Monographs in Environmental Education and Environmental Studies. Volume VIII. The North American Association for Environmental Education, Troy, Ohio.

Weitzman, E.A. & Miles, M.B. (1995). *Computer Programs for Qualitative Data Analysis.* A Software Sourcebook. California: SAGE Publications.

Wigblad, R. (1997). *Karta över vetenskapliga samband.* Orientering i den samhällsvetenskapliga metoddjungeln. Lund: Studentlitteratur.

Wisara ya Elimu ya Taifa (1969, reprinted 1977). *Muthasari ya Mafundisho ya shule za Msingi (madarasa I–VII). 6. Maarifa ya Nyumbani*, pp. 75–162. Chapa ya Nne, 1977. Dar es Salaam.

Wisara ya Elimu ya Taifa (1977?). *Muhtasari ya Mafundisho ya Shule za Msingi: Elimu ya Siasa I–VII, Historia IV–VII, Jografia III–VII, Sanaa na Ufundi I–VII.* Dar es Salaam.

Wisara ya Elimu ya Taifa (1980). *Muthasari wa Malezi ya Taifa Stashaha*da. Dar es Salaam.

Wisara ya Elimu ya Taifa (1982). *Muhtasari wa Sayansi kwa Shule za Msingi.* Darasa III–VII. Dar es Salaam.

Wisara ya Elimu ya Taifa (1982). *Muhtasari ya Mafundisho ya Kilimo kwa Shule za Msingi.* Dar es Salaam.

Wizara ya Elimu (1984). *Jamhuru ya muungano wa Tanzania.* Mfumo wa Elimu Tanzania.

Wizara ya Elimu (1986). *Kiongozi cha Mkaguzi wa Shule.* Dar es Salaam.

World Bank (1990). *Staff Appraisal Report. The United Republic of Tanzania. Education Planning and Rehabilitation Project.* Report No 7998-TA. Southern Africa Department. Population and Human Resources Division. (Restricted distribution document—received by hand at the World Bank office in Dar es Salaam.).

World Bank (1991). *United Republic of Tanzania. Teachers and the Financing of Education.* Confidential Report No. 9863-TA. Southern Africa Department. Population and Human Resources Division.

World Bank (1995). *Tanzania. Social Sector Review.* Confidential Report No. 14039-TA. Washington DC 20433.

World Commission on Environment and Development (1987). *Our Common Future.* Oxford: Oxford University Press. ('The Brundtland Report').

Wort, M.A.A. (1998). *Distance Education and the Training of Primary School Teachers in Tanzania.* Uppsala: Acta Universitatis Upsaliensis. Uppsala Studies in Education 74.

Yin, R.K. (1994). *Case Study Research. Design and Methods.* 2nd ed. Applied Social Research Methods Series. Volume 5. Thousand Oakes: SAGE Publications.

Yinger, R. and Hendricks-Lee, M. (1993). Working Knowledge in Teaching. In Day, C., Calderhead, J. and Denicolo, P. (eds.) (1993). *Research on Teacher Thinking: Understanding Professional Development.* London: The Falmer Press.

Zeichner, K. M. (1994). Research on Teacher Thinking and Different Views of Reflective Practice in Teaching and Teacher Education. In Carlgren, I., Handal, G. and Vaage, S. (eds.) (1993). *Teachers' Minds and Actions: Research on Teacher Thinking and Practice.* London: The Falmer Press.

Zint, M. (1996). *Science education as a means for improving Great Lakes citizens' risk decision making skills and predicting teachers' intention to incorporate risk education: A comparison of the theories of researched action, planned behaviour and trying.* Ph.D. thesis. Michigan State University.

Östman, L. (1995). *Socialisation och mening. No-utbildning som politiskt och miljömoraliskt problem.* Uppsala: Acta Universitatis Upsaliensis. Uppsala Studies in Education 61.

Personal communication

Johansson, Barbro (1994). Experiences from Tanzania 1946–1985. Former teacher and headmistress. Former MP for Bukoba and Mwanza 1961–65 and 1980–85. Honorary doctor at the University of Gothenburg, Sweden 1968. Head of Section, Adult Education, Ministry of Education, DSM 1973–75. Counsellor of the Tanzanian Embassy in Stockholm 1970–73. Member of the Presidential Commission on Education up to year 2000 1980–82. Personal communication in April 1994.

Appendix

APPENDIX 1
Examples of categorisation in Table 1, Chapter 1

Table 1 a: Technical interest:
A basic orientation towards controlling and managing the environment through rule-following action based upon empirically grounded laws. Congruent with the *empirical-analytical sciences*.
Key word: *causal explanation*.
Education for *management and control*.

Issue: Field-based instructions' effects on students' conceptions (Lisowski & Disinger 1991).
Aims: To explore the nature of ideas and beliefs held by students. Method: Development and use of a student ecology assessment instrument. Results: Prior knowledge is a significant predictor of post-test scores; gains in conceptual understanding are positively related to instructional emphasis and field-based programmes in the sciences are effective in assisting students' understanding and retention of selected ecological concepts.

Issue: Transfer of knowledge from child to parent (Sutherland & Ham 1991).
Aim: To examine the transfer of environmental information and ideologies from Costa Rican children to their parents. Method: Ethnographic data collection. Field pre-test and post-test. Result: Transfer is generally rare and situation specific.

Issue: Assessment of teachers' attitudes (Lane, Wilkie, Champeu and Sivik 1994).
Aim: An assessment of Wisconsin teachers' perceived competencies in attitudes toward and class time devoted to teaching about the environment. Method: valid and reliable survey instrument was developed and mailed to 1,545 randomly selected elementary and secondary education teachers. Results: Lack of training in environmental education is a major reason teachers do not infuse environmental education concepts. Teaching was done about the environment.

Issue: Definition of variables for responsible environmental behaviour (Cottrell & Graefe 1997).
Aim: To examine predictors of general responsible environmental behaviour and specific environmental behaviour, indicated by the percentage of raw sewage discharged by boaters. Method: Mail survey that included a number of measures drawn from prior studies of environmental and boating behaviour. Result: Eight predictors explained 46 percent of the total variance. Three background variables education, boat length and years of boat experience were predictors of specific behaviour. Specific issue category (knowledge of water pollution issues etc.) of variables contributed most to the variance.

Table 1 b: Practical interest:
A fundamental interest in understanding the environment through interaction based upon a consensual interpretation of meaning. Congruent with the *hermeneutic* concept of application (promoting knowledge and action which is a subjective process).
Key word: *understanding*.
Education for *environmental awareness and interpretation*.

Issue: Teachers' perceptions of nature (Simmons 1993).
Aim: To explore classrooms teachers' perception of nature and their association to suitable educational activities. Method: Interviews with 39 teachers in Chicago. Result:

Responses are based on past experiences or expectations and that teachers need training to learn what can be accomplished in different settings.

Issue: Student-teachers' conceptualisation of the environment and human-nature relationships (Robertson 1995).
Aim: To explore student-teachers' pre-instructional perspectives on the environment and environmental education. Method: Interviews and a phenomenographic approach. Results: Students' pre-instructional beliefs exhibit important elements of conceptions of environment and environmental education. Their conceptualisations traverse a range of eco-philosophical perspectives.

Issue: Science education as a political and environmental-ethical problem (Östman 1995). PhD thesis.
Aim: to develop a content analysis, based on curriculum theory, of the political and environmental-ethical dimensions of education. Method: text analyses of textbooks, in-service training literature and syllabi. Result: Science education in Sweden can be characterised as scientific-rational, with two selective traditions: the academic and the romantic. Science education during the 1980s can be seen as an education for the elite.

Issue: A phenomenological study of the thinking of children and young people about environment (Alerby 1998). PhD thesis.
Aim: To clarify the way in which young people think about our environment, based on their experiences. Method: phenomenological analysis of drawings of children 7 to 16 years of age and interviews with a smaller group. Result: The children's thinking is multi-faceted. Four themes of thoughts were reflected in the drawings and eight in the interviews.

Table 1 c: Emancipatory interest:

A fundamental interest in emancipation and empowerment to engage in autonomous action arising out of authentic, *critical* insights into the social construction of human society (through processes of self-reflection).
Key word: *reflection.*
Education for *sustainability.*

Issue: Research issues in Southern Africa (van Rensburg 1995). Ph.D. thesis.
Aim: To identify research priorities in environmental education within the context of Southern Africa. Method: Action research. Result: Research priorities as three orientations with main focus on a reflective perspective in and on environmental education.

Issue: Reflective practice (Fien & Rawling 1996).
Aim: A case study of a professional development programme for environmental education at Griffith University in Queensland, Australia. Method: Participatory research and critical reflection. Result: The study revealed that the students derived a number of benefits from developing their reflective practice skills, including heightening political awareness, a strong sense of the influences and limitations of the social context on their ideas and environmental education practices, increased self-confidence and a desire to continue in a reflective practice group.

Issue: Teacher action development (Wals & Alblas 1997).
Aim: To develop the environmental dimension of teachers' teaching.
Method: By critically examining their own teaching practice and materials and in collaboration with an external researcher, four teachers from a secondary agricultural school used action-research model . Result: Jointly they became engaged in a process of problematising their own teaching practice, analysing key issues of mutual concern, generating potential solutions, confronting the selected solution with the everyday practice of teaching and evaluating the results.

Issue: Teachers as learners in the context of their environmental education (Axelsson 1997). PhD thesis.
Aim: to find out and analyse the process within the project of Environment and School Initiatives, based on how the teachers change their teaching approaches. Method: Action research. Result: Empowerment of students and environmental knowledge are seen as equally important for learning for sustainable development. This demands changes in content repertoires which do not in a similar way lead to changes in teaching repertoires.

APPENDIX 2
Chronology of Education and Politics in Tanzania. Adapted from Samoff (1990) and extended

Year	Economy, Policy, Society	Education
1961	Independence. Three-Year Plan for Economic Development.	University College, Dar es Salaam opened.
1962		Initial decolonialisation of curriculum.
1964	Army mutiny. Union with Zanzibar—First Five-Year Plan (FFYP) for Economic and Social Development.	FFYP major emphasis placed on high-level skills training by the educational system, particularly secondary schools and the university. Secondary school fees abolished.
1965	One-Party Interim Constitution adopted.	Swahili becomes language of instruction in primary schools. Phasing out of Standard VIII and Standard IV examination and merging of upper and lower primary schools begun.
1966		University students demonstrate against required National Service.
1967	Arusha Declaration: clarifies and strengthens Tanzania's commitment to Ujamaa socialism; nationalisations; leadership code. Creation of Permanent Labour Tribunal, limiting workers' ability to strike and negotiate contracts.	Education for Self-Reliance Policy: emphasis on mass education, particularly primary schools—both increasing enrolment and changing curriculum to provide skills for rural agricultural development strategy. Phase out of Standard VIII completed. National Literacy Test: 69 % illiterate.
1968		Entrance examination to Standard V eliminated. UNESCO/UNDP-supported World Oriented Adult Literacy Project—Mwanza Functional Literacy Project—initiated.
1969	Second Five-Year Plan (SFYP).	SFYP directs that all primary schools will become adult education centres and directs that the main emphasis of adult education will be on rural development. National Education Act: government assumes control of all schooling. First mass education campaign: Plan is to Chose.
1970	Workers' Councils established in every public corporation/enterprise.	Party declares 1970 Adult Education Year. Second mass education campaign: The Choice is Yours. University of Dar es Salaam created.
1971		Six Districts Literacy Campaign TANU 15th Biennial Conference: Resolution 23 calls for eradication of illiteracy in the next four years and directs that worker education be carried out within working hours. Third mass education campaign: A Time for Rejoicing. National Forms IV and VI examination replace Cambridge examinations.
1972	Decentralisation policy adopted.	National Literacy Campaign planned for three years. Fourth mass education campaign: Politics is Agriculture.
1973		Primary school fees abolished. TANU 16th Biennial Conference: Resolution 29 declares that students in classes VI and VII should be taught skills directly useful for work in villages. National Examination council established. Fifth mass education campaign: Man is Health.

Year	Economy, Policy, Society	Education
1974	TANU National Executive Committee (Musoma) Resolution. Villagisation campaigns.	Musoma Resolution directed accelerated progress toward universal primary education (by 1977), elimination of illiteracy (by 1980), and self-sufficiency in high-level skills (by 1980); instituted vocational orientation in all secondary schools; required village or factory work experience and recommendation and party endorsement for admission to university.
1975	Third Five-Year Plan postponed.	Folk Development Colleges established. Sixth mass education campaign: Food is Life and Death. National Literacy Test: 39 percent illiteracy.
1976	Third Five-Year Plan.	Universal primary education accelerated. Adult literacy progress extended and intensified.
1977	Chama Cha Mapinduzu (CCM) formed. Collapse of the East African Community.	National Literacy Test: 27 percent illiteracy.
1978	War with Uganda (1978–79).	
1980		Presidential Education Commission (PEC) formed to evaluate past nineteen years of education and plan the next twenty.
1981		National Literacy test: 21 percent illiteracy.
1982		PEC reports to president and party.
1983		National Literacy Test: 15 percent illiteracy.
1984	Cost Recovery Programme.	Shifting part of the responsibility for primary school construction to the communities, introduction of school fees in primary schools and secondary school, purchase of textbooks and exercise books by the students and self-reliance projects at all levels. Education for manpower development. Sokoine University of Agriculture opened.
1985	Ali Hassan Mwinyi succeeds Julius K. Nyerere as President.	Initial implementation of approved recommendations of PEC, including introduction of secondary school fees, plan to double the number of government secondary schools, and encouragement of private secondary schools. Emphasis on academic, vocational, science and technical sectors.
1986	Economic Recovery Programme	Development of a market-driven society in which public and private initiatives would be blended. General cuts in the extent of state expenditure and economic activity. National Literacy test: 9.6 percent illiteracy.
1989	Enhanced Structural Adjustment Programme.	Continued development of a market-driven society and general cuts in the extent of state expenditure and economic activity.
1990	The Task Force on Education System for the 21st Century formed.	
1993		The Task force reports.
1995		The Tanzania Education and Training Policy (TETP) formed. Increased role of the private sector, liberalisation, partnerships in provision of education, solutions to be found at local levels.

APPENDIX 3

Comparison between Education for Self-Reliance, Tanzania Education and Training Policy and internationally accepted aims of Environmental Education

Education for Self-Reliance, (1967).	Tanzania Education and Training Policy, (1995) – general aims.	Environmental education (EE), internationally accepted aims.
The aim is socialism based on equality and respect for human dignity, sharing of resources which are produced by communal efforts, work by everyone and exploitation by no one.	Education for development of the society. Human dignity and human rights. Individual initiative.	EE is not neutral but is value based – it is an act for social transformation (Treaty 1992).
Using resources to the best advantages.	Sustainable development.	Sustainable use of species or ecosystems (IUCN 1980).
Social goal of commitment to the community – spirit of co-operation. Schools (especially primary schools) should be an integral part of the community/village.	Increased power for local authorities and parents.	Emphasise local, regional, national and global perspectives and the need for co-operation to solve environmental problems (UNESCO 1978, Tbilisi Declaration). EE should empower all peoples and promote opportunities for grassroot democratic change and participation (Treaty 1992).
Good farmers who are able to think for themselves, to make judgements on issues affecting them. Implement decisions in the light of local circumstances. Learn basic principles of modern agriculture and adapt them to solve their own problems. For a predominant rural economy.	Self-Reliance.	EE must consider the economical, social and ecological realities in each society (UNESCO 1978, Tbilisi Declaration). EE should be grounded in critical and innovative thinking in any place or time, promoting the transformation and construction of the society (Treaty 1992).
An inquiring mind.	A inquiring mind.	Develop critical thinking and problem-solving skills. (UNESCO 1978, Tbilisi Declaration).
Pupils' participating in planning is very important.		Involve students in decision-making and the planning of their studies (UNESCO 1978, Tbilisi Declaration).

Education for Self-Reliance, (1967).	Tanzania Education and Training Policy, (1995) – general aims.	Environmental education (EE), internationally accepted aims.
Theory and practice should be joined in the school subjects as well as in the practical (farm) work. Every teacher and every pupil is also a farmer. Pupils should do the cleaning in school and other service duties – both boys and girls. Self-reliance as the basis for development. Through self-reliance projects children contribute to the upkeep of the school. Learning by doing. Learning by experience.		Use diverse learning approaches to teaching/learning, especially practical activities and first-hand experience (Tbilisi Declaration) View EE as an interdisciplinary life-long experience (UNESCO 1978, Tbilisi Declaration) EE must integrate knowledge, skills, values, attitudes and actions. It should convert every opportunity into an educational experience for sustainable societies (Treaty 1992).
Learn judgement of the appropriateness of new methods and tools so that they do not lead to rapid destruction of land (including properties of fertilisers, their use and limitations, proper grazing practises, terracing and soil conservation methods).		Develop an understanding of the symptoms and root causes of environmental problems (UNESCO 1978, Tbilisi Declaration).

APPENDIX 4

Primary School—Agriculture Syllabus

The environmental education components are found in the topics of soil science and natural resources in Standard (Std) IV–VII:

Objectives related to environmental education in the topic of soil science in the agriculture syllabus, Std IV–VII (issued in 1982, reprinted in 1990)

Soil Science objectives in Std IV	In Std V	In Std VI	In Std VII
1. Understand various types of soils and their characteristics	Know micro- and macro-elements	Know various methods used to fertilise soil and to maintain its fertility	Know causes and disadvantages of soil erosion
2. Recognise sand soil, clay and loam soil	List both micro- and macro-elements	Use these methods at home and school	Know various types of soil erosion
3.	Recognise signs of deficiency of NPK in plants	Uses and how to put on various types of fertilisers	Know methods of controlling soil erosion and use them

Objectives related to environmental education in the topic of natural science in the agriculture syllabus, Std IV–VII (issued in 1982, reprinted in 1990)

Natural Science objectives in Std IV	in Std V	in Std VI	in Std VII
1. name the meaning and advantage of forests	understand various types of fishes and their advantages	know types and advantages of bees	select the best method to keep bees
2. know various types of fruit trees	list four advantages of fish	distinguish between the three types of bees	make a beehive
3. prepare a nursery, grow seeds, plant seedlings and care for them	know types of ponds		collect honey
4.	select an appropriate site for a pond		
5.	dig out and maintain a fish pond		
6.	keep fish and preserve fish		

Primary School—Domestic Science Syllabus

Topics, objectives related to environmental education in the domestic science syllabus, Std IV–VII (issued in 1969, reprinted in 1977)

Standard	Topic
Standard I	Cleanliness of the surroundings. In the classroom and in the school compound. How to keep a garden. Weeding and watering of plants. Toilets. How to use and clean toilets.
Standard II	Cleanliness of the surroundings. The school compound. Gardening. Planting of seedlings, watering and weeding. How to prepare the seedbeds.Cleaning of the classroom. Cleaning of toilets. Cleaning of houses in villages and towns. How to do it and what to use. How to remove rubbish . How to weed the gardens and take care of them. How to clean the kitchen.
Standard III	Cleaning of the place where they live. Stores, kitchens, dining rooms and the surroundings. Drinking water and its uses. Diseases. Types of diseases carried by water. Teutaneus, malaria, cholera, eyes diseases, bilharzia.
Standard IV	Cleaning of the kitchen. Health. How to avoid flies. Mosquitos, how to prevent breeding. Rats, how to get rid of them. Small insects (the use of DDT is mentioned)
Standard V	General cleaning of a house. Cleaning of surroundings. Where to put rubbish in the villages and towns (digging of pit).Cleaning of dustbins. Cleaning of bath houses. Water. Importance, how water is contaminated. Boiling of water. How to keep water. Garden. Preparation of gardens. Organisation of pupils' gardenwork.
Standard VI	Toilets and bathing places. Importance in schools and villages. Types of toilets. Where to build them. How to avoid smells and how to clean the toilets. How to dig pit latrines. Prevention of flies, mosquitos. Clean the houses everyday. Daily inspection of school surroundings. The use of kerosene and hot water, mosquito coils, DDT, fire. Storing of food in a proper dayway. Cleaning of beds. Cleaning of houses.
Standard VII	No topics that can be said to be related to environmental education.

Primary School—Geography Syllabus

Topics, objectives related to environmental education in the geography syllabus, Std IV–VII (issued during the 1970s)

Topic	Objective, procedures and activities
Std IV Agriculture	To enable the students to know how man can use various ways to upgrade his life and his economy by using the environment appropriately.
Std IV National parks	To enable the students to realise the importance of national game reserves as one of the ways to help our economy. Natural vegetation in these reserves. Various animals that attract tourists. Importance of these reserves for the nation.
Std VII Tanzania, Agriculture	Soil, types of soil, problems of soil (erosion), methods of soil conservation. Students should practice various methods of conserving soil in their school farm.
Std VII, Tanzania, Forests	Natural forests like Buyungu, Lungonya and Nvido. Artificial forests such as Mtibwa, Matogoro, Sao Hill, Meru etc. Various activities of planting and conserving trees. Advantages of trees/forests. Project: Pupils should participate in planting trees and conserving them in school and in their village.

Topics, objectives related to environmental education in the geography syllabus, Std IV–VII (issued in 1990)

Topic	Objective, procedures and activities
Std IV Soils	Lead pupils to observe and differentiate different soil samples. Lead them to identify what crops grow on different types of soil. Lead them to mention factors of soil erosion. Lead pupils to outline the different methods to conserve soil and control soil erosion.
Std IV Fisheries	Lead the pupils to discuss bad fishing methods. Conservation of fishing grounds.
Std V Mining	To show how mining activities in some areas affect the environment.
Std VII Natural vegetation	To discuss environmental destruction. To be able to discuss methods applied to conservation of natural vegetation. To be involved in a project of tree planting activity in the school or the village.

Primary School—Science Syllabus

Topics, objectives related to environmental education in the science syllabus, Std III–VII (issued in 1982)

Topic	Objective, procedures and activities
Std III General Hygiene	Pupils should know the importance of clean food, water and environment.
Std IV Soils	Soil formation, soil composition (air, water and living things), types of soil: clay, sand and loam, typical characteristics of each type of soil.
Std IV Diseases	Types, how diseases are spread, prevention of diseases (students should practice to clean environment, boil drinking water and to destroy breeding places of mosquitoes).
Std V and VI Soil and soil erosion	Elements that play a part in soil formation (temperature, plants, animals). Definition of soil erosion, types of soil erosion, disadvantages of soil erosion.
Std VI Soil	Methods of preventing soil erosion: Terracing, planting trees, good agricultural practices etc., fertilisers.
Std VII Ecology	Environmental management, how living things manage their environment, how living organisms interact with their environment, the inter-relationship amongst animals e.g. a lion and an antelope, inter-relationships amongst plants, plant-animal relationship.

APPENDIX 5
Secondary School—Agriculture Syllabus
Environmental education components in agriculture, syllabus issued 1976

In Form I
The topic Introduction to Agriculture has the sub-topics:
1 b) Physical Environment of Agriculture in Tanzania (Ministry of National Education: Applied Sciences pp. 5):
— Rainfall distribution.
— Altitude and temperature.
— Soil types.
— Ecological zones.
3) Soil Types and Classification (Ministry of National Education: Applied Sciences pp. 7):
— Classification of soils by physical characteristics
— Soil formation
— Soil properties and constituents:
  Soil constituents
  Soil texture
  Soil structure

In the topic Crop Science Production (Ministry of National Education: Applied Sciences pp. 14) there were such components as:

7 e) Principles of crop production: choice of suitable land; timely land preparation; soil conservation, timely planting, spacing or thinning; manure and fertiliser application; mulching, weeding and weed control; crop rotations; timely harvesting; processing, storage; pests, vermin and disease control, diversification. Stress use of recommended seeds; discuss various pests and disease control methods: cultural, biological, chemical, physical (e.g. control of army worms).

In Form II
The topic Soil Science (Ministry of National Education: Applied Sciences pp. 21–23):
1) Soil fertility, productivity and plant nutrition:
— Basic plant nutrients.
— Functions of mineral elements in plants.
— Loss of soil fertility: natural and artificial causes; effect on yield returns.
— Manures and fertilisers and their role in replenishing soil fertility:
  Meaning and importance of manures and fertilisers.
  The importance of preservation of organic matter in relation to C/N ratio.
  The carbon and nitrogen cycles and how they affect soil fertility.
  Organic manures: green manures, poultry manures, kraal or boma manures, compost manures.
  Inorganic fertiliser: nitrogenous, phosphatic and potassic fertilisers.
  Minor and trace elements.
  Fertiliser storage.
— Soil conservation.
  Basic importance of conservation of soil fertility.
  Various methods used in conserving soil.
  Mention methods used in soil conservation: strip farming, terracing, bunds, cut-off drains, grassed water ways, contour farming and ridging, use of cropping systems as control measures: forests, rotations, special grasses and mulching, legal enforcement of erosion control methods. Meaning and importance of manures and fertilisers.

The topic Livestock Science/Production (Ministry of National Education: Applied Sciences pp. 25):
2b ii) Fodder conservation:
Hay and silage making; dry season grazing; wet season grazing; zero grazing; tethering.

In Form III
The topic Crop Science/Production (Ministry of National Education : Applied Sciences pp. 43–44):
7) Soil and Water Conservation:
— Objectives; meaning,; methods used in soil and water conservation.
  Land capability classes.
  Meaning of erosion.
  Irrigation.
  Surveying.

In Form IV
The topic Crop Science/Production 64 periods (Ministry of National Education : Applied Sciences pp. 48–49):
1) Forest and Forest Products:
— Introduction to forestry: value, importance and potential of forestry as raw material for the economical development of Tanzania.
— Ecology of the forestry: factors affecting forestry production including Ujamaa wood lots.
— Familiarisation to some local and exotic tree species and their value.
— Silvicultural systems and tending operations.
— Simple planning and management of forests, including wood preservations.
— Beekeeping: the importance and potential of the beekeeping industry in Tanzania; traditional and modern methods of beekeeping in Tanzania including their comparative advantages; different types of bees found in Tanzania, their characteristic features; simple beehive construction; bee management; apiary protection.

Secondary School—Biology Syllabus

Environmental education components in biology, syllabus issued 1976

In Form I
1. Introduction to Biology:
1.2. Objectives of studying Biology.
2. Value living things and the balance of nature (Ministry of Education; Biology Syllabus pp. 2).

In Form II
11. Plant nutrition../..
10. Discuss the importance of photosynthesis in nature (Ministry of Education; Biology Syllabus pp. 38).
5.3.2 Loss of water from plants../..
7. Discuss the positive and negative effects of transpiration (Ministry of Education; Biology Syllabus pp. 45).

In Form IV
12. Soil and plant growth (Ministry of Education; Biology Syllabus pp. 166–118).
12.3 Soil Fertility and Productivity (objectives to differentiate between organic and inorganic manures, explain the meaning of compost manure, green manure and farm yard manure, describe the method of preparing compost manure, discuss the merits and demerits of using compost, farm yard and green manure).
12.4 Soil erosion (objectives to explain the meaning of soil erosion, discuss the factors affecting soil erosion and the human activities which enhance soil erosion, discuss the methods of controlling soil erosion and the effects of soil erosion in relation to plant growth, discuss the factors which may lead to loss of soil fertility).
16.0 Ecology (last topic in Form IV):
16.1 Energy flow and nutrient circulation in the ecosystem.
16.2 Interdependence of organisms (to include symbiosis, parasitism, predation, mutualism, commensalism).
16.3 Population growth and control.
16.4 Natural Resources.
16.5 Pollution (Ministry of Education; Biology Syllabus pp. 128–131).

Secondary School—Geography Syllabus

Environmental education components in geography, syllabus issued 1976

Form II
Physical geography:
2. Forces that Affect the Earth's Surface:
b) External forces:
iii) Erosion and Deposition by:
(1) Running water: features produced by running water.
(2) Wind-resulting features.
(3) Ice-resulting features.
(4) Ocean-resulting features.
(Whenever possible field observation to be undertaken by the pupils).
4. Soil:
a) Formation and factors of soil formation.
b) Properties.
c) Simple classification.
d) Soil erosion:
i) Factors causing soil erosion.
ii) Soil conservation (Ministry of National Education: Social Sciences pp. 13–14).

In Form IV
The topic of East Africa, Tanzania:
2. Economic Geography: .../..
d) Forestry:
i) Natural and planted forests, hard wood and soft wood.
ii) Uses of forests.
e) Wildlife and its conservation: The tourist industry.
j) Energy:
i) Oil fuels. Study the importance of Tipper Refinery.
ii) Electricity:
a) Thermal.
b) Hydro: Study the development of H.E.P. and its distribution. (Ministry of National Education: Social Sciences pp. 28–29).

Secondary School—Home Economics Syllabus

Environmental education components in home economics, syllabus issued 1976.

In Form I
4. Kitchen Hygiene.
5. Food Hygiene.
6. Food storage (Ministry of National Education: Applied Sciences pp. 129).

In Form II
1. Cleaning of a House:
2. Cleaning Agents:
3. Daily Cleaning of a House:
4. The House Compound:
Care of the compound. The need for a vegetable and fruit garden. Useful vegetables and fruit trees to grow. The importance of having a flower garden.
5. Water Supply:
Sources of water supply and collection of water. Care of wells, springs, tanks, dams, lakes, rivers and reservoirs. Qualities of pure water, contamination of water supply. Waterborne diseases and their prevention.
6. Refuse:
Classification of house refuse. Dangers of refuse to health.
Types of lavatories:
— Conservancy system:
   Pail or tub closets.
   Pit latrines. Earth closets.
— Water carriage systems:
   Water closets.
House, drains and sewage disposal. Dustbins—use and care. Ash-pits (incinerators) and compost pits. Discuss how they are made and used (Ministry of National Education : Applied Sciences pp. 131–133).

General House Craft.
1. Cleaning of a House:
The essential equipment for efficient cleaning of the home. Choice, care and storage of brooms, brushes, mops, rags, dusters, buckets etc. Classification of dirt. Methods of removing dirt (Ministry of National Education: Applied Sciences pp. 131).

APPENDIX 6

Teacher Training—Geography Syllabus

Environmental education components in the syllabus of Geography, syllabus issued 1980

Topic	Topic objectives	Learning—Teaching Strategies
1.2 Water.	— identify and distinguish the sources of water	Lectures, seminars and tutorials. Fier. Discussions.
1.21. Surface Water.		
1.21.1. Rivers — the hydrological cycle. — the catchment area — (river basin) and its management — river regime — river profile.	— make a logical analysis of the hydrological cycle, catchment area and its management, river regime and profile—appreciate catchment area management — draw a long and cross profile of a river.	Lecture, seminar and tutorials. Discussion. Individual and group tasks followed by discussions.
1.3 Soils.		
1.31 Formation (active and passive soil formers).	— describe processes of soil formation.	Lectures, seminars and tutorials. Field study of soil properties and profile.
1.32 Composition — organic matter, inorganic, water, air and biological organisms.	— analyse soil composition.	
1.33 Texture and structure.	— distinguish between texture and structure.	
1.34 Classification and distribution of soil. — criteria, order and main types of soils in East Africa. — describe the major types of soils and their distribution. — give specific examples of the economic importance of soils.	— define criteria for classification.	
1.35 Soil erosion and soil conservation.	— state and explain factors of soil conservation.	
2.31.2 Forestry — natural and manmade.		
2.31.21 Extent and distribution.	— distinguish types of forests and describe their extent and distribution.	Lectures, seminars and tutorials.
2.31.33 Development of forests.	— give specific examples of environmental and economic advantages of forests.	Guest speaker from the forest department.
2.31.22.1 Exploitation of forests and problems.		

Topic	Topic objectives	Learning—Teaching Strategies
2.31.22.2 Afforestation.	— give specific examples of problems related to afforestation.	A visit to a local factory.
2.31.23 Conservation of forests.		Group or individual assignments followed by discussions.
2.31.27 Beekeeping.	— assess the economic importance of beekeeping in EA and describe its distribution.	
2.31.3 Fisheries.		
2.31.35 Conservation and national policies including law of the sea.	— state and analyse national policies for the fishing industry.	
2.31.4 Wild life.		
2.31.43 Significance of wild life (products, attraction, national heritage e.g. educational).	— assess the importance of wild life and give examples of problems related to wild life.	
2.31.44 Conservation and related problems.	— be aware of conservation measures and related problems.	

APPENDIX 7

Elimika. A Primary School example in 1995

The Elimika school is situated on the slopes of the mountain in the village of Aminika. The surroundings are green and filled with trees, banana plants and coffee plants. The altitude is about 1000 meters above sea level and there is seldom a lack of water. The distance to the regional capital Bweni is about 40 kilometres.

The school was a practise school for the nearby teacher training college. It had about 580 pupils from Standard I to VII, and 40 in the pre-primary class. The children came from the village and most of their parents were farmers.

Physical structures

The school consisted of five buildings with 12 classrooms, one staff room, one bookstore and an office for the headmaster. Standard I A and B were sharing one classroom and so were Standard II A and B. One stream of classes came in the morning and the other in the afternoon. The school buildings were of comparatively good standard; spacious and with glass windows. The pupils sat two or three at each desk meant for two (c.f. a nearby primary school, where they sat five to a desk). There was a blackboard in each classroom.

The pre-primary class was located in a building with walls, floor and roof but no windows. This building was also used as a lunchroom for the pupils.

The domestic science department had a shed where they cooked, using fire wood as the energy source. The lunch for the children was also prepared here.

The school yard had grass, trees and flowers but large parts of it consisted of bare soil, where the pupils walked, ran and played.

Staff

There was one head teacher, one second head teacher and 25 teachers (two held grade A diplomas and 23 held grade B certificates). They worked in nine departments. Each department had a head who was responsible for material, books, control of the teachers' schemes of works as well as examination questions, and other general responsibilities for the subject in question.

The teaching load varied depending on the number of available teachers. The variation was as great as 16 to 25 lessons per week. Each teacher taught two to three different subjects.

The teachers were mostly in the school from 8.00 in the morning to 4.00–4.30 in the afternoon with one and half hour for lunch. Very few were transferred from this school. They were fortunate to be able to collect their salaries from the nearby Teacher Training College (TTC). In other schools the collection of salaries included travelling, wasting 2–3 days each month.

Performance
In the previous year 13 of 67 Standard VII leavers were admitted in secondary education, i.e. 19.4 percent. For the country as a whole, about 10–15 percent of the primary school leavers continued to secondary schools (governmental and private).

Resources
The local government provided the school with textbooks, exercise books (two per pupil each year) and chalk for the blackboard. The Ministry of Education and Culture paid the salaries for the staff.

The parents contributed 200 Shillings (0.3 USD) per child and year. Besides that, they were asked to contribute 2,500 Shillings per year (4.1 USD) for school lunches and additional money for desks and other needs. The school had asked for contributions for building new latrines, but so far the parents had not responded.

The pupils were given lunch at the school but they had to pay for it. This money was used for buying beans, cooking oil and other such items. Maize was grown at the school shamba (farm field). Teachers were also able to buy lunch. The diet consisted mostly of maize porridge (ugali) and beans.

Cash obtained by the school came from the self-reliance projects.

A school farm of approximately 3 hectares surrounded the school. It had banana plants, a few coffee plants and a number of gardens with different vegetables growing (when they were able to afford the seeds). The school had another farm of 5 hectares about 4 km away, where maize was grown. All of these agricultural activities were part of the self-reliance project. The maize and the vegetables were used for the school lunches. Generally, they were not enough for the whole school year. The bananas, on the other hand, were sold and the profit was used for buying stationery for the pupils, maintenance of the school, entertainment of guests and the fares for the head teacher when he had to go to town for meetings. Because there were no insecticides and pesticides, the coffee gave very little harvest. The pupils did the work on the farms.

The school had the opportunity to use the library at the Aminika Teacher Training College (TTC) for preparation of lessons. At times, too, the TTC gave them some additional stationery.

The subjects of science, agriculture and history were well provided with books. In mathematics there was no textbook in Standard VI, and in Standard V and VII there were no geography textbooks. There were no textbooks in Standard V in domestic science and in English textbooks were missing in Standard V and VI. The new subject called civics (the substitute for political education) had neither syllabus nor textbooks.

Management
There was a school committee which met twice a year. The members were parents and teachers. All parents met and chose their representatives for a period of two years. The school committee discussed matters of concern related to teaching. When the school had a problem, it was presented to the chairman of the school committee or to the village chairman. They in turn alerted the parents.

The head teacher had been in his position since 1990. It was his first assignment as head teacher. The principal of the TTC made certain decisions. The school staff were considered college workers. The school was visited by a school inspector in both 1993 and 1994. The inspector also made classroom visits.

Environmental Education
According to the head teacher, neither the school committee nor the school inspector had discussed the matter of environmental education. The only one who had done so was a geography tutor from the nearby TTC. He provided the agriculture class with trees and plants.

General observations on a particular day
Minutes before school started, the three teachers on duty went out to the yard and chased any pupils who were late. They punished the latecomers by beating them with sticks on the hands or the back. The pupils ran to avoid the beating and headed for their classrooms.

Just before 8 o'clock a.m. the second head teacher gave each teacher a piece of chalk in the staff-room. Afterwards he placed the box in a locked cupboard.

At 8 o'clock there were few pupils in the yard. In the classrooms, where the teacher had not yet arrived, the voices of the pupils were loud and I could see them moving or running around in the classroom. But when a teacher had arrived, the pupils became silent.

The time schedule included six to eight periods per day. From Standard III, the teaching was done by subject teachers. The time table had the following distribution: 8–8.40, 8.40–9.20, 9.20–10.00, 10.30–11.10, 11.10–11.50, 11.50–12.30, 2–2.40, 2.40–3.20. After 3.20 there were other activities that went up to 4.00 such as UVT or EWW (youth organisations), games, hobbies and baraza (discussion).

The attendance of the pupils was noted for every day in a special book.

The atmosphere in the staff room was friendly and many laughs could be heard. Pupils came in now and then to collect or return exercise books at the desk of their teachers. The elder teachers were greeted with respect.

When the teachers left the staff room to go to the classrooms, they generally carried an exercise book or some loose pages (well worn) with them. Those that I had an opportunity to look at were ones with mathematical problems or lesson notes. When there was an available text book, the teacher carried one.

In the staff room there were some simple posters hanging on the wall. A few traditional musical instruments were stored on top of a cupboard together with a very old globe which had lost most of its different colours.

There was a counting frame that was made locally of bottle caps from soft drinks on strings (the pre-primary school children come to school with a necklace made of 50 bottle caps, which they use when they are learning how to count). There were three new flip charts (called flash cards) in biology, agriculture and health hanging on the walls.

APPENDIX 8

Chuma. A Secondary School example in 1995

The school is built on the slopes of a mountain. It was built by missionaries and became governmental in the 1970s. The view from the school is breathtaking. Behind the school you see the peaks of the mountain. Below the school you see the plains. The surroundings were lush green from the shambas of the peasants. Bananas, coffee, maize and trees of different kinds could all be seen.

The school was built for 300 pupils. Now it had 650. Like most of the secondary schools, it was a boarding school. The girls slept three in a bed (meant for one) and some also slept on the floor in the dormitories. There was a fire in one of the dormitories in January 1993 after which the pupils had to sleep in the dining hall. After more than one year, the roof had now been reconstructed and the dining hall was no longer used for sleeping.

There were three streams in Form I–IV and one stream in Form V–VI. In Form II–IV there were at minimum 50 pupils in each stream and around 60 in Form I.

Physical structures
The school consisted of an older and a (comparatively) newer part. The older part had six buildings with classrooms, including three rooms for home economics classes and two rooms for physics and chemistry. There was a school library. There were also buildings for storage, dispensary, kitchen, laundry and two dormitories. There was one chapel which was also used as an assembly hall.

The newer part had one building with four classrooms and three offices for teachers, two dormitories and one dining hall. A new dormitory was under construction since years back, but there were no funds to complete it. It used to be a teacher training centre but was taken over by the secondary school. The buildings looked new at that time. In the school compound there were also staff houses.

The land and some of the houses belonged to the Lutheran church.

Staff
There were 39 teachers, covering all subjects. There was a shortage of teachers in biology, physics and mathematics.

Performance
The performance in the national examinations was good. In the previous year 58 of 128 (45 percent) Form IV leavers were admitted to Form V. This was above the national average. In total, about two percent of the pupils went from Form IV (O-level) to Form V (A-level).This performance record was one of the reasons why so many pupils tried to transfer to this school.

Resources
There were 13 subject departments. The departments of fine art and music each had only one teacher.

The school had a library but no librarian. It was supposed to be opened until 10.30 p.m. but that depended on the availability of electricity. The books in the library were both academic and fiction (a small amount). Over the years they were poorly classified and categorised because of lack of expertise. Two teachers were now responsible for the library.

In 1995, tuition was 15,000 Shilling per year (24.5 USD). This money was collected and used by the school itself. The pupils bought their own exercise books, pens and other necessary materials. The text books were very expensive and it was rare to find that pupils had bought them. If possible, they borrowed from relatives.

For expenditures like exercise books, the school received a small sum from the Ministry of Education and Culture (10–15,000 Shillings). It was also to cover some material for the teachers (for example, paper for schemes of work and exercise books for lesson plans).

The government allocated 90 Shillings (0.15 USD) per day and per pupil to each school for food. There was also a minor allocation for electricity, post, telephone and maintenance. Of course, this sum of money was far from sufficient.

The school had a number of self-reliance activities. The profits in Tsh from the projects in 1994 were as follows:

Milk from the cows	Shop	Garden	Shamba	Pigs	Needle work	Bakery
740	893,558	95,730	−56,700	100,600	1,564,523	4,110

Most of the cattle were bulls, and medical treatment such as cattle dips were expensive. The maize in the shamba had not been successful in the previous year. The first planting was eaten by worms so they had to plant a second time. Then there was no rain so there was very little harvest. The needle work project was a school uniform making project. The girls made the uniforms under the supervision of teachers.

In 1994, the school made a total profit of 2,602,561 Shillings (4,266.5 USD). The school was allowed to decide upon the use of the money. Formerly the profit was supposed to be handed in to the government.

It was predicted during the year I was there that the harvest of maize and beans would be good, but the profit was expected to balance the previous year's loss. Seven full days were spent on the shamba, the entire school participated and the teaching was cancelled.

The vegetables from the garden, mainly cabbage, helped to improve the students' diet. The normal food was ugali (maize porridge) and beans, but this was not always available toward the end of the term.

Management
The head mistress was assisted by a second head master and an academic dean. On the notice board, there was a schedule of all meetings during the term including staff meetings, school meetings (inclusive of students), class meetings (class teacher and subject teachers), school board meeting and self-reliance committee meetings.

The school board consisted of village elders, members appointed by the head mistress and the regional education officer, staff representatives, the head mistress and the second head master. There was no fixed time for serving on the board.

There had been no visit from the school inspectorate during the past six years.

Environmental education activities
In Form III the pupils could choose a topic for a project that was to be handed in during Form IV. It was expected that the project would be written and form part of the national exams. The teachers at the school assessed the reports and sent the three best to the National Council of Examination. The pupils were able to choose between social, pure science, and language topics. They worked in groups of 5–15 on each project. Some of the topics were related to the environment (which in East African includes health and hygiene aspects), such as AIDS, pollution, energy sources and energy conservation. The most popular topics the previous year had been AIDS and malnutrition. Nobody had chosen pollution.

The school has had a Malihai Club (M.C.) since 1982. At the time of my visit, there were 30 members, which was the maximum. One of the teachers, Mr M, was the patron of the club. The club meetings (which had been lagging behind) were to be once a week on Wednesdays. But the teacher in charge wanted to shift to Saturdays, because he felt that there would be fewer interruptions than on schooldays. The main concern of the club was the environment with an emphasis on conserving and protecting the natural surroundings.

Through its School Maintenance Programme, DANIDA had assisted in establishing a quite large, fenced-in nursery with a small store for equipment and a well for watering purposes. Here, the club was growing tree seedlings for the prevention of soil erosion, as wind breakers and for shade. Every year, the students planted a tree fence around the school compound. They had also been planting at the school farm. A forester came occasionally to give advice to students and teachers about the activities in the tree nursery. They had prepared a planting calendar, but they did not keep strictly to it. The club members occasionally cleared the bush in the school compound.

The club was supposed to be self-funding by selling seedlings to the school or the community. The club had a drama group and they sang songs to motivate farmers. Posters with environmental messages were placed on the walls around the school. The students were to produce these posters. When the financial situation permitted, they sometimes made trips to national parks or went mountain climbing.

General observations on a particular day
In the morning the teachers on duty stood with their sticks to control and send the pupils into the classrooms. Assembly was at 7.15 a.m. and afterwards, they ran or walked to their respective classrooms. Some of the girls did not attend the assembly but instead were cleaning the classrooms.

Classes were supposed to start at 7.30 but by 7.45 many of the classes were still without the teacher. When I made a visit to the library at 8.40 some 15 girls were reading in books, notes or studying the newspaper. All the students were expected to take the seven basic subjects but it was not compulsory to take optional subjects.

There were very few teachers in the staff room in the mornings. The few that were there, were reading or preparing lessons. Most of the teachers arrived at teatime – 10.15-10.30 a.m. From my experience, I noticed that the tea break lasted longer than 15 minutes! One day a representative for the trade union visited the school and that day nobody left the staff room before 11.00 o'clock.

On the board there were several cards, including invitations to weddings and so on. There was also a card from a former pupil which read: 'My good performance has been greatly influenced by my good teachers! Thank you!' On the board there was also a timetable for tuition in the evenings. Normally the pupils paid an extra fee for that.

The closest neighbours were a church and a primary school. The church had a women's group that had several activities, among them were growing of vegetables, bananas and coffee. The vegetables were grown on (not so perfect) terraces. The women were making stoves that consumed a third of the fuel wood compared to the traditional ones. One type was made of clay and grass, another of tins filled with saw dust. The primary school cultivated vegetables (an ESR project) on well kept terraces. Every child cultivated seedlings, mostly coffee plants, for selling.

APPENDIX 9

Aminika Teacher Training College (TTC)

Aminika TTC is situated in the Aminika division, on the slopes of a mountain in green and lush surroundings. The villagers were peasants or business people.

The college was established in 1902, but at another location, namely Kibweta – Old Bweni. It was a seminary started by Lutheran Evangelical missionaries and at first accepted only 10 male students from a certain tribe. It was closed down in 1905 and reopened in 1912 in Aminika, where it is now. The location had once been a German substation. The school opened with 42 students and more subjects were introduced later. It had to be closed down in 1915 but was reopened in 1926 during the British colonial era.

In the beginning, the college was run by two missionary groups, one from Germany and one from the USA. In 1926 the colonial government agreed to share the cost. It paid 75 percent of the two native teachers' salaries. The school was renamed Aminika Teachers' Training School and was run entirely by the German missionaries. All of the students were Lutherans.

The school was closed again in 1940 and re-opened in 1942, when it started to admit female students. In 1954, the school was named Aminika Teachers' Training Centre.

Ten years later, the college got its first African principal and a year later it initiated a large construction programme producing the library, three dormitories, classrooms, departmental blocks and a number of staff houses. As a result the number of students attending the college rose from 120 in 1961 to 439 in 1967. In 1970, the college was handed over to the government.

Physical structures

The college has not expanded since the 1960s and the buildings were in an acute state of decline since there was hardly any maintenance .

Staff

The college had 34 tutors organised in 10 subject departments. There was a shortage of tutors in almost every department but the most severe shortage was felt in the Education Department. The shortage was of two kinds: the number of tutors and qualification of tutors (very few had graduated).

Courses

The college had a two year certificate programme for primary school grade A teachers, and a two year diploma programme for teachers in primary and lower secondary schools. The normal academic year was from 30 July to the first week of June with a break in December-January. Due to financial problems the college experienced, an earlier closure of the terms was seen as necessary. This resulted in the courses losing about 25 percent of their time. There were about

490 students in the certificate programme and about 175 students in the diploma programme. Recruitment had been nation-wide earlier but due to the financial constraints of the last few years, students tended to come mainly from the immediate region.

As a British Council supported project, a one-month in-service course in English was given every second month, making a total of six per year.

Performance
The students at Aminika TTC had for a number of years performed among the five best colleges in the country in the national examinations. Sometimes they were number one. This demonstrates that very few students failed in the examinations.

In the 1994 examinations, ten students received A in Geography, 54 received B and only five received C (the scale ran from A to F). There were no failures. It is likely that performance in the 1995 examinations was even better. In 1994 on the whole, geography was the best scoring subject in the college.

Resources
Two primary schools, Dauma and Elimika primary schools, were linked to the college as practice schools. They were situated on the outskirts of the college compound and were partly under the local government and partly under the Ministry of Education and Culture. Compared with other primary schools that were unable to use the facilities of a TTC, they were better equipped and had more opportunities for academic assistance. This did not mean, however, that they had no problems. The schools were used for demonstration and single lesson practice.

The TTC had a library with about 60,000 books. Most of them were old. The school could not afford to buy books but received donations, from, for example, the British Council and private donors.

There were two farms which were owned by the college. One was 30 acres and maize and beans were cultivated there. The farms (shambas) were situated in dry areas below the mountains. The college was very dependent on the farm products in order to give the students lunch and dinner. In 1993, the harvest reaped almost nothing, due to lack of rain. The students had to be sent home while the college tried to find funds with which to purchase food.

There were also gardens in the self-reliance project and these products were sold. Of the cows, only one remained. She produced up to nine litres of milk per day.

In previous years, there were severe problems with the realisation of the teaching practice periods for the students. The TTC did not get sufficient funds from the Ministry of Education and Culture. It was the same problem for all TTCs in Tanzania. Instead of a total of eight weeks teaching practice, students were only able to give two single lessons in the schools that were within walking distance.

In May 1995 the students were sent home with a letter to the head masters/ mistresses and head teachers in the areas where they lived. The principal of Aminika TTC asked the schools to allow the students to practice teaching and be assessed by each school's administration. Other TTCs had asked the students for a contribution of 20,000 Tsh to pay for teaching practice.

Management
The administration staff was headed by a principal. The financial problems had been acute for the previous three years.
The last school inspection had been in 1994.

Environmental Education
The most visible activities of environmental education were those of the Malihai Club. It was a non-governmental organisation aimed at secondary schools and teacher training institutions. The headquarters were in Batiza town. From the beginning the club was mostly interested in wild life but had now expanded their area to encompass conservation in general.

One of the tutors in geography, Mr K., was the leader of the Malihai Club (M.C.) at the TTC. The M.C. at the college was increasingly co-operating with the M.C. at two secondary schools nearby. There were 42-50 members. Many students wanted to join the club, but the recommended number was 40. The limit also served the purpose of seeing to it that there were members in the other clubs at the college as well (the debating club, agricultural club, history club etc.).

M.C. was the most active club, according to Mr K. It met once a week for one period on Friday afternoons. Members tended the tree nursery where different species were raised and later planted tree seedlings in the compound. They also discussed various environmental issues. Occasionally, the club received magazines from the East African Wildlife Society, the Tanzania Wildlife Protection Association and the Malihai Clubs of Tanzania. Club members read the English-language newspaper, Daily News, which had articles once a week on environmental issues. They discussed the nature of the problem and what measures could be taken.

Sometimes they wrote educational articles about the environment. The best article was put on the Aminika Wall Magazine (board). Also, in a 1995 issue of the magazine of the Malihai Clubs, one of the students had his article published.

The club had a very active choir and they composed songs. At the time of my visit, they had seven good songs which carried a message on environmental awareness. In 1993, they performed for the president and several ministers at an awareness week in Batiza organised by the Tanzania Wildlife Association.

The club also had a drama group. They had written and performed two plays. One was about a villager that set fire to the forest when collecting honey. The fire spread all around in a water catchment area and the streams dried up. This was a typical problem in the area, Mr K. said. Further (in the play), villagers cut down trees to get fire wood and a forest officer visited the village and discussed what could be done about the problems. They decided to be educated on how to collect honey without setting fire to the forest and also the need to plant a tree when cutting one down. An agreement was reached to the effect that the forest officers would bring tree seedlings to be planted. This play had been performed several times and was also video taped by the M.C. headquarters.

The club planned to perform in villages. Representatives from the national park nearby volunteered to provide transport on such occasions.

Sometimes field study trips were organised. Thus, the club once went to Bweni to visit industries. They had also planned to visit a dam. In 1993, they climbed the mountain and studied the rain forest and a cave. In 1994, they climbed even higher and were able to see different climate and vegetation zones.

Finance, of course, continued to be a problem. Mr K. was always collecting seeds to be grown in the tree nursery. They received a small amount of money from the college fund to buy a particular seed. Another source of income was to ask for a modest entrance fee, 30 shillings (= 0.05 USD) when they performed the play. The hope was that they would be able to sell seedlings to the surrounding farmers.

In 1992, three courses in environmental science were run with 30 participants in each. The course length was three months and the target group was primary school teachers in the Northern Zone. The course had an agricultural emphasis and was financed by German funds and the Tanzanian Ministry of Education and Culture.

In July 1995, there was a one day seminar, organised by Schools Partnership World-wide (SW), on the subject of A Joint Initiative for Environmental Education, which had been developed during the year with the aim of assessing environmental problems in Tanzania and the level of environmental awareness of the local population. The initiative had been taken by a mixed group of Tanzanian and British school leavers who had travelled around Tanzania for four months looking at various environmental issues in different areas of the country. Tutors from the college participated in the seminar.

General observations
During the 17 days I visited the college, I observed several staff members sitting around discussing for a long time during the day. They were not on leave, but waiting for the courses to start. One of them called the area where they participated in discussions, 'the jobless corner.' Many reported in the morning and returned to their homes to work on something else, e.g. their private projects (cows, chicken etc.).

The English Department was very active. They had an in-service course running and I observed the teachers during evenings, weekends and holidays as they prepared their lessons. The timing was mainly due to when electricity was available. When it was on, they made their preparations (electricity has been rationed in Tanzania since 1992).

When the students started to arrive on Sunday August 13, they were registered immediately. The vice principal and the dean of students remained in their offices while some teachers walked to and from the administration building.

In the evening I asked some of students I met if they had been able to get some teaching practice. Some said no. The reasons they gave were that the schools were closed. Others said yes. They had been able to teach for two weeks.

APPENDIX 10

Frequency distribution of answers to question 1 and 3–11

Table 1: *Frequency distribution of questionnaire scores;* primary schools, n=672

Question	Score 0	Score 1	Score 2	Score 3	Total
1. What is meant by 'environment'?	120	199	324	29	672
3. Why is knowledge about the environment important?	78	270	299	25	672
4. How can you reduce soil erosion?	52	50	156	186	444[a]
5. Give some examples of endangered animals (animals threatened by extinction) in Tanzania!	114	263	230	65	672
6. Give three examples of pollution of the environment!	220	316	114	22	672
7. What is the 'green-house effect'?	668	4	0	0	672
8. What is an ecosystem? Please give an example.	255	235	163	19	672
9. Where should a garbage dumping site be situated? Explain why.	120	234	315	3	672
10. Why is it forbidden for fishermen to use dynamite to catch fish?	281	344	45	2	672
11. What are the causes of deforestation?	28	115	510	19	672
Total	1 936	2 030	2 156	370	6 492

[a] The answers from the first school were omitted since the question was re-phrased.

Table 2: *Frequency distribution of questionnaire scores; secondary schools.* n=738

Question	Score 0	Score 1	Score 2	Score 3	Total
1. What is meant by 'environment'?	27	263	395	53	738
3. Why is knowledge about the environment important?	55	195	434	51	735
4. How can you reduce soil erosion?	31	63	108	489	691
5. Give some examples of endangered animals (animals threatened by extinction) in Tanzania!	229	213	219	74	735
6. Give three examples of pollution of the environment!	268	274	121	72	735
7. What is the 'green-house effect'?	714	15	5	3	737
8 What is an ecosystem? Please give an example.	364	103	199	72	738
9. Where should a garbage dumping site be situated? Explain why.	410	174	147	7	738
10. Why is it forbidden for fishermen to use dynamite to catch fish?	387	256	81	14	738
11. What are the causes of deforestation?	306	165	224	43	738
Total	2 791	1 721	1 933	878	7 323